Cognitive Poetics

'A masterly presentation of the 'cognitive turn' in literary reading and analysis, providing a radical re-evaluation of literary activity. ... an invaluable text and an important contribution to the emerging field of cognitive poetics as a literary science.'

Margaret H. Freeman, Los Angeles Valley College, USA

'In this book, Peter Stockwell presents a delightful combination of theoretical enlightenment with a deep concern for practical analysis and understanding.'

Willie van Peer, Munich University, Germany

Cognitive poetics is a new way of thinking about literature, involving the application of cognitive linguistics and psychology to literary texts. This book is the first introductory text to this growing field.

In *Cognitive Poetics: An Introduction*, the reader is encouraged to re-evaluate the categories used to understand literary reading and analysis. Covering a wide range of literary genres and historical periods, the book encompasses both American and European approaches. Each chapter explores a different cognitive poetic framework and relates it to a literary text. Including a range of activities, discussion points, suggestions for further reading and a glossarial index, the book is both interactive and highly accessible.

Cognitive Poetics: An Introduction is essential reading for students on stylistics and literary-linguistics courses, and will be of interest to all those involved in literary studies, critical theory and linguistics.

Peter Stockwell is Senior Lecturer at the University of Nottingham. His publications include *Sociolinguistics: A Resource Book for Students, Contextualized Stylistics: An Introduction to the Nature and Functions of Language* (with Howard Jackson) and *The Poetics of Science Fiction*.

D1336247

Cognitive Poetics
An introduction

Peter Stockwell

London and New York

First published 2002
by Routledge
2 Park Square, Milton Park, Abingdon, Oxon OX14 4RN

Simultaneously published in the USA and Canada
by Routledge-Cavendish
270 Madison Avenue, New York, NY 10016

Routledge is an imprint of the Taylor & Francis Group, an informa business

© 2002 Peter Stockwell

Reprinted 2007 (twice), 2008, 2009

Typeset in Sabon by
Bookcraft Ltd, Stroud, Gloucestershire
Printed and bound in Great Britain by
the MPG Books Group

British Library Cataloguing in Publication Data
A catalogue record for this book is available
from the British Library

Library of Congress Cataloging in Publication Data
A catalog record for this book has been requested

ISBN 0–415–25895–2 (pbk)

ISBN 978–0–415–25895–1 (pbk)

Contents

Acknowledgements

In the beginning, it was all Peter Verdonk's idea. Several years ago, at a restaurant in a Hungarian forest, he suggested with his usual quiet wise smile that I should write a textbook on cognitive approaches to literature. The conception of the book has changed quite a bit since then, and the field itself has acquired a name and a firmer set of borders, but the shape of this book and its mere existence owe a great deal to the inspiration and influence he has exerted over all that time.

I have also been encouraged by many other people who were there on that occasion, and who have helped me with their work, ideas and discussions ever since. Many thanks to Michael Burke, Charles Forceville, Don Freeman, Margaret Freeman, to Katie Wales for being there in spirit and to Louisa Semlyen for her support and foresight in commissioning this book and its companion volume.

I am fortunate in the generosity of my colleagues and friends. Through the Poetics and Linguistics Association (PALA), I have benefited from many and late discussions with the best minds and their most precise criticism. I am especially grateful to my fellow committee members over the years: Tony Bex, Urszula Clark, Catherine Emmott, Keith Green, Lesley Jeffries, Willie van Peer, Martin Wynne and Sonia Zyngier. For specific ideas and startling discussions, I am indebted to Jayne Carroll, Peter Crisp, Szilvia Csabi, Jonathan Culpeper, Monika Fludernik, Ray Gibbs, Laura Hidalgo Downing, Rocio Montoro, Mary Ellen Ryder, Elena Semino, Mick Short, Paul Simpson, Gerard Steen, Michael Toolan, and particularly Reuven Tsur; and I would like to acknowledge with fond memory conversations with the late Paul Werth.

The academic community at Nottingham University has been a rich source of ideas and inspiration. The philosophy here of language study in a radical, engaged and humane context makes it one of the most fruitful and exciting places to work and think. In particular I have learnt more than they would realise from my colleagues Robert Adlington, Svenja Adolphs, Robert Cockcroft, Janette Dillon, Zoltan Dörnyei, Val Durow, Craig Hamilton, Mike McCarthy, John McRae, Louise Mullany, Bill Nash, Mark Robson and Norbert Schmitt. This community owes much to the astonishing energy of Ron Carter and I am grateful for all his support and the apparently boundless enthusiasm and intellectual rigour which sustains the study of modern English language at Nottingham. I have developed many ideas and had my own thinking sharpened by my research colleagues Dany Badran, Ida Bahar, Tracy Cruickshank, Christiana Gregoriou, Ernestine Lahey, Ahmed Meliebary, Salwa Nugali, and by the students who took my cognitive poetics course, out of which I wrote this book.

I have been supported, encouraged and loved through all my work and thinking by my wife Joanna Gavins. This book is as much hers as mine.

Not all of these people agree with my ideas or the way I have shaped the book, but as Don Freeman once said to me, the only real criticism comes from your friends. I have incorporated many changes as a result of this friendly fire. Though of course I am responsible for all my schematic readings of their ideas, I hope the book emerges in a form they would recognise and approve.

Finally, I am grateful to the following for permission to reproduce copyright material: the estate of Ted Hughes, and Faber and Faber publishers, for 'Hill-stone was content', and Bill Nash for *Vakum clenere* and 'Milkmen everywhere'. While every effort has been made to contact copyright holders, we would be pleased to hear of any that have been omitted.

1 Introduction
Body, mind and literature

Cognitive poetics is all about reading literature. That sentence looks simple to the point of seeming trivial. It could even be seen simply as a close repetition, since *cognition* is to do with the mental processes involved in reading, and *poetics* concerns the craft of literature. But in fact such a plain statement is really where we need to start. In order to understand exactly what this book is about, we will first need to be clear what we mean by 'reading' and what we mean by 'literature'. The answers to these questions will take us to the heart of the most important issues facing us as individual, conscious, intelligent, critical people, sharing with each other a facility for language and perception. In the course of exploring these ideas, we will not be satisfied with asking important and difficult questions; we will also try to provide either answers or at least directions towards solutions.

In order to consider what happens in literary reading, we need at least an object that is a literary text, and a process of reading, which of course requires a reader. Here is part of a literary text:

> We that had loved him so, followed him, honoured him,
>   Lived in his mild and magnificent eye,
> Learned his great language, caught his clear accents,
>   Made him our pattern to live and to die!

Since you have just read these four lines, we also have a reading, which is what is in your mind right now. Our first option is just to leave what you think of this passage in your mind without any further discussion. In truth, this is what mainly happens when the vast majority of people read the vast majority of literary texts: they read them for themselves, and are happy neither to discuss them, nor work out the craft in their construction, nor intellectualise them, nor fit their understanding into a theoretical framework out loud for other people to read or hear. This is 'reading' as it happens most of the time, 'reading' as an object in the world. This is reading as an entirely natural phenomenon.

We are all readers like this. But this book is *about* reading literature. We can read literature any time we want to, but when we want to *think about*

what we are doing when we read, when we want to reflect on it and understand it, then we are not simply reading; we are engaged in a science of reading. The object of investigation of this science is not the artifice of the literary
text alone, or the reader alone, but the more natural process of reading when
one is engaged with the other. This is a different thing altogether from the
simple and primary activity of reading. Literary texts are artefacts, but 'readings' are natural objects.

In scientific terms, readings are the data through which we can generalise
patterns and principles across readers and texts. However, understanding what
we do when we engage in reading literature need not be an abstract or highly
and purely theoretical exercise. Though a clear and precise understanding is the
aim of any scientific exploration, the means of discovery involves considering a
great deal of messy and perhaps contradictory data. We need, then, to attend to
the detail and quality of many different readings. Particular readings are important for us; they are not simply the means to an abstract end. Indeed, it is in the
detail of readings that all the interest and fascination lies.

So what did you make of those four lines of literature above? What are
they about? What do they mean? What do they mean for you? What do you
understand by them? Of course, these questions are all the same question,
asked from slightly different perspectives. Perhaps you have read the lines
before, and are wondering why they have been reproduced here? You might
know the author, or the source, or the historical background. You might
recognise the lines as being in a particular form that you can give a name to,
or you might be able to describe the pattern in the sounds of the lines when
read aloud using a technical term that you know.

All of these questions are to do with *context*, and this is a crucial notion for
cognitive poetics. The questions in the context of this book are different from
what they would mean if I were to ask you while we were sitting together on a
bench in a park, or standing as tourists in front of them written on a grave-
stone somewhere, or even if we were in a university or college seminar. In the
last case, we would both understand that some of the questions and their
answers would be appropriate in the situation, and some would not. For
example, if you were to tell me that the lines sounded to you like a eulogy for a
dead hero, that would be something I would probably develop in a seminar
discussion. If you told me, honestly, that the lines reminded you of a much-
loved family cat that had recently died, both you and I and probably the rest of
the people in the seminar would regard that as irrelevant and a bit eccentric.
But why is it? The four lines might mean exactly that to you, and you could
certainly make a case for that reading based on the textual evidence given here.
Why are some responses appropriate and acceptable, while others are
regarded as personal and therefore irrelevant in a seminar context? Why does
it seem so easy for me to equate personal responses with irrelevance here?

What you do with the lines depends very much on the context in which
you find yourself with the text. There is nothing universal or unchanging
about the meaning of these lines: indeed, there are as many meanings as there

are different contexts for different readings. But the status that is attached to each reading also depends on context and the assumptions that underlie the question being asked. It is usual when discussing literature within an institutional setting to apply assumptions that belong to the discipline of literary study. One of these assumptions is that idiosyncratic and personal meanings are not worth discussing with anyone else. However, at your cat's shoebox funeral in your garden, you might feel it appropriate to read these lines at a small ceremony attended by your like-minded friends and family.

These decisions of appropriateness and status apply within all the different branches of literary studies. For example, if we take a view of literary reading in which history is foremost, then I could assert that your opinion that the lines are a eulogy for a dead hero is simply wrong. In the historical moment of the poem's construction, the lines belong to a poem called 'The Lost Leader', written by Robert Browning in 1845, about Wordsworth's shift with age from revolutionary radical to arch-conservative. Though the poem draws on elegy and eulogy, Wordsworth is still alive to be accused of betrayal by Browning:

> Just for a handful of silver he left us,
> > Just for a riband to stick in his coat.

And Wordsworth's change of heart means that there will be

> Never glad confident morning again!

In this approach from literary history, readings are acceptable or not depending on their conformity to these accepted historical 'facts'. A reading that claimed the poem was about Milton, or Coleridge, would simply be wrong. It would be as wrong as claiming that the poem was about a twentieth-century politician.

Alternatively, the poem, and these lines in particular, can be used within a purely textual approach as an example of a particular pattern in metrics. The lines create a 'dactylic tetrameter' (four repetitions of one accented and two unaccented syllables) in the first line – go back and read it out loud to hear this. Then the subsequent lines introduce minor irregularities to disrupt the pattern: omitting the last two unaccented syllables at the end of lines two and four in order to place heavy emphasis on 'eye' and 'die'; or twice omitting one of the unaccented syllables in the third line to create a heavy pause in the middle of the line. The emphases of the word-meaning can be created and confirmed by these metrical patterns, and illustrate the expert craftsmanship in the poem.

The textual and historical approaches can even be brought together, if you recognise that hexameter (called 'Alexandrine') was a prominent pattern in heroic Greek verse such as the *Iliad,* the *Odyssey* and the *Aeneid.* Then you might read Browning's disruptions of the dactyl and reduction of the repetitions from six to four in the line as offering a debasement of the heroic that parallels the fall of Wordsworth as a hero-figure.

What about a personal and idiosyncratic reading? I must admit that I only learnt about the historical construction of the poem several years after I first read it. My first contact was when I heard these lines quoted, out of context, in a political analysis programme on the BBC after the 1992 British election. At that time, the Labour Party had been widely expected to win, rejuvenated and modernised by its leader, Neil Kinnock, after three election defeats. They lost, and Kinnock immediately resigned. The lines from 'The Lost Leader', quoted in a new context, took on a different and poignant meaning for a Labour supporter like me. In this selective reading, Kinnock was the lost leader not, like Wordsworth, out of choosing betrayal, but because of electoral misfortune. 'Never glad confident morning again' was to apply to the next five years of Tory government. From this angle, the poem *can* be about a twentieth-century politician.

From a historical perspective, one that privileges the context of production, my reading of these lines is a misquotation, a selective use that is just plain wrong. However, it is one of the many uses to which this poem must have been put over the years. It seems to me that it is important to reconnect the different readings of literary texts between the academic and the everyday, and to recognise that readings have status not objectively but relative to their circumstances. When I ask what does the poem mean, I am really asking what the poem does, which is another way of asking what is it being used for. Meaning, then, is what literature does. Meaning is use.

The key to understanding issues of literary value and status and meaning lies in being able to have a clear view of text and context, circumstances and uses, knowledge and beliefs. Cognitive poetics offers us a means of achieving this. It has a linguistic dimension which means we can engage in detailed and precise textual analysis of style and literary craft. It offers a means of describing and delineating different types of knowledge and belief in a systematic way, and a model of how to connect these matters of circumstance and use to the language of the literature. It also demonstrates the continuities between creative literary language and creative language in everyday use. In short, cognitive poetics takes context seriously. Furthermore, it has a broad view of context that encompasses both social and personal circumstances.

The foundations of cognitive poetics obviously lie most directly in cognitive linguistics and cognitive psychology, together forming a large part of the field of cognitive science. We need to understand the basic premise that behind these innovative disciplines all forms of expression and forms of conscious perception are bound, more closely than was previously realised, in our biological circumstances. Most simply, we think in the forms that we do and we say things in the ways that we do because we are all roughly human-sized containers of air and liquid with our main receptors at the top of our bodies. Our minds are 'embodied' not just literally but also figuratively, finally clearing away the mind–body distinction of much philosophy most famously expressed by Descartes. To give a simple example (suggested by my colleague Tony Bex), one possible cognitive reason why we chop trees *down* but we chop wood *up* is that trees are bigger than us but are on the ground below us once they have been felled. Another cognitive solution sees these directional features as deriving from an underlying metaphor in which 'good is up' and 'bad is down'. Trees are unified 'good' wholes when they are upright, and firewood is more usefully 'good' when it is chopped from fallen trees.

This example is a neat one because it indicates that even the completive particles of phrasal verbs ('down' and 'up') are essentially bound up in our cognitive condition. The notion of embodiment affects every part of language. It means that all of our experiences, knowledge, beliefs and wishes are involved in and expressible only through patterns of language that have their roots in our material existence. The fact that we share most of the factors of existence (requiring food, having a heat-regulation system, seeing in the visible spectrum, living in three dimensions under a sun that transits in a day, and so on) accounts for many of the similarities in language across humanity. The fact that some communities have different factors of existence (such as men's and women's different reproductive functions, for example, or different levels of technology, environment or lifestyle around the world) can also account for habitual differences in expression. Cognitive poetics has the potential to offer a unified explanation of both individual interpretations as well as interpretations that are shared by a group, community or culture.

Whether through oral or documentary 'literature', most cultures hold verbal expression as a high status form of art. The relevance of patterns emerging from cognitive psychology and especially cognitive linguistics is obvious for the field of literary study. Cognitive poetics, then, is clearly related also to the field of literary criticism. Within that discipline, the focus of attention has shifted around the triangle of 'author–text–reader', with different traditions placing more or less emphasis on each of these three nodes. Cognitive poetics can be overlaid onto this scheme, in the sense that it is not restricted to one or other of the points. Concerned with literary reading, and with both a psychological and a linguistic dimension, cognitive poetics offers a means of discussing interpretation whether it is an authorly version of the world or a readerly account, and how those interpretations are made manifest in textuality. In this sense, cognitive poetics is not simply a shift in emphasis but is a radical re-evaluation of the whole process of literary activity.

A trivial way of doing cognitive poetics would be simply to take some of the insights from cognitive psychology and cognitive linguistics, and treat literature as just another piece of data. In effect, we would then set aside impressionistic reading and imprecise intuition and conduct a precise and systematic analysis of what happens when a reader reads a literary text. Given this methodological perspective, we would probably be mainly interested in the continuities and connections between literary readings and readings of non-literary encounters. We would not really have much to say about literary value or status, other than to note that it exists. We would regard the main concerns of literary criticism, for example, as irrelevant to our concerns, as part of a different set of disciplines that just happened to be focusing on the same area of interest, but that were at best unimportant to us and at worst an irritating and wrong-headed opposition. In our different disciplines, it would be as if we were surfers, fishermen, wind-turbine builders and watercolour artists all looking at the same bit of beach.

In my view, treating literature only as another piece of data would not be cognitive poetics at all. This is simply cognitive linguistics. Insights from that discipline might be very useful for cognitive poetics, but for us the literary context must be primary. That means we have to know about critical theory and literary philosophy as well as the science of cognition. It means we have to start by aiming to answer the big questions and issues that have concerned literary study for generations. I think that cognitive poetics offers us a means of doing exactly that. This entire book will try to answer the question of what cognitive poetics is by showing you examples of it.

As I said, taking 'the cognitive turn' seriously means more than simply being interested in the psychology of reading. It means a thorough re-evaluation of all of the categories with which we understand literary reading and analysis. In doing this, however, we do not have to throw away all of the insights from literary criticism and linguistic analysis that have been drawn out in the past. Many of those patterns of understanding form very useful starting points for cognitive poetic investigation. Some of them require only a little reorientation to offer a new way of looking at literary reading. Occasionally, this might seem to be no more than recasting old ideas with new labels. I would argue (along cognitive linguistic lines) that new labels force us to conceptualise things differently.

In any case, this is a textbook, and such schematising is essential in order to present complex ideas in a way that is accessible and usable. In undertaking this 'operationalising' of terms, I have tried to simplify the presentation without simplifying the concepts, though of course it is a delicate balancing act. To help you with new terms, there is a glossarial index at the back of the book that directs you to a definition in context. I thought this would be more useful than a set of definitions out of context. It is important, though, to recognise that descriptive terminology is a starting point for your thinking and a way of arranging your thoughts systematically, rather than simply being a set of labels. Throughout this book, I encourage you to move the terms around, redefine them, argue with them and handle them until they are comfortable. Though there are many different frameworks from cognitive science, cognitive poetics is essentially a *way of thinking* about literature rather than a framework in itself.

Within the different sub-disciplines of literary criticism, cognitive poetics is most closely connected with stylistics (sometimes called 'literary linguistics'), and you might even see it called 'cognitive stylistics' in some places. The common impression of stylistics is that it is concerned with giving a descriptive account of the language features of a text in a rather mechanistic and non-evaluative way. However, most good stylisticians have always recognised the importance of the context of literature in exploring the literary effect and value of a particular text. The problem for them up until twenty-five years or so ago was that linguistics was mainly focused on providing analytical frameworks for phonology, syntax and semantics. This meant that it was mainly (shorter) poetry that got analysed, and then the analysis tended to be rather decontextualised and somewhat pedestrian. As linguistics developed frameworks for understanding the contextual effect on meaning (in the form of pragmatics, text- and discourse-analysis, and conversation analysis) so stylistics was able to produce more complex and richer discussions of extended prose fiction and non-fiction, and drama. In recent years, stylistics has seized on developments in cognitive linguistics in order again to reassess its exploration of the workings of literary language.

There is some debate in stylistics at the moment over the status of a stylistic analysis of a piece of literature. Like the uses of cognitive linguistics, stylistics has its linguistic and its literary sides. Linguistic stylistics is often concerned not just with literary texts, but sees itself as a branch of language study with literature as one among many sets of language data. Literary stylistics arises out of literary analysis, but uses approaches and frameworks developed by linguistics in non-literary contexts. Since it has been demonstrated many times that there is nothing inherently different in the form of literary language, it is reasonable and safe to investigate the language of literature using approaches generated in the language system in general.

More debatable is the status of the findings of cognitive poetic and stylistic exploration. On the one hand you could argue that readers reach a primary interpretation before any analytical sense is made apparent. The purpose of a cognitive poetic analysis would then be to rationalise and explain how that reader reached that understanding on that occasion. In this perspective, cognitive poetics has no predictive power, and cannot in itself produce interpretations. The advantage of this view is that the readings themselves, if held honestly, can only be argued against by reference to the common currency of the cognitive poetic framework and its terminology: it means the discussion can continue systematically on the basis of a common language.

An alternative view would suggest that the process of engaging in cognitive poetic analysis offers a raised awareness of certain patterns that might have been subconscious or not even noticed at all. Cognitive poetics in this view has a productive power in at least suggesting a new interpretation. This perspective is more attractively radical but its challenge is that it seems to suggest that some interpretations are only available to analysts who have a knowledge of cognitive poetics. This has the unfortunate consequence of implying that prior interpretations were faulty, and only cognitively aware analyses are valid.

These two positions leave cognitive poetics either as a highly limiting and deterministic approach which closes off many interpretations as being invalid, or as an infinitely open and non-predictive framework which, in allowing any interpretation at all, ends up being a model of nothing very substantial. A way of resolving this problem is to notice a distinction between the terms 'reading' and 'interpretation'. Interpretation is what readers do as soon as (perhaps even partly before) they begin to move through a text. Their general sense of the impact of the experience could range over many different impressions and senses, some of which are refined or rejected. It is this later, more analytical process that produces a reading. Some interpretations (especially those rejected early) can be simply wrong: mistakes, errors, miscues that are demonstrably not supported by any textual evidence at all. Readings, however, are the process of arriving at a sense of the text that is personally acceptable. These are likely to combine individual factors as well as features that are common to the reader's interpretative community. Cognitive poetics – in having the power to combine both the individual and communal effects of language and experience – offers a means of squaring this circle. Cognitive poetics models the process by which intuitive interpretations are formed into expressible meanings, and it presents the same framework as a means of describing and accounting for those readings.

Unlike literary criticism, cognitive poetics does not have to focus exclusively on minute differences between readings. Most readers even from vaguely similar interpretative communities tend to agree on readings of literature far more than they disagree. Literary criticism has focused on the minutiae of disagreement because deviance is more interesting, but an unfortunate consequence of this is that literary criticism has emphasised difference, ambiguity, ambivalence and irresolution to a disproportionate extent. Cognitive poetics can encompass matters of readerly difference, but these are set into a general context of the various and varying cultural, experiential and textual constraints around real readers reading literature in the real world.

Cognitive poetics is still relatively new as a discipline, though it makes clear reconnections back to much older forms of analysis such as classical rhetoric. The phrase 'cognitive rhetoric' was briefly used recently, and in fact the discipline combines the classical scholarly trivium of rhetoric, grammar and logic. Again I must emphasise, however, that the major consequence of taking 'the cognitive turn' seriously involves a radical re-evaluation of all of these terms. Choice of words, forms of textual structures, and patterns of reasoning are all three intimately inter-related to each other when viewed through a science of cognition. 'Poetics' in modern literary theory has come to mean a 'theory' or 'system', but I also like the associations with the related word 'poetry' that the term suggests, implying the practical creativity inherent in the thinking in this area.

As with all new fields, different traditions have already begun to emerge within cognitive poetics. The phrase itself was used in a very precise and particular sense by Reuven Tsur in his theory of poetry and perception. It has also been more broadly applied to any approaches to literary craft that take models from cognitive science as their descriptive frameworks. This textbook necessarily takes the broad view of the discipline, and even so cannot of course claim to be exhaustive. For example, though there are illustrative analyses of poetry in this book, a thorough account of cognitive poetics in the narrow sense is beyond its scope. You are referred first of all to the list of key texts in cognitive poetics that I have listed after the final chapter. These works are a good place to go after you finish this book.

The different approaches in the field have placed their emphases in stylistic and persuasive patterns (rhetoric) on the one hand, or in the grammatical representation of conceptual structures (grammar and logic) on the other. While being complementary to each other, several scholars have addressed similar questions and have developed different ways of resolving the issues. The understanding of cognitive poetics in America has centred very closely around cognitive linguistics, which for institutional reasons has become a major means by which linguists can engage in language study that does not follow the Chomskyan generative tradition. The American model has been highly influential around the world, not least in promoting the attraction of cognitive poetics for colleagues in areas of literary study. Its main concerns have been to do with metaphor, conceptual structures and issues of reference.

Traditionally, the discipline of stylistics has flourished in Europe and Australia, and has had limited appeal so far in America. Since it has been through stylistics that cognitive poetics has found its main enthusiasts outside America, it is not surprising that it is elsewhere that cognitive poetics has been conceived more broadly. Also, practitioners of cognitive poetics have not had to fight the same institutional battles in their departments in Europe and Australia, as generativism as a linguistic paradigm does not have the same hold here as in America. This cognitive poetic tradition encompasses the concerns of the American approach, but also sees the field as including issues of world-representation, reader interpretation and evaluation, and other concerns that are traditionally literary, such as in narratology and reception theory. As the field develops, the contact and familiarity of these two camps will no doubt increase. It is interesting to note that in those parts of the world where European and American influence is felt (especially in the Far East), a rich blend of cognitive poetic practice is apparent.

In this book, I have tried to represent the field in as broadly conceived a way as possible. Each chapter takes a major theoretical feature from cognitive linguistics as its focus, and I first set out the key ideas and terms in outline. These cognitive linguistic concepts are related to the literary context in order to produce a cognitive poetic emphasis, and to develop a clear sense of how the particular area of cognitive poetics can address major literary issues. I attempt throughout to blend key issues of literary reading (such as tone, literariness, character, narrative, metaphor, plot, and so on) with the cognitive model that best encompasses the feature.

In the next chapter, I use the basic cognitive phenomenon of figure and ground as an illuminating pattern that informs literary theory. Then Chapter 3 explores the usefulness of prototypes for the notion of categorisation of literary movements. Narrators, authors, readers, characters and poetic voice are the subjects of Chapter 4, understood through a cognitive twist on deixis. Cognitive grammar informs an evaluation of close stylistic analysis in the next chapter, and then Chapter 6 uses one of the early cognitive theories of scripts and schemas as a means of discussing literary expectations and genre. World theory has been highly influential in cognitive poetics, and Chapter 7 focuses on discourse worlds, possible worlds and mental spaces in terms of fictionality, reality and reference. Chapter 8 outlines the power of conceptual metaphor in the literary construction of value-systems, and Chapter 9 develops and extends this through the idea of parable. In Chapter 10 I return to the idea of world-theory to look at narrative structure and plot, and this is given a dynamic and procedural turn in Chapter 11, on the process of reading and tracking episodes and characters.

It should be noted throughout the book that I have presented each area of cognitive poetics within a clear and definite framework. Sometimes, this is reasonable where the approach coincides with the work of a single author or a set of colleagues working closely together. At times, however, I have had to decide how best and most accessibly to present an approach where there is disagreement or contention involved. Rather than confuse you by simultaneously introducing a concept and also calling it into question, I have outlined the ideas in as plain a way as possible. Where there are alternative views, I have tried to draw these out under application to literature. This practice, in any case, seems to me to capture the practical nature and value of cognitive poetics as an essentially *applied* form of exploration. In the further reading section at the end of each chapter, you will be able to track down for yourself the detail of the ideas presented.

The structure of each chapter is similar. First, there is a descriptive outline of a cognitive poetic framework. This is presented with a few examples to illustrate the key terms and ideas, and it is linked with the main literary concerns. Some questions for consideration and points for discussion follow this section. I have made these questions deliberately difficult or open-ended in order to generate as wide a discussion as possible. Then, in each chapter, I have written a new cognitive poetic analysis of a literary text to exemplify the discussion. These analyses are primarily for illustration and so cannot be as detailed as they might be given a lot more space. For more detailed and intricate case-studies of cognitive poetic analysis, you should read *Cognitive Poetics in Practice* (edited by Joanna Gavins and Gerard Steen). Also published by Routledge, this is the companion book to *Cognitive Poetics*; it presents readings in cognitive poetics, all of which are new studies by a wide range of key figures, and the chapter headings correspond with the chapters in this book so that you can read them alongside each other. Finally, each of my chapters ends with suggestions for further study, or advice on following your own exploration, together with further reading in the specific area of the chapter to enable you to develop your knowledge of cognitive poetics.

I have tried to cover as wide a range of literary genres and historical periods as possible in the analyses. This seemed important to me if the textbook is to be usable across a range of literature. I also think that cognitive poetics is only worth anything if it is able to be addressed to more than just literary texts that seem amenable to it. The analyses presented in this book are exemplary, but we should also be tackling more difficult and challenging texts, the ones which do not fit easily into cognitive poetic theory. Those are the situations in which we will be forced to develop new frameworks for cognitive poetics, and it is these sorts of analyses that you will find in the companion book.

The last chapter of this book collects together more recent trends in the field, and speculates on the future directions of cognitive poetics. The glossarial index that follows will allow you to check quickly on key words and terms (which are emboldened on first mention in the text), and find cross-references and definitions in their context. Other technical terms appear in italics. My aim throughout is to encourage you to ask questions, engage with the ideas, and rediscover in your own thinking the excitement of connecting scientific principles with a love of literature.

This is one of the first textbooks in a new and emerging field. Some of the areas outlined in the following chapters will develop into major areas of research and exploration; some of the areas will seem less important in years to come. Here I am staking out the territory and sketching an early map for future explorers. My own feeling is that cognitive poetics offers a lifeline to everyone working in literary studies, and has the potential to make the discipline and the institution of literature more accessible and more connected with the world outside university and college life. It is all about reading literature, and it represents nothing less than the democratisation of literary study, and a new science of literature and reading. Cognitive poetics is rapidly developing its main strands of research and is in the process of maturing as a discipline, but at the moment it is possible to reach the edge of research very quickly in your study: everything is still provisional, new and exciting, filled more with potential than masses of study as yet. It is into that glad confident morning that this book takes its first steps.

2   Figures and grounds

Preview

Look at the two famous images below:

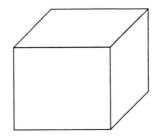

The image on the left can be seen either as a black vase on a white background, or as two human profiles facing each other against a dark background. The image on the right can be seen either as a box on the floor or as the top corner of a room where the walls meet the ceiling. In both cases, you can flip your perception from one view to the other, reversing the figure that you see with everything else that is in the background, but it is very difficult not to see one as *figure* and the rest as *ground*.

The notion of figure and ground is a basic and very powerful idea in cognitive linguistics, and it has been used to develop a detailed grammatical framework for close analysis, as well as very general and abstract ideas across whole discourses. This chapter outlines both of these applications: first in using the figure/ground idea as a means of understanding general literary critical concepts, and then as a means of exploring specific patterns in prepositions. I will also develop the connected idea of *attention* in order finally to present an analysis of literature: a poem by Ted Hughes.

Links with literary critical concepts

Deviance, devices, the dominant, defamiliarisation,
foregrounding, imagery, literariness, literary competence, style

The most obvious correspondence of the phenomenon of figure and ground is in the literary critical notion of **foregrounding**. Certain aspects of literary texts are commonly seen as being more important or salient than others. Though this is partly a subjective matter, it is also largely a matter of the cues that the text provides. For example, the opening to Charles Dickens' novel *David Copperfield* contains masses of information of the circumstances of the main character's birth, including what became of his infant shawl, how much it cost and who bought it. All of this information remains in the background by never being mentioned again, while the central plot-advancing elements of Copperfield's life are foregrounded by several **devices**: placed as a topic in the chapter heading ('I am born'), and repeated several times throughout the passage.

More generally, the literary innovations and creative expression can be seen as foregrounding against the background of everyday non-literary language. In this view, one of the main functions of literature is to **defamiliarise** the subject-matter, to estrange the reader from aspects of the world in order to present the world in a creative and newly figured way. This can even be seen as a means of identifying *literariness*, though of course this is a slippery notion since many non-literary uses of language contain creative and striking elements too.

Foregrounding within the text can be achieved by a variety of devices, such as repetition, unusual naming, innovative descriptions, creative syntactic ordering, puns, rhyme, alliteration, metrical emphasis, the use of creative metaphor, and so on. All of these can be seen as *deviations* from the expected or ordinary use of language that draw attention to an element, foregrounding it against the relief of the rest of the features of the text. **Deviance** has also been seen to be one of the important elements in literariness, or at least in literary value.

The feature that is determined to be the organising element, or seems most striking in the text, has been called the **dominant**. The dominant – though obviously having a subjective aspect – is a formal feature of the text: it could be the fourteen lines and metrical pattern that determine the sonnet form, or the alliteration of Anglo-Saxon poetry, or the imagism evident in the poetry of T.S. Eliot, or the inescapable absurd situations in *Catch-22*, or even the silences in the plays of Harold Pinter. The dominant is a sort of 'super-foregrounded' figure, around which the rest of the literary text is dynamically organised.

The relationship between the formal devices in the text and the part of the experience that strikes you most strongly lies in the description of figure and ground. This is a dynamic process because elements of the text are thrown into relief in the course of reading or 'actualising' the text. The devices are available for stylistic description and analysis, so the processes of 'figuring' and 'grounding' as you read the text can be tracked quite precisely as they emerge.

Figure and ground

The initial observations of figure and ground were made by gestalt psychologists in the early twentieth century. If we did not have the facility for creating a difference between figure and ground, then we would only be able to perceive a 'flat' field of interlocking shapes and colours in our environment. However, we see, hear and move in stereo three dimensions, and so the cognitive capacity for making figure and ground is clearly and literally an embodiment of this human condition. Furthermore, since figure and ground are differentiated on the basis of traits or features that we perceive in the objects in view, our orientation in the world fundamentally depends on our ability to perceive *style* and stylistic differences in objects. Figure and ground are therefore the basic features of literary stylistic analysis too.

The part of a visual field or textual field that is most likely to be seen as the figure will have one or more of the following features that make it prominent:

- it will be regarded as a self-contained object or feature in its own right, with well-defined edges separating it from the ground;
- it will be moving in relation to the static ground;
- it will precede the ground in time or space;
- it will be a part of the ground that has broken away, or emerges to become the figure;
- it will be more detailed, better focused, brighter, or more attractive than the rest of the field;
- it will be on top of, or in front of, or above, or larger than the rest of the field that is then the ground.

All of these different stylistic traits confer **prominence** on the figure that differentiates it from the ground. All of these have been confirmed by experimental results on visual fields, but they all have correspondences in the linguistic field of literary texts.

In most narrative fiction, for example, characters are figures against the ground of their settings. They have boundaries summarised by their proper names ('Beowulf', 'Hamlet', 'Winnie the Pooh'), and they carry along or evolve specific psychological and personal traits. Stylistically they are likely to be the focus of the narrative, moving through different settings, and are likely to be associated with certain verbs of wilful action by contrast with the attributive or existential sorts of verbs used descriptively for the background. Occasionally, the setting can thematically become the figure, emerging out of the background to assume a figure status in the text: Mars in Ray Bradbury's *The Martian Chronicles* or Egdon Heath in Thomas Hardy's *The Return of the Native* achieve prominence and come to be seen as character 'figures' by some readers.

Alternatively, dominant features of style are seen more easily as figures when they are identified, labelled and patterned within a rigorous stylistic analysis. The set-piece songs in Hollywood musicals or the concert-piece arias in operas are obviously stylistically set apart from the ground of the rest of the speaking part or libretto, achieving prominence as a result. The first-person narrations of Vladimir Nabokov's *Lolita* or F. Scott Fitzgerald's *The Great Gatsby* are stylistic factors that are strong elements in the success of those novels. Particular patterns of point of view and focalisation have been used by stylisticians to explore the texture of James Joyce's *Ulysses* or Samuel Beckett's *Molloy*. In these cases, the technical stylistic analysis has led the critics to an awareness of prominent and 'figured' features in the texts.

Characters are also figures because they move across the ground, either spatially or temporally as the novel progresses, or qualitatively as they evolve and collect traits from their apparent psychological development. Movement tends to be stylistically represented through verbs of motion and through locative expressions using prepositions ('over', 'through', 'under', 'from', 'up', 'down', 'into' and so on). In cognitive linguistics, locative expressions of place (and, metaphorically, time) are understood as **image schemas.**

Image schemas are mental pictures that we use as basic templates for understanding situations that occur commonly. We build up image schemas in our minds, and we tend to share particular image schemas with the community in which we live, on the basis of our local bodily interaction with the world. Like figure and ground and many other concepts in cognitive linguistics, image schemas are embodied: we have a physical and material picture of image schemas such as JOURNEY, CONTAINER, CONDUIT, UP/DOWN, FRONT/BACK, OVER/UNDER, INTO/OUT OF, and others (image schemas are conventionally written in small capitals like this).

Locative expressions, such as in the following literary titles, are expressed with prepositions that can be understood as image schemas: 'Sailing to Byzantium' (W.B. Yeats), *The Man in the High Castle* (Philip K. Dick), *One Flew over the Cuckoo's Nest* (Ken Kesey), *Out of Africa* (Isaak Dinesen/Karen Blixen), 'Under Milk Wood' (Dylan Thomas), *Behind the Scenes at the Museum* (Kate Atkinson), *The Voyage Out* (Virginia Woolf), *Love in a Cold Climate* (Nancy Mitford). The image schemas underlying these prepositions all involve a dynamic movement, or at least a final resting position resulting from a movement ('in the High Castle', 'Behind the Scenes'). For example, the title of Kesey's novel has a moving figure ('One') which can be pictured as moving from a position to the left of the ground ('the Cuckoo's Nest'), to a position above it, to end up at a position to the right of it. In this OVER image schema, the moving figure can be seen to follow a **path** above the ground. Within the image schema, though, the element that is the figure is called the **trajector** and the element it has a grounded relationship with is called the **landmark.**

Trajectors on paths in relation to landmarks are the general elements in image schemas. They represent a general and abstract conceptual structure which underlies all actual textual manifestations of the image schema. In other words, all 'over'-type locative expressions are like each other (and they are conceptually like 'in'- and 'out'-type image schemas too). Our image schemas have variations known as elaborations. For example, the following literary uses of 'over' represent different paths taken by the trajector in relation to the landmark:

> Over hill, over dale,
> Thorough bush, thorough briar,
> Over park, over pale,
> Thorough flood, thorough fire,
> I do wander everywhere
> > (*A Midsummer Night's Dream,* William Shakespeare)

> Trajector (I, the speaker Puck) takes a path flying above the landmark (hill, dale, park, pale).

> Underground, overground, wombling free,
> The Wombles of Wimbledon Common are we
> > (*The Wombles,* BBC children's programme theme music)

> Trajector (we Wombles) comes to be in contact with the landmark (the ground).

> I am going to turn over a new life and am going to be a very good little girl
> > (*Journal,* Marjory Fleming)

> Trajector (my new life) covers and replaces the landmark (existing life).

> Thine azure sister of the spring shall blow
> Her clarion o'er the dreaming earth
> > ('Ode to the West Wind', Percy Bysshe Shelley)

> Trajector (from clarion blast) covers and pierces the landmark (earth).

> And saw in sleep old palaces and towers
> Quivering within the wave's intenser day,
> All overgrown with azure moss and flowers
> > ('Ode to the West Wind', Percy Bysshe Shelley)

> Trajector (moss and flowers) ends up covering and enveloping the landmark (palaces).

> That's the wise thrush; he sings each song twice over
> > ('Home-Thoughts, from Abroad', Robert Browning)

> The original trajector (singing the song) becomes the landmark replaced by a new trajector (the song sung again).

> it gets run over by a van
> > ('Your Dog Dies', Raymond Carver)

> The trajector (van) crushes the landmark (your dog).

In each case, the image schema is basically the same, but the elaboration is specified in slightly different ways. It is in the elegant and subtle variations of these elaborations that the literary expressions of commonly understood image schemas are interestingly and poetically varied. The creative elaboration of image schemas can be seen as the striking or unsettling re-cognition of familiar patterns: that is, defamiliarisation.

Attention

The counterpart of the prominence of a linguistic feature is the readerly **attention** that it attracts. Reading a literary text is a dynamic experience, involving a process of renewing attention to create and follow the relations between figure and ground. Cognitive psychology has discerned several different facets of attention that are useful in considering literary reading.

Attention is *selective* rather than an undiscriminating blanket phenomenon. Certain elements in a visual field are selected for attention, and these will typically be the elements that are regarded as figures. This means that the ground of a visual field is deselected, or characterised by **neglect**. Cognitive psychologists have used the metaphor of the 'spotlight' as a means of understanding the focus of attention. Whatever is in the spotlight at a certain moment will receive all the interest and processing focus of the viewer or reader: all the expectations based on prior experience with that attended figure will be cued up and ready in order to follow the activity of the figure.

In cognitive psychological theory, five general issues have been proposed as a means of exploring attention in the visual field. These can also be applied to the literary context of cognitive poetics:

- how is space represented?
- what is an object?
- what determines the shape of the spotlight?
- how does selection occur within the focus of attention?
- how does selection between objects occur?

These questions have correspondences in literary reading that will emerge throughout this section. A literary text uses stylistic patterns to focus attention on a particular feature, within the textual space. The precise nature of these patterns will vary according to circumstances, but attention will only be maintained by a constant renewal of the stylistic interest, by a constant process of renewing the figure and ground relationship. This is because attention is typically caught by movement (in the visual field); in fact, elements in view that remain static are swiftly lost to attention. In textual terms, this means that 'newness' is the key to attention: literature is literally a *distraction* that pulls attention away from one element onto the newly presented element. I will call these objects or devices **attractors** in this context.

The loss of attention to static or unchanging elements is known as the

inhibition of return. Attention is focused on an object – which is typically a character in a fictional narrative or a building or other setting in a lyrical poem, for example – and attention follows that object if it moves (that is, as the text develops). In the visual field, perceptual grouping attracts attention more effectively than locational grouping: objects (figures) are more attractive than backgrounds. Attention does not remain tied to the original location, since it seems that our cognitive faculty has already tagged the information there and is on the lookout for new stimuli. In other words, attention is paid to objects which are presented in topic position (first) in sentences, or have focus, emphasis, focalisation or viewpoint attached to them. Objects can be bundles of features, as long as they are perceived as composing a unified thing, such as a character, or a theme, or a place, or the continuity offered by an action such as a chase or a puzzle.

But what about when there is a rich complex of potentially interesting objects vying for attention? Then the 'spotlight' moves depending on which object is the most interesting: textually, which is placed in the most focus, or has the majority of text-space allocated to it, or is expressed with the most noticeably deviant words or phrases. I would like to suggest that inhibition of return is overcome in this way primarily by action, by clear and explicit character development, and by strikingly deviant style. These aspects also seem to be in balance with one another. We pay attention to characters (objects) rather than their locations, because we want to track their apparently changing experience. A character that does not develop at all is, in effect, a static object and our natural inhibition of return is likely to mean that we lose interest in this boring character. One way that texts can compensate for this is by increasing the newness of one of the other primary factors: in science fiction, for example, undeveloped characterisation (the 'everyman' token) is typically counterbalanced by a distracting emphasis on thrilling action; in lyricism, neglect caused by lack of action or characterisation is mitigated by stylistic inventiveness; in many contemporary 'literary' novels, the fact that nothing much happens is compensated by attention to intricate and subtle characterisation or style.

Where our attention is divided (typically by a complex literary text with several interesting characters, themes and a blend of stylistic features), there are various ways of understanding which parts we find most interesting. We tend to neglect features where there is *redundancy* – that is, where the element is stereotypical and expected – in order to focus attention on features that are new to us. Also, as part of our social and literary experience, we have learnt to privilege some patterns over others. As a simple test of this, you could use a red pen to write the word 'green' on a piece of paper. Then ask a friend to say what colour the ink is, and show them the paper. Answering quickly, they will almost always say 'green' rather than 'red', because in this case the processing of the word is more prominent than the colour. In literary reading, we are similarly conditioned to regard certain patterns as being more worthy of literary attention than others.

This suggests that attentiveness is partly a matter of experiential learning and, with certain patterns, is a skill. In the past, the acquired skill of recognising conventions in literary reading has been called **literary competence**. Just as we become accustomed to things that we once found difficult (like riding a bicycle, driving a car, playing a computer game, reading) without paying much attention now, so we tend to lose interest in 'formula' literature that seems simply to repeat patterns that we have seen previously. This **automaticity** in cognitive psychology is the counterpart of the sense of 'automatisation' that the Russian Formalists thought that literary defamiliarisation (or de-automatisation) addressed.

So far I have been locating attention mainly in the attractiveness of text features; however, we can also exercise deliberate *control* over the attention that we pay. It takes an effort of will to focus attention on the ground, for example, 'reconfiguring' it as the figure and the object of interest. Nevertheless, this is the sort of thing professional critics or trained students do within the disciplinary parameters of literary study. Deliberately repositioning attention produces new (and thus interesting) readings. Professional literary readers do not require as much distraction, being able to focus attention to be satisfied with subtle complexity beyond the primary distractions of action, character and style. Minute features of textuality can then become the object of attention, interest and discussion.

Discussion

Before you proceed to my analysis below, you might like to have a discussion of the effects these ideas have on your own conception of the literary context. You could begin by considering the following questions:

- Do you agree that the main function of literature is its power to defamiliarise? Think of examples of texts that do this, and also try to think of examples where this feature is not an issue. Are the latter somehow less literary?
- Consider the subjective nature of perceiving figure and ground, and paying attention. Can you list the ways in which a text might encourage or 'cue' particular patterns of attention and inhibit others?
- How far do you think your literary training up to now has altered your capacity for attention?
- How might you apply the ideas above in a close stylistic analysis of literature? Choose a poem, for example, in which the topic and setting, or the location, or the prepositional structure seem important, and examine the poem in terms of figure and ground. What other binary patterns might be amenable to being perceived as figure and ground?

Cognitive poetic analysis

The following poem is by Ted Hughes, from the collection *Elmet* (1994), the name for an area of West Yorkshire which was the last Celtic kingdom in England.

Hill-stone was content

To be cut, to be carted
And fixed in its new place.

It let itself be conscripted
Into mills. And it stayed in position
Defending this slavery against all.

It forgot its wild roots
Its earth-song
In cement and the drum-song of looms.

And inside the mills mankind
With bodies that came and went
Stayed in position, fixed like the stones
Trembling in the song of the looms.

And they too became four-cornered, stony

In their long, darkening, dwindling stand
Against the guerrilla patience
Of the soft hill water.

Like all cognitive poetic analyses, the discussion that follows is a matter both of textual patterns and an interpretation, which in this case is mine. My attention is caught first of all by a variety of attractors, primarily the personification of 'Hill-stone' in the title which runs over into the first stanza. The usual pattern of a human figure against a hill-stone moorland ground is reversed by this. The personification is effected in the usual way by attaching a human predicate ('was content') to the inanimate noun ('hill-stone'). However, this personification creates a paradoxical balance in foregrounding the passivity of the stone ('content') using an active verb-form, against the activity of the humans embedded as the unnamed agents in passive grammatical form ('to be cut, to be carted / And fixed'). Right from the beginning, a pattern of reversal of expectations is being set up.

Second, my attention is caught by another stylistically deviant feature: the presence of several striking phrasal metaphors ('wild roots', 'earth-song', 'drum-song of looms', 'guerrilla patience'). Attempting to assimilate these into my reading so far, I can place them as part of the figure that is personification and reversal: they animate the stone as a plant with roots, or as being capable of singing; they attribute singing similarly to the looms; and they give intentions to the 'soft hill water'.

Having noticed the part played by the active and passive grammar, I am also encouraged to attend to the syntactic structure of the sentences in relation to the stanzas. Brought out of the title, the first sentence is constrained within the limits of the first stanza (which I treat altogether as three lines). The second stanza exactly fits in two fairly short sentences, again of three lines. The third stanza is composed entirely of a single sentence, of three lines once more. In all of these tightly contained sentences, the hill-stone is the topic and focus, placed as the figure against which the unnamed humans, the landscape and the mills are all left as the ground.

After that, though, the sentences become longer (the last two sentences fill almost half the poem) and the syntax moves noticeably away from everyday patterns. The main clause amounts to 'Mankind stayed in position', but this is broken up with several adjuncts composed mainly of prepositional phrases. The syntax of this four-line stanza leaves the referent of 'they' (in 'And they too became four-cornered') ambiguous. The automatic and primary reading is probably that 'they' means 'mankind'. However, several of the preceding nouns are available for co-reference, and I can focus my attention on any of them: 'the mills', 'mankind', 'bodies', 'the song of the looms', or 'the looms'. Each of these offers a different general reading, placing in turn industrialisation, or dehumanisation, or the continuity of history, or industrial decay, or the continuity of landscape and people, as the thematic figure against the ground of the other, neglected, readings. The final sentence is broken over a stanza break, and is extended by a lengthy adjunct packed with adjectives, which makes the reading slow down and run on over the edges of the lines to the water at the end.

In all of this, the reversals that are composed of several attracting devices are based on figure and ground transpositions. The hill-stone is the initial figure, literally cut out of its ground and moved away. The human activity at this point remains part of the ground. The violence ('cut') is presented as military discipline ('conscripted', 'in position', 'defending', 'drum-song', 'guerrilla') with, to my mind, a strong association with social class hierarchy ('in its … place', 'slavery'). These facets of industrialising human societies are brought out of the ground and attached to the figure of the hill-stone. The human/stone figure-ground reversal is complete as the animate stone moves towards the unnamed and almost inanimate workers, to the point where what is a simile ('like the stones') shifts into a transformed identity ('And they too became four cornered, stony').

At the end of this section, I will return to consider the figure–ground reversal of the final stanza, but for now, I am going to focus attention on the prepositions, which for me represent the dominant in the text. There are numerous structures featuring prepositions throughout the poem:

fixed *in* its new place
conscripted *into* mills
stayed *in* position
defending this slavery *against* all
forgot … *in* cement and the drum-song *of* looms
inside the mills
with bodies
stayed *in* position
in the song *of* the looms
in their long … stand
against the guerrilla patience
of the soft hill water

What is immediately noticeable here is the large incidence of different elaborations of the basic INTO image schema. The dominant image schema across the poem is one of containment. In this conceptual structure, the trajector traces a path from an initial position outside the landmark to a final resting position in which the landmark contains the trajector. In general, this image schema underlies many concepts involving not only movement but also transformation and identity. Essentially, the figure becomes part of the ground. In the poem, the particular expressions in which each trajector and landmark are realised are subtly important. The first two examples from the list above (varying 'in' and 'into') express the movement stage of the image schema, in which the hill-stone trajector is moving towards its landmark 'new place' in 'mills'. The next two INTO examples express the final static part of the image schema, when the hill-stone trajector rests 'in position' 'in cement'. So solidly has this figure become identical with the ground, that the next preposition ('inside the mills') has the hill-stone already part of the factory ground, with 'mankind' now acting as the new trajector. This is reinforced by the repetition of the same phrase ('stayed in position'), and the reversal of figure and ground is demonstrated in the fact that the trajector in each occurrence of these identical phrases has changed (hill-stone to mankind).

The final INTO example ('In their long, darkening, dwindling stand') has the static (and military and wearying) 'stand' as landmark. The trajector could be either 'mankind' or 'the stones'. Because of the ambiguous reference illustrated above, and because of the reversal and identification of hill-stone and mankind, by this point figure and ground, stone and man, have merged as a single, fused, identical trajector. A point about people, landscape, roots and industry, and the hardness of hierarchy and work has been powerfully made. However, in the last few lines, the poem delivers what is its wonderful final reversal.

A different image schema, AGAINST, has already been placed into the poem. In general, the trajector traces a path up to the landmark, finishing adjacent to it and blocking it. Earlier in the poem, the hill-stone trajector defended its slavery 'against all'. At this point in the poem, the landmark oppositional 'all' seems to consist of the unnamed masters who cut and carted the stone.

At the end of the poem, 'all' and the hill-stone have become identical: workers were no longer just 'like the stones' but 'became' stone. In the closing image schema expressed by the final 'Against', the two main figures in the poem are thrown into the ground, faced by the overwhelming and even more irresistible trajector figure of 'the soft hill water'. Human industry and landscape might borrow some of the hardness of the hills, but its true place in geological time is put firmly into perspective.

Of course, such an analysis as this does not remotely exhaust possible readings of the poem, not even just in a cognitive poetic approach. My analysis has been concerned to illustrate in particular the workings of figure and ground at both the thematic and close grammatical levels. But the poem itself is also a figure in the foreground of the collection, *Elmet*, in which it sits. Furthermore, I am conscious of the foregrounding of this collection and this poet against my own sense of English 'northern-ness'. No doubt some of the attention that I have given to the analysis has been informed by ideological and social experience, and that is partly conscious and controlled, part of my learned literary competence that is attracted to continuities between earth and work in a Northern industrial and moorland landscape. Factors such as this place the literary text as figure against the ground of readerly experience, and are part of the discussion as well.

Explorations

1   Write a short text that is highly defamiliarising. You could choose an object in the room or randomly in a dictionary as the topic of the text. The estrangement could be on the basis of a shift in viewpoint, perspective, language, time and history, ideology, and so on. When you have finished, trace the linguistic strategies you used, and compare them with other people's texts. Which are the most literary?

2   Find a love poem and trace the workings of figure and ground through as many patterns as you can find. How does your analysis support your initial interpretation or intuitive feeling about the poem?

3   Explore an anthology of literature for some examples of personification. How is this effected linguistically, and what is the cognitive role played by figure and ground in personification? Alternatively, you could look (for example in war literature) for examples of dehumanisation to see whether figure and ground were being manipulated differently.

4   Using a specific example of a piece of literary prose, list the ways in which a text can attract your attention to certain elements. How is neglect used in the text?

5   How do foregound and background, attention and neglect work in a dramatic production? Think about these categories in relation to characters, scene, on-stage and off-stage action, live action and reported action, speaking and silent characters, actors' parts and stage directions in the

text, and so on. You might also consider the different configurations offered by different types of staging of drama: in a traditional theatre, in the round, with audience participation, as a walk-around experience, as a cinema movie, as a television drama, and so on.

Further reading and references

The work of the gestalt psychologists is reviewed by Boring (1950) and represented by Beardslee and Wertheimer (1958). The cognitive linguistic work on figure and ground is introduced in Ungerer and Schmid (1996: 156–204); see also Haber and Hershenson (1980). For image schemas see the overviews by Lakoff (1987) and Johnson (1987), and Gibbs and Colston (1995). Langacker (1987, 1990, 1991) gives the detail of cognitive grammatical applications of all these notions.

Attention is surveyed in detail by Styles (1997); the five key questions are from Logan (1996, see also 1995), and the 'red/green' trick is called a Stroop test, after Stroop (1935); visual attention, selection and neglect can be found in Posner (1989), Baddeley and Weiskrantz (1993); see also Smyth, Collins, Morris and Levy (1994).

Defamiliarisation is a term (*ostranenie* = estrangement) used by the Russian Formalists: see Garvin (1964), Erlich (1965), Lemon and Reis (1965), Matejka and Pomorska (1971) for translated collections. The *dominant* is discussed by Roman Jakobson in the Matejka and Pomorska collection. On the modern application of the formalist notion of foregrounding (*aktualisace* = actualisation) to literature, see van Peer (1986) and Short (1996). The idea of literary competence was introduced by Culler (1975). Carter and Nash (1990) and Carter (1997) revisit the notion of literariness using modern linguistics.

3 Prototypes and reading

Preview

One of the most radical areas of thought affected by cognitive science has concerned the fundamental issue of categorisation. The way that we divide the world up and name it to ourselves determines what we think the world is, and, even more importantly, how we think that we think at all. Suggesting a new understanding of categorisation is therefore not a trivial undertaking. What cognitive science proposes is not simply a different pattern for categorising mind, body, language and thought, but a revolutionary re-cognition of the notion of categorisation itself.

The traditional dominant view in western philosophy has regarded reason as a product exclusively of the mind, and the rational mind has been treated as being separate from the material body. Cognitive science calls this distinction into question, arguing, as I have pointed out already, that reason (as well as perception, emotion, belief and intuition) are literally **embodied** – inextricably founded in our bodily interaction and experience with the world. Our physical orientation as humans and our perception of common material processes were shown in the last chapter to be at the root of concepts such as figure and ground and image schemas.

In this chapter, I introduce the cognitive reconception of categorisation, and show how it has consequences for our perception of certain details of language in literary reading. I also demonstrate how recasting the notion of categories has implications for the ways in which literature itself is categorised, and I include an analysis of some literature in which boundaries and genre are an issue.

Links with literary critical concepts

Action, creativity, genre, influences and sources, intertextuality, literary history, mind-style, modes of writing, movements, open and closed texts, parody, periodisation, point of view, reading, reception

In the previous chapter I mentioned the twentieth-century issue of classifying literature and literary language as opposed to non-literary uses of language. Within literary study, the preoccupation with labelling and classifying different sub-groups of literature has been ongoing since ancient times. The most obvious way of grouping a body of texts is by their common author-ship, where a single person, or perhaps a small 'school' or well-defined group, is the source of the texts. In this case, phrases such as 'We're going to see some Shakespeare' or 'Have you got the latest Iain M. Banks?' make sense. We can even talk of **mind-style** as a means of categorising the partic-ular way in which an author tends to write. Where a self-defined group writes as part of a project, we can label them and talk of 'the Bloomsbury set', 'the metaphysicals', 'the surrealists', 'the beat poets' and so on.

Another easy way of classifying literature is simply by carving history up into periods such as 'the nineteenth-century novel', 'poetry of the 1930s', or by tying texts to political events: 'Restoration theatre', 'First World War poetry' and so on. It becomes more contentious when texts overlap the periodisation: should we call Spenser a late medieval writer or a Renaissance poet; Thomas Hardy lived till 1928 but we tend to think of him as a nine-teenth-century novelist; the poet Gerard Manley Hopkins died in 1889 but his poems were first published in 1918. The debates really begin when the lit-erary *movement* is based on a critically loose sense of common ideology or imaginative or political purpose or style: where are the boundaries of Romanticism, post-Romanticism, Modernism, post-Modernism, Imagism, Symbolism, Vorticism, Futurism, Absurdism?

The issue at stake here is **genre**. This word, meaning 'class' or 'kind', has been applied to several different levels of classification. It has been used simply to differentiate poetry, prose and drama (though I would call these **modes** of writing); or to refer to thematically grouped works such as comedy, tragedy, horror, romance. *Sub-genres* such as sonnets, ballads, slasher novels, bodice-rippers, capuccino fiction, and so on have been identified. The phrase 'genre fiction' has even been used, perhaps disparagingly, to cover formulaic exam-ples of science fiction, detective fiction, fantasy and so on.

From all of the examples given above, it is apparent that what counts as a genre and what gets included within a genre depends on what you think a genre is in general, and which common feature of its elements you have decided to foreground as being most salient. Genres can be defined socially, historically, functionally, authorially, politically, stylistically, arbitrarily, idiosyncratically, or by a combination of any of these. The rest of this chap-ter will present a means of understanding these sorts of choices.

Prototypes

Try this magic trick to amaze your friends. Folding a square of paper, write down the words 'apple' and 'orange' on each half. Then hide this, and ask the person next to you quickly to name you an example of a fruit. When they say either 'apple' or 'orange' (as they almost certainly will), you can produce the half of the paper with the same word on, taking care to keep your hand over the other word. This will fail only perhaps once out of every twenty times you try it.

The reason that almost everyone gives 'apple' or 'orange' as their first choice is because the category of fruit displays **prototype** effects. Moreover, these effects are a characteristic not just of the category of fruit but of the cognitive capacity for categorisation in general. Essentially, oranges and apples are very good, central examples of fruit. Ask people to give you a list of fruit, and they will come up with other good examples such as pears, bananas, lemons, limes (these two always seem to go together), peaches, plums, then strawberries, blackberries, gooseberries (and so on through the roll-call of berries), until you get to kiwi fruit, lychees, passion fruit, star fruit, and then debatable ones such as tomatoes, avocados, cucumbers, courgettes/zucchini – or maybe you have strong feelings about these?

It seems that our cognitive system for categorisation is not like an 'in or out' filing cabinet, but an arrangement of elements in a **radial** structure or network with **central** good examples, **secondary** poorer examples, and **peripheral** examples. The boundaries of the category are fuzzy rather than fixed. You can test this by considering which is more 'fruity': potatoes or cabbages? Both are obviously not good examples of fruit, but it is likely that you will be able to pick one of these, and even give reasons: cabbage, because it grows above the ground, and is commonly eaten raw; or potato, because it is round and self-contained, and is more fleshy than a cabbage, and so on.

Effects such as this have been observed in a range of experimental studies, especially focusing on how people classify elements at the fuzzy boundaries of categories: where flat cups blend into high-sided bowls, or low chairs become small tables, or bluey-green becomes greeny-blue. It is important to remember that we cannot say that an apple is the protype of a fruit, since, as we will see below, centrality and peripherality judgements are not always fixed, and in any case behavioural patterns cannot always be seen as being a direct mirror of mental structures. Nevertheless, we can say that *prototypicality* is the basis of categorisation, with central examples acting as **cognitive reference points** in the middle of a radial structure.

You can try these effects on a range of other categories: furniture, road vehicles, emotions, garden plants, birds, rock music, holiday destinations, Romantic poets, and many others. Of course, these categories are to some extent conventional and you can appeal to 'expert' authority by consulting a furniture store catalogue, transport legal statute, psychological text, horticultural directory, ornithological manual and so on. Such 'scientific' classifications, however, even those that appear to be based on 'natural kinds', are still representational conceptual systems with ideological parameters in the determination of the prototype structure. All concepts, even ones that seem exclusive binary choices, can display prototype effects under the right circumstances, indicating that what is accepted as a 'true' picture of the world is as much a matter of representation as everything else.

Items that display prototypicality within a structure can be seen to be **chained** through the notion of radiality. Within the category of furniture, a kitchen chair shares some of the **attributes** of a stool and an armchair, but also shares features (either inherent or functional) with a settee/sofa/couch, a chaise-longue, a park-bench, a dentist's chair, an aeroplane seat, a beanbag, a bicycle saddle and so on. A dining table is chained with a coffee table, a sideboard, a dresser for plates, a dressing table with a mirror, a worktop, a foldaway picnic table, a gambling table and so on. There is not much similarity between a bike saddle and a dressing table, but they are part of the same category through a series of chain links. These links offer a **family resemblance** that explains how two apparently dissimilar items can nevertheless belong to the same genre. John Webster's *The White Devil* (1612) and Alfred Hitchcock's *The Birds* (1963) share generic features of drama and horror, and there are similar generic connections through science fiction across such dissimilar texts as Thomas More's *Utopia* (1516), Mary Shelley's *Frankenstein* (1818), H.G. Wells' *The Time Machine* (1895), and Kim Stanley Robinson's *Red Mars* (1992). Literary critical viewpoints can be revised by seeing certain generic attributes as more or less prominent.

Even categories that are not familiar or fixed like those above seem to display prototypicality. Faced with categories such as 'things to take from one's home during a fire', or 'what to get for a birthday present', or 'what to do for entertainment on a weekend', people still have a sense of central items and less good examples in these cases. Here, it seems that general conceptual **goals** are used to determine the prototype structure and come to a decision that appears rational and defensible. It seems that part of our literary competence at recognising conventional genres is also an advanced ability to discern new genres in, or attach new texts to, our understanding of different genres.

Of course, prototypicality can also be applied to categories of language. Cognitive linguists have noticed that a prototypical subject acts as both topic and agent. Taking, for example, the opening of the Ted Hughes' poem from the last chapter,

Hill-stone was content to be cut, to be carted and fixed in its new place,

the subject 'hill-stone' here is not prototypical (in some grammars it is not even called a subject) since although it is the topic, it is not the agent of the action. The agents here are omitted by Hughes using the passive form. Consider how different it would have been if the sentence had been followed with: 'by the mill-builders'. Or how the poem would fall apart if it had begun prototypically:

The mill-builders cut, carted and fixed the contented hill-stone in its new place.

Prototypicality in clause structure thus allows us a means of identifying and measuring stylistic *deviance*, parallelism and adherence to discoursal norms.

Categories

The categories set out above display prototypicality structure on the basis of our **experience** and the *embodiment* of conceptual patterns. Structures with very strong or definite arrangements tend to be the basic, human-scale features with which we are most familiar. It seems that we think in terms of **basic level categories**. For example, 'dog' is ordinarily regarded as a basic level category, rather than 'poodle', 'collie', 'beagle', which are seen as subtypes, or even 'border collie', 'Welsh collie', and 'long-haired collie'. This accounts for why certain word-choices seem appropriate or not in context: 'I'll take the dog for a walk' is usual; 'I'll take the terrier for a walk' would sound strange unless it was being used to single out one dog among many; 'I'll take the mammal out for a walk' would be humorous or facetious. The **context dependency** involved here demonstrates that prototype effects and categorisation are not fixed but are socially and historically specified. The line from Webster, 'But keep the wolf far thence that's foe to men' (*The White Devil*, 1612) is altered by T.S. Eliot to, 'O keep the Dog far hence that's friend to men' (*The Waste Land*, 1922) in the middle of a twentieth-century city setting.

The basic level tends to be the level at which we most commonly interact on a human scale with the category. We distinguish basic level objects at the point where they seem to have the most discontinuities with other objects in the world. Terriers are not as different from collies as dogs are different from cats. The basic level is also where most of the attributes of a category are optimally available – we tend to have more of a sense of 'dogginess' than 'collie-ness' or 'mammal-ness'. These hierarchies of superordinacy and subordinacy are what allow us to use and recognise **over-** and **under-specificity**. Over-specificity is a common means of expressing sarcasm and ridicule: 'What's the weather like? – Two centimetres of rainfall over a 6 hour period with atmospheric pressure of 998 millibars falling to a low of 980'. Under-specificity conveys evasiveness, obstructiveness or plain rudeness in characters' speech: for example, at a dog-show, 'What's that over there? – A dog'.

Recognising categories seems to be a two-stage process, involving a *holistic* perception of the category as an object (a 'gestalt' whole) followed, if necessary, by an analytical **decomposition** of the object into separate chained subtypes or attributes. These stages can be seen as analogous to the process of the literary reading experience. A recognition of the literary text in its entirety is an act of **interpretation** – a holistic understanding of the literary work that begins in our culture even before we begin to read the actual text. This act of interpretation, or primary understanding, is what all readers do when encountering literature, when the experience is ongoing and as yet unexpressed. As soon as readers become aware of what they are doing, this more analytical stage of recognition can be differentiated as **reading**. Critical analysis and discussion is part of reading in this sense. It is at the stage of reading that interpretations are rationalised and salient attributes picked out for attention and prominence.

In gestalt psychology, a discrete object is recognised on the basis of five principles:

- principle of proximity;
- principle of similarity;
- principle of closure;
- principle of continuation;
- principle of functionality.

In the visual field, this means that something is likely to be regarded as a unified object if its elements are close together, similar to each other, differentiated from surrounding non-category elements by a perception of closed boundaries, seen to be related to each other without many disjunctions, and seen to share a role or single function. Try this first with the objects 'dog', 'book', 'chair', 'rose'; and then 'democracy', 'happiness', 'friendship'; and now 'nineteenth-century literature', 'gothic novels', '*Dracula*'.

The first few of these objects are fairly easy to interpret as coherent wholes, read off into their composite attributes which can then be related according to the five principles above. Where there is likely to be little disagreement over the analysis of the first group, you might find more debate over the middle group. Similarly, the literary group of objects can be read into many attributes largely depending on your familiarity with the concepts. Expert literary readers know about more attributes and so the potential for defining the objects in a variety of ways increases.

Of course, you might see some of these as **compound categories**. Typically, compounds are expressed with two or more words, such as 'wheel chair', or 'head waiter' or 'gothic novel'. In these cases, attributes are joined to produce a new unified object. However, the concepts underlying compounds are often more than the sum of the parts. None of these items could be understood simply by knowing the constituent words, and sometimes extra knowledge of the world is required to make sense of them. Similarly, when faced with a new term that is unfamiliar, we tend to guess at an understanding of the concept by borrowing attributes that appear to be close to it. Where the two elements are strikingly unrelated in existing understanding ('electric spiders' – Ray Bradbury; 'the heron-priested shore' – Dylan Thomas), there is a sort of 'leakage' of attributes between the source objects, and the object takes on many other attributes from other categories in being understood. Essentially what is constructed and drawn on here is no longer a simple object but a **conceptual model**, also called a **cognitive model**.

Cognitive models

Essentially, the image schemas that were outlined in the last chapter are a common and very powerful part of cognitive models. These are idealised and generalised patterns which find their manifestation or actualisation in a variety of linguistic expressions. **Idealised cognitive models** (ICMs) are the structures with which we organise our knowledge. Cognitive models consist of relations between categories, set up socially, culturally, and on the basis of individual experience, as our means of understanding and negotiating the world and our lives through it.

Cognitive models are what cause prototype effects and our sense of basic categories. They can consist of image schemas and propositional structure relating certain elements to others, and they can be enriched or reconfigured by the action of conceptual metaphor and metonymy (see Chapter 8). They are the basis of the way that cognitive science squares the circle between individual and social factors in language and thought.

The meanings of concepts do not lie wholly in the words that are used to express those concepts, but in cognitive models which are cued up by words and which add rich and complex understanding in a communicative situation. To take a famous example, 'bachelor' does not simply mean *an unmarried man*. It would be inappropriate to call the Pope, or other Catholic priests, or a widower, or a man in a long-term but unmarried partnership, or a teenage male a 'bachelor'. In order to agree that this is inappropriate, we must be applying other, socially rooted definitions and circumstances to our understanding of 'bachelor'. We know about the working practices of the Catholic church, and the social norms, addresses and politeness surrounding personal relationships, and the social ideology that regards 'bachelor' as a useful term. All of this knowledge is contained in a series of cognitive models which we employ when we use or understand the word 'bachelor'. Fundamentally, words (and semantics) cannot be reduced to logical or decontextualised or asocial or non-cognitive denotations.

Cognitive models which are shared become **cultural models**. These can be specified on the basis of *context dependency*, as introduced above. For example, I have found that the 'apple/orange' magic trick does not work in Singapore or with some of my Japanese students in Britain, where one of the first fruits mentioned was 'durian' – a spiky green fruit native to south-east Asia with an overpoweringly terrible smell. Similarly, elements in the categories of furniture, vehicles, breakfast foods, and so on, are likely to be radically differently arranged in their prototype structure.

Cultural models are shared by social groups, and so patterns of categorisation can vary not only by virtue of nationality and environment but also along the lines of common understanding or purposes. We can talk of the cultural model shared by an interpretative community – a group who can be said to share a similar way of understanding and reading. The cultural model displayed by my colleagues who are experts in Renaissance literature produces readings of Shakespeare that are radically different from those produced by cinema audiences or even by new students in the field. Expertness and authority are largely determined by this display of the cultural model patterns that are valued in the interpretative community in question. In one of my own experiments, I found that people who were more-experienced readers of science fiction tended to include more within the genre and to see science-fictional elements in things that others would classify as fantasy, horror, mythology, post-modernism, surrealism and so on. Inexperienced readers restricted their classification to monsters, flying saucers and rayguns.

We can see, then, that patterns in genre are socio-culturally based but nevertheless cognitive matters. In genre studies, a hierarchy has been suggested as follows:

mode	poetry, prose, drama, conversation, song ...
genre	comedy, tragedy, gothic, surrealism ...
sub-genre	mock-epic, comic opera, airport fiction, war novel, political memoir ...
type	sonnet, ballad, email, one-act play, short story ...
register	reporting language, letter-writing, narrative, lyricism ...

Applying prototype theory to this, 'mode' seems to be the basic level category, or (put the other way round) the categories that people tend to use most readily and which often consist of one-word descriptions are then seen as the basic genre level. I can imagine linguists and literary critics taking issue with this, and perhaps for them 'genre' is basic, but I would argue that the cultural models that they share as experts means that their judgement in this regard is non-normal.

Instead we can use the notion of **discourse communities** as a broadening of the idea of an interpretative community. A discourse community is a group that is defined in relation to their uses of language and texts, and of course this is a fluid matter as we shift from role to role in the course of our lives. I can read as an academic, but I can also read as a train-passenger, and in each place I belong to a different discourse community. How these communities define and use distinctions of genre is determined by their respective socio-cognitive cultural models.

Discussion

Before proceeding, you might like to have a discussion of the effects these ideas have on your own conception of literature and different sorts of literature. You might start with the following questions:

- What is a genre? Consider some literary genres and decide on what basis the texts that compose them are grouped together.
- Faced with a new text, how do you decide whether it counts as literature or not, and how do you decide to which genre it belongs? Can a single new text create a new genre? How far can you give detail to the ideas of literary competence, interpretative and discourse communities?
- Do you agree with the distinction made above between 'interpretation'

and 'reading'? How might these two aspects of the process of cognition be better expressed and how do they affect your ideas of what literary reading involves?
*   How might you distinguish the following closely related set of categories, in the light of a cognitive understanding of categorisation: *parody, travesty, pastiche, satire, spoof, imitation, allusion, intertextuality*?

Cognitive poetic analysis

The use of prototypicality as a means of specifying linguistic deviation was mentioned above: a prototypical subject acts as both topic and agent, and alternative clause-patterns represent a deviation away from this norm. This application can be extended to other linguistic realisations.

A 'fully formed' proposition in traditional grammar can be said to be **actualised** if it is expressed with all of the following linguistic features:

predication	must have a noun phrase and a verb phrase;
past tense and finite verb form	to locate a completed action or event;
positive polarity	since negatives do not make a claim about reality;
declarative mood	cannot be interrogative, imperative, exclamatory or moodless;
definite reference	indefinite reference ('a', 'some') cannot be verified.

So these sentences represent degrees of deviance, respectively:

'London. Michaelmas Term lately over, and the Lord Chancellor sitting in Lincoln's Inn Hall. Implacable November weather.'
(*Bleak House*, Charles Dickens) – no predicates.

'Philomel, with lullaby, lulla, lulla, lullaby'
(*A Midsummer Night's Dream*, William Shakespeare) – non-finite.

'I know not whether Laws be right,
Or whether Laws be wrong'
('The Ballad of Reading Gaol', Oscar Wilde) – not positive polarity.

'Look on my works, ye Mighty, and despair!'
('Ozymandias', Percy Bysshe Shelley) – an imperative.

'Someone must have been telling lies about Joseph K., for without his having done anything wrong he was arrested one fine morning.'
(*The Trial*, Franz Kafka) – not definite.

The list is an assertion about the degree to which a surface sentence can actualise a claim about the world, but we can also understand it cognitively as a way of seeing 'good' and 'less good' examples of 'fully formed' sentences: in other words, as a measure of stylistic deviance. The list constitutes a scale of the prototypicality of actualisation, with non-predication being most deviant, down to indefiniteness as less deviant. In each of the examples above, the deviance has a thematic or functional cause that you could identify by reading the entire text.

The following sentences are some distance away from prototypical sentences in this sense.

> Fog everywhere. Fog up the river, where it flows among green aits and meadows; fog down the river, where it rolls defiled among the tiers of shipping, and the waterside pollutions of a great (and dirty) city. Fog on the Essex Marshes, fog on the Kentish heights. Fog creeping into the cabooses of collier-brigs; fog lying out on the yards, and hovering in the rigging of great ships; fog drooping on the gunwhales of barges and small boats. Fog in the eyes and throats of ancient Greenwich pensioners, wheezing by the firesides of their wards; fog in the stem and bowl of the afternoon pipe of the wrathful skipper, down in his close cabin; fog cruelly pinching the toes and fingers of his shivering little 'prentice boy on deck. Chance people on the bridges peeping over the parapets into a nether sky of fog, with fog all round them, as if they were up in a balloon, and hanging in the misty clouds.
>
> (*Bleak House*, Charles Dickens)

These are relatively un-actualised. 'Fog everywhere' lacks predication, and thus necessarily lacks many of the other possible features in the list. Where there are some verb-forms later on ('creeping', 'lying', 'wheezing'), they are not cast in declarative form. There is even a case to be made and tested here for the cognitive effort involved. It is an easy matter for the reader to perceive the non-prototypical patterns as a theme to be communicated, concerning the overwhelming, stultifying and motionless nature of the fog. Neverthless, the text is reasonably open to *readerliness* in interpretation here; Dickens does not state the matter in clear asserted prototypically actualised propositions. In general, the less prototypical the style, the more potentially **open** the text is for readerly intervention and activity in interpretation. Writerly texts, which present prototypical expectations at every level, are more **closed** to readerly work. It is more open to the reader to generalise the fog's heavy oppressiveness onto the social and legal system in which the rest of the novel is set.

In the rest of this section I will discuss the general issues of genre where it is most flexible and uncertain, using an example of **parody**:

> Milkmen everywhere. Milkmen up the Avenue; milkmen down the Grove. Milkmen on the High St, where it winds between banks of shops stacked with plastic footwear and cut-price washing machines; milkmen in the alleys that meander past the dirty backyards of dormant pubs. Milkmen

rattling their bottles in areas and basements; milkmen wheedling incorrect sums from harassed housewives; milkmen with dejected horses; milkmen with electric floats, stuck at the traffic lights where the main road forks left past the grim grey majesty of the multi-storey car park.

(Nash 1985: 99)

This was produced in a seminar on composition; Nash calls it a 'pseudoparody', since it simply echoes some of the stylistic features of the original. It does not constitute a thorough stylistic **imitation** and it would be difficult to match the rhetorical effect with the Dickens. Likewise it is not close enough to the original to count as a **travesty**. It is perhaps closest to a **pastiche**.

All of these related terms from the critical literature on *parody* can be understood prototypically. The obvious 'best example' of the original (perhaps we should start saying 'originating text', or **originator**, as opposed to 'author') is the originating text. Nothing is closer to *Bleak House* than *Bleak House* itself. From that cognitive reference point we can discern less and less good examples through a prototype structure. In accordance with radiality, we can see some chained examples: an imitation is a better example of the originator than a **spoof**, and a spoof is closer to the originator than an *allusion*. We can also discern elements that can be delineated more easily in relation to the core than to each other: a parody and a **satire** might be equally distant from the originator, but sit in a complex relationship with each other.

Here is an example of a spoof, again from Bill Nash, which is in the form of a pastiche of a Middle English song, but which has subject matter that is impossible for a medieval writer.

Vakum clenere

Ha, vakum clenere, synge thi songe,
A luvsum laye hyt ys, I wene.
Wyth brethynges amorous and stronge
Thow makest mone a mornynge longe
Til al mi hows ys clene.
    Then welcum, welcum, vakum-wight
    That suckest uppe the mucke aright.

A serpente ys thi luvelie necke,
Thi bodie ys a litel bulle;
On duste thow dynest, manye a pecke,
Thow gobblest everie spotte and specke,
Til belye waxeth fulle.
    Then welcum, welcum, vakum-wight
    That suckest uppe the mucke aright.

Foteless thow farest thurgh mi halle,
Thow grazest on the grittie grownde,
And, grettest wondyrment of alle,
This tayle thow pluggest yn a walle,
Yf anye poynte be fownde.
   Then welcum, welcum, vakum-wight
   That suckest uppe the mucke aright.

A derksum closet ys thi den,
Wherin thow liggest stocke-stille
Til hit be Saterday, and then
Thow farest foorth, and alle men
Cryen, wyth gode wille,
   Ha, welcum, welcum, vakum-wight
   That suckest uppe the mucke aright.
                            (Nash 1992: 91–2)

Nash calls this 'Muddle English', and notes that many academic colleagues – especially medievalists – feel obliged to draw attention to the infelicities of Middle English grammar and spelling, and to note the lines that do not scan. In the cultural model of this discourse community, the poem is a travesty, with the anachronistic vacuum cleaner subject-matter revealing the bad intentions of the writer. For less-experienced readers, who are not aware of the technical inconsistencies, the poem is a funny spoof. Indeed, even if we were aware of the flaws, we would see them as evidence that the poem was intentionally parodic and non-serious. In each case, the same observed 'facts' can fit perfectly into different cultural models.

Most loosely in the prototype structure, we can see the notion of **inter-textuality** as the most distant element. Here, literary sources and influences are items in the attributes of the concept. The shadow of other texts becomes available to the reader as the text in hand is read, and clearly the scope of this perception is also a subjective and discourse communal matter too. The proximity of the text to the originator provides a measure of generic centrality and literary tradition. For example, tracing the features of prox-imity and similarity in the utopian and dystopian science fiction of the 1970s can illuminate their links with Thomas More's original *Utopia*. Engaging in this sort of analysis can also help you to draw out distinctions between true utopias, dystopias, and complex hybrid forms which have been called 'heterotopias' or 'critical utopias'. In this way, prototypicality could also give us a means of understanding genre-distinctions, and a stylistic means of analysing the prototypical distance in intertextuality.

Finally, faced with a new text that cannot easily be placed into any of our existing cognitive models of genre-types, we use a cognitive *goal* as a means of resolving the issue. Russell Hoban's *Riddley Walker* is written in a dialect that echoes Middle English, but also archaic rural accents of south-east England:

On my naming day when I come 12 I gone front spear and kilt a wyld boar
he parbly ben the las wyld pig on the Bundel Downs any how there hadnt
ben none for a long time befor him nor I aint looking to see none agen.

(Hoban 1982: 1)

Here we might have a goal of understanding the novel in order to write an
analysis of it, or making sense of the style in order to get to the end of it, or
simply resolving the deviance so we can enjoy it more. We pick out attributes
to support strategies in achieving these goals: in my own case, I place the
novel as science fiction, in the sub-genre of post-apocalyptic SF. It is set in the
future, in a landscape and society broken by nuclear war. However, my
cognitive model of the sub-genre is altered and widened to include the attributes brought by this novel, unlike any other I have previously read. The
process of reinforcing and refining our cultural models through reading is the
process of increasing our literary competence.

Explorations

1 Prototype patterns could be applied to any graded scale in language or
   literary study. How might you adapt cognitive linguistics to the following?

   - the apparently binary notion of figure and ground
   - degrees of perceived politeness (see Brown and Levinson 1987)
   - types of speech and thought presentation in fiction (see Leech and
     Short 1981)
   - types of point of view and 'involvement' in the narrative (see
     Simpson 1993)
   - distinctions between central and marginal characters in novels (see
     Culpeper 2001).

2 Investigate the conceptual models underlying genre decisions in:

   - an academic publisher's catalogue (available in paper or on the web)
   - the arrangement of shelves in your local bookshop
   - the course structure and module/seminar divisions in your college
   - a published history of literature.

3 Think of one of the genres contained in any of the places listed in (2), and
   decide what, for you, are the central attributes and the peripheral attributes of the genre. Compare your thinking with other people's ideas.

4 Write down a list of genres on pieces of paper. Take a famous literary
   text that is well-known to you, and then pick a piece of paper randomly.
   You must then find a way of re-cognising the text so that you can argue it
   is 'actually' an example of the genre. You might, for example, have to
   argue that *Dracula* is primarily a detective story, or *To The Lighthouse*
   is a thriller. Trying this with a list of sub-genres is even more challenging:

Mansfield Park as a gardening manual, *The Canterbury Tales* as a tourist guide (and see the final section of Carter and Nash (1990) for many more examples). Examine the processes that you have to go through, and see if any of your random arguments turn out to generate new literary critical insights.

5   Find a text which is obviously deviant in some linguistic way. Try to produce a detailed analysis of the language that uses insights from cognitive poetics to account for the meaning and impact of the literary text.

Further reading and references

Prototype theory was developed by Rosch (1975, 1977, 1978, summarised and reviewed 1988), by Rosch and Mervis (1975), Mervis and Rosch (1981), Rosch, Mervis, Gray, Johnson and Boyes-Braem (1976) and in Rosch and Lloyd (1978). It is most easily accessible through Lakoff (1987: 5–153), Ungerer and Schmid (1996: 1–113), and Taylor (1995). Family resemblance is discussed by Wittgenstein (1958); ICMs in Lakoff (1987: 68–76); new categories and goals also in Lakoff (1987: 45–6) and Barsalou (1983, and context-dependency 1982). The 'bachelor' example is in Fillmore (1982); see also Sweetser (1990).

The notion of mind-style comes from Fowler (1977, 1996). The use of prototypes in linguistic categories is addressed by Lakoff (1987: 64–7), citing Bates and MacWhinney (1982), and Van Oosten (1984). I took the list of 'actualisations' of propositions from Leech (1981: 154–6). My SF experiment is in Stockwell (2000a), where there is also an analysis of the extended *Riddley Walker* passage. I develop the interpretation/reading distinction from Gadamer (1989; see also Hoy 1997 and Warnke 1987) and Ingarden (1973a, 1973b), and use it to address Fish's (1980) notion of interpretative communities. Open, closed, writerly and readerly texts come from Eco (1981) and Barthes (1977). Swales (1988, 1990) describes discourse communities and writes on genre; see also McCarthy and Carter (1994) and Bex (1996) for an overview.

For discussions of parody and its variants, see Nash (1985, 1992), Kuester (1992: 3–23), Simpson (2002) and the papers in Müller (1997). The classic discussions are in Bakhtin (1984), Hutcheon (1985), Rose (1993), and recently Genette (1995, 1997a, 1997b).

4 Cognitive deixis

Preview

When people talk about the experience of reading literature, they describe the feeling of being immersed in the world of the text, relating to characters, scenes and ideas in a way that happens rarely in non-literary reading. It seems as if a threshold is crossed and readers can project their minds into the other world, find their way around there, and fill out the rich detail between the words of the text on the basis of real life experience and knowledge.

Such a projection involves a means of understanding how closely word choices are tied to context. If *you* were to say, 'I am here now', it would mean something utterly different compared with me saying it. 'I' would mean you, not me; 'here' would be where you are, not where I am; and 'now' means your present, which is some point in my future. Even in reading those last two sentences, you are interpreting 'I/me' and 'you' exactly the opposite way round from the way I am writing them. The capacity that language has for anchoring meaning to a context in this way is called deixis (meaning 'pointing'), and deictic patterns can be tracked through a text.

Deixis has been discussed in philosophy and linguistics for many years, with each approach both resolving and creating many key questions about meaning and understanding. Deixis, of course, is central to the idea of the embodiment of perception, and a cognitive approach offers the possibility of a new and unified answer to these questions. In this chapter, I outline the current understanding of deictic categories, and then present a cognitive linguistic model of deixis. I illustrate the centrality of deixis with a cognitive poetic discussion of literary personae.

Links with literary critical concepts

Author, character, focus, implied author, narratee, narrator, persona, perspective, point of view, voice

The following diagram assimilates the work of many theorists in trying to delineate different roles in the process of reading literature.

real author

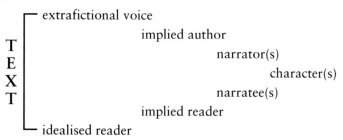

real reader

In the real world, we have a real flesh-and-blood author who lived a life, some of which was taken up in producing a literary text. We also have real flesh-and-blood readers, people like us who spend some of our time reading literature. As **real readers**, we have no access to **real authors** through their textual remains; the vast majority of real authors are dead. We only have access to those few we might know personally.

However, I have a belief, for example, in a real historical person who wrote *Frankenstein*. I call her Mary Shelley. I know that she composed the novel partly as a result of a story-telling and drug-taking session by Lake Geneva with Percy Shelley, Byron and his doctor John Polidori, in 1816. In spite of the fact that the novel is narrated largely by Victor Frankenstein, I know that this **narrator** is an invention of Mary Shelley, and that in fact she arranged all the paragraphs and chapters. Still, I have no direct access to the real Mary Shelley. The Mary Shelley I know about is an **extrafictional voice** which I have pieced together from her writing, from literary criticism and from reading historical accounts.

My idea of the real Mary Shelley in general is different from the **implied author** of *Frankenstein*. My re-creation of a persona generating and arranging the novel is specific to this novel published in 1818: my sense of the implied author of *The Last Man* (1826) is not the same Mary Shelley. There are different concerns and writing style in the later work, a different implied author.

Within the novel, Frankenstein is the main *narrator*. However, there is a framing narration around him, in the form of letters written by Captain Robert Walton. Victor Frankenstein's story (the majority of the novel) is narrated to Walton who then writes it down and posts it back to his sister. Frankenstein is also a **character** in the novel, and there are other characters who also narrate parts of the story, either in the form of direct speech or by having their letters reproduced. The monster that Frankenstein creates is a further embedded narrator when he recounts his own part of the story, at the centre of the novel. We can see that some of the categories in the diagram can overlap, but it is still useful to see where different roles are being enacted. In autobiography, for example, implied author and narrator and extrafictional voice can overlap.

Characters speak to other characters, and narrators narrate to an addressee: this addressee at any particular point is the **narratee**. Letters within *Frankenstein* are addressed to other characters; Victor Frankenstein himself narrates the whole story to Walton, a polar explorer and scientist. Of course, there is an **implied reader** of Frankenstein's narrative who sees all of the elements directed at different narratees. This is the reader to whom the novel is directed.

Finally, we must recognise that there are many different possible readings of the novel, foregrounding different elements, and so we can collect all possible readings together into a sort of **idealised reader**. This has variously been called the 'model reader', or 'informed reader', or 'super-reader'. All of the possible readings (a potentially very large but, I argue, finite number) available from the novel are represented within the idealised reader.

Each one of these entity-roles is made manifest in the text and can be described and tracked through an understanding of deixis.

Deixis

The prototypical deictic categories in speech are founded on the originating **deictic centre** or *zero-point* or *origo*: the speaker ('I'), place ('here') and time of utterance ('now'). Many theorists have limited the discussion of deixis to these *egocentric particulars* (Bertrand Russell), also called *indexicals* (Charles Peirce), *occasional terms* (Edmund Husserl) or *shifters* (Roman Jakobson). The deictic centre allows us to understand uses of words in context such as 'come' and 'go', 'this' and 'that', and egocentrically determined locatives such as 'left' and 'right', 'above' and 'below', 'in front' and 'behind', and so on. Deixis is obviously the central concept in the context-dependency of speech. However, others have argued that the prototypical speech situation can be extended into written language, and applied equally well in literary or fictional situations.

One way of understanding how we can shift our viewpoint to see things as others do or as characters in literature would, is by recognising our capacity for **deictic projection**. We can project a deictic centre in saying things like 'on your left', or, 'it's behind you', or,

> I met a traveller from an antique land,
> Who said – 'Two vast and trunkless legs of stone
> Stand in the desert ... Near them, on the sand,
> Half sunk a shattered visage lies, whose frown,
> And wrinkled lip, and sneer of cold command,
> Tell that its sculptor well those passions read
> Which yet survive, stamped on these lifeless things,
> The hand that mocked them, and the heart that fed;
> And on the pedestal, these words appear:
> My name is Ozymandias, King of Kings,
> Look on my Works, ye Mighty, and despair!

Nothing beside remains. Round the decay
Of that colossal Wreck, boundless and bare
The lone and level sands stretch far away.'
              ('Ozymandias', Percy Bysshe Shelley)

Here, I can project the deictic centre that says 'I' in the first line, and then
project the viewpoint of the traveller 'in the desert' within the direct speech,
and then project another embedded deictic centre to understand the 'my' and
'ye' of the pedestal inscription. We can follow the three different persons,
two different places (the implicit 'here' and 'the antique land'), and three
different times: a time implicit in the present tense of 'met' and 'said'; the
time in which the traveller was in the desert, chronologically in the past but
deictically projected as a present tense 'stand' and 'these words appear'; and
a deictic projection to the ancient time of the inscription when 'is', 'look' and
'despair' were written while Ozymandias was alive. All of the locating
expressions follow the deictic centre in each case: 'near them' is spatially
related to the traveller standing in the desert; 'those passions' and 'these life-
less things' are centred on the traveller looking at the shattered face; 'far
away' is understood relative to the site.

However, the deictic elements here go beyond person, place and time.
There is a **relational** aspect to the participants within the text, in terms of how
they are socially related to each other, and how each perceptual deictic centre
seems to regard the other participants. This is a matter of deixis in the sense
that characters in a scenario are socially anchored not absolutely but in relation to each other. For example, the narrator calls the other character 'a traveller', summarising him by this role rather than by personal name or a longer
description. The traveller uses certain aspects of *evaluation* to encode his attitude to the objects he finds, choosing expressions such as 'sneer', 'cold',
'mocked', 'decay' and so on. There are acts of evaluation here that are encoded
in the traveller's modality: it is obvious he admires the sculptor, who is in turn
set into a social hierarchy below the 'Mighty' and below the 'King of Kings'.
Attitude and social structure are encoded through relational deixis.

There is also a **textual** deictic dimension to be considered. The poem draws
attention to itself as a textual language event in a variety of ways. The poem
inscribes the craft of sculpting and refers to the 'sculptor', his hands and heart,
and begins with 'I', collapsing narrator and implied author to make a parallel
between the sculptor and the poet. This inevitably draws a link between the
ruined statue and the text as an artefact, and the generic word 'Works' is used
to link the remains of artistic production explicitly. The poem draws attention
both to the process of production and to the act of reading: the traveller reads
the inscription, and reads it back to the narrator, who reads it back to us in the
form of a poem, and the sculptor 'well those passions read'. Even the printing
process is perhaps echoed in the use of 'stamped'.

All except the first line is a report of direct speech. The main point of the
traveller's tale focuses on the written inscription on the pedestal, and it is

here that the ironic effect between the various deictic centres is most concentrated. The impact of the words is completely different when read from the different imagined vantage points of the original Egyptian audience, Ozymandias, the sculptor, the traveller, the poetic persona, the implied author, the nineteenth-century reader, and us.

Lastly, there is a deictic aspect in the **compositional** quality of the text. Certain generic patterns in word-choice, syntax and register in general have been selected in order to place the poem, to anchor it in a literary tradition, which inevitably is located in relation to other literary works. The artifice of the poem is foregrounded if you realise that the pedestal inscription would of course not be written in English in the time of Ozymandias (Pharoah Rameses II, 1279–1213 BC). The poetic licence applied here is apparent in 'ye', a self-conscious archaism even when the poem was published in 1818, coincidentally the same year as *Frankenstein*.

The poem is in a form which can be seen as a poor prototypical example of a sonnet (a weak gestalt, in psychological terms): although of fourteen lines, its prosody does not quite match either the Shakespearean or Italian sonnet pattern. It could be argued that this blurred pattern represents a dialogue between speaker and addressee that is also compositionally deictic. There is, too, relational deixis that encodes Shelley's aristocratic early nineteenth-century accent in rhyming 'stone' and 'frown', and 'appear' and 'despair', which do not rhyme in my accent. Even the frequent alliteration ('stone ... stand ... sand ... sunk', 'cold command', 'boundless and bare', 'lone and level') establishes that we are in the presence of literary conventions. We might even recognise that a prototypical sonnet form often has its most dramatic final flourish in the last two lines (sometimes rhymed, as in Shakespeare's sonnets). However, Shelley places his most dramatic pair of lines ('My name is Ozymandias ... and despair') five lines before the end, in order further to emphasise their multi-centred and polyvalent nature. The inconclusiveness of the form is matched, of course, by the very weak sense of closure in the final line ('The lone and level sands stretch far away'), which also takes the scene spatially away from the deictic centre of the ruin.

To summarise, I have outlined the following categories of deixis as adapted to the literary context:

- **Perceptual deixis** – expressions concerning the perceptive participants in the text, including personal pronouns 'I/me/you/they/it'; demonstratives 'these/those'; definite articles, definite reference 'the man', 'Bilbo Baggins'; mental states 'thinking, believing'. I include some elements (such as third person pronouns and names) here that are seen by some as part of reference; I argue that taking cognition seriously means that reference is to a mental representation and is a socially located act and is therefore participatory and deictic.
- **Spatial deixis** – expressions locating the deictic centre in a place, including spatial adverbs 'here/there', 'nearby/far away' and locatives 'in

the valley', 'out of Africa'; demonstratives 'this/that'; verbs of motion 'come/go', 'bring/take'.

- **Temporal deixis** – expressions locating the deictic centre in time, including temporal adverbs 'today/yesterday/tomorrow/soon/later' and locatives 'in my youth', 'after three weeks'; especially tense and aspect in verb forms that differentiate 'speaker-now', 'story-now' and 'receiver-now'.

- **Relational deixis** – expressions that encode the social viewpoint and relative situations of authors, narrators, characters, and readers, including modality and expressions of point of view and focalisation; naming and address conventions; evaluative word-choices. For example, the narrating author of Henry Fielding's *Tom Jones* is very polite to the reader in direct address, and adopts different stylistic tones of 'voice' in relation to the different characters in his novel.

- **Textual deixis** – expressions that foreground the textuality of the text, including explicit 'signposting' such as chapter titles and paragraphing; co-reference to other stretches of text; reference to the text itself or the act of production; evidently poetic features that draw attention to themselves; claims to plausibility, verisimilitude or authenticity.

- **Compositional deixis** – aspects of the text that manifest the generic type or literary conventions available to readers with the appropriate literary competence. Stylistic choices encode a deictic relationship between author and literary reader.

It is important to state that even single words, expressions and sentences can display all of these facets of deixis. They are only determinable *as* deixis, of course, if they are perceived as such by the reader, if they are seen as anchoring the various entity-roles in participatory relationships. Because occurrences of deictic expressions are dependent on context, reading a literary text involves a process of context-creation in order to follow the anchor-points of all these deictic expressions. Reading is creative in this sense of using the text to construct a cognitively negotiable world, and the process is dynamic and constantly shifting.

Deictic shift theory

It should be evident from the discussion above that it is almost impossible to talk plausibly about deixis without considering cognition. One fully worked out approach to cognitive deixis is **deictic shift theory** (DST), and this section will outline its key concepts. DST mainly restricts itself to the prototypical deictic situation of egocentric person, place and time. It can be extended, however, along all six of the dimensions I have outlined above for the written literary context. Its fundamental advance in deictic theory is to place the notion of deictic projection as a cognitive process at the centre of the framework.

DST models the common perception of a reader 'getting inside' a literary text as the reader taking a **cognitive stance** within the mentally constructed world of the text. This imaginative capacity is a **deictic shift** which allows the reader to understand projected deictic expressions relative to the shifted deictic centre. In other words, readers can see things virtually from the perspective of the character or narrator inside the text-world, and construct a rich context by resolving deictic expressions from that viewpoint. The notion of the shifted deictic centre is a major explanatory concept to account for the perception and creation of *coherence* across a literary text.

The key areas of investigation for DST are how the deictic centre is created by authors in texts, how it is identified through a cognitive understanding of textual patterning, and how it is shifted and used dynamically as part of the reading process. The world of a literary text consists of one or more **deictic fields**, which are composed of a whole range of expressions each of which can be categorised as perceptual, spatial, temporal, relational, textual and compositional in nature. A set of expressions which point to the same deictic centre can be said to compose a deictic field. They are usually arranged around a character, narrator or narratee, the relatively central entity-roles in the text, though of course animals, plants, landscape elements and other objects can also form deictic centres in imaginative literature.

When a deictic shift occurs, it can be either 'up' or 'down' the virtual planes of deictic fields. In other words, a novel which begins with the deictic field centred on a narrator might shift its deictic centre 'down' to a point earlier in the narrator's life (shifting deictic centre on the basis largely of the temporal dimension), or to a different spatial location, or even to the deictic centre of a character in the novel (with perceptual deixis prominent). Borrowing a term from computer science, this type of deictic shift is a **push**. In my scale of entity-roles near the beginning of this chapter (see p. 42), pushing into a deictic centre in the text is a movement towards the right of the diagram. Moving from being a real reader to perceiving yourself in a textual role as implied reader or narratee, or tracking the perception of a narrator or character, all involve a deictic shift that is a push into a 'lower' deictic field. Entering flashbacks, dreams, plays within plays, stories told by characters, reproduced letters or diary entries inside a novel, or considering unrealised possibilities inside the minds of characters are all examples of pushing into a deictic field.

By contrast, moving up a level is a **pop**, leftwards in my diagram. You can pop out of a deictic field by putting a book down and shifting your deictic centre back to your real life level as real reader. Within a text, you can pop up a level if the narrator appears again at the end to wrap up the narrative, or if the narrator interjects opinion or external comment at any point within the narrative. These involve shifts from the character who is the current focus of attention up to the deictic centre of the narrator. Equally, popping out from the narrative level to ascribe features of the deictic centre to the extrafictional voice is what enables readers to identify and locate irony. The characters in Jane Austen's *Pride and Prejudice* are unaware of their ironic position. However, an ironic motivation is usually ascribed to 'Jane Austen' and this sense

is a product of the juxtapositioning of events, the arrangement of plot structure, and compositional mismatches between content and expressions in register (such as the famous opening, 'It is a truth universally acknowledged that
a man in possession of a fortune is in want of a wife'). All of these patterns
represent choices by the extrafictional voice.

Usually, we expect pops and pushes to be balanced: flashbacks usually
return us eventually to the current time; plays within plays do not take over the
entire narrative; we do not read a book forever! However, when some literary
texts break this norm, it is noticeable and we like to make an issue or theme
out of it. 'Ozymandias' begins with a push to a narrating 'I', but the deictic
centre pushes immediately down to the traveller who recounts a past experience in a distant land (the deictic centre shifts perceptually, spatially and
temporally). Though there is a further push, into the words of Ozymandias,
we pop out of this. However, we never pop back to the narrative level. The
poem ends deictically stranded at a distance from our own readerly deictic
centre, and it is tempting to equate this feature with the ruins of the king,
stranded alone in the desert, or the poem as artifice, cut off from its creator
and left as isolated remains.

Perhaps the most famous similar example is the opening of Shakespeare's
The Taming of the Shrew. This is prefaced by an 'Induction', in which a
drunk, Sly, is left asleep 'before an alehouse on a heath'. A Lord and his reti-
nue, passing by, decide to play a trick on him by carrying him off comatose to
awaken in a fine bedroom with music, artworks, and perfume, attended by
servants and a page-boy pretending to be his wife. In an admirable display of
quick deictic shifting, he exclaims:

> Am I a lord? and have I such a lady?
> Or do I dream? or have I dreamed till now?

The servants convince him he has been in a dream for fifteen years, and to
celebrate his return, a play is organised. The play he settles down to watch is
Act I, Scene 1 of *The Taming of the Shrew*. The themes of comedy, and the
inversion of social hierarchy associated with festival carnivalesque, as well as
gender role reversal and the replacement of reality with dream/fiction, are all
taken up in the play within a play. Curiously, though, the usual function of
carnival as an affirming closing re-imposition of the social order is not sustained. The play within a play ends with no pop out to the initial framing
level. This thematisation of subversion has led some readers to give an ironic
feminist interpretation to the uncharacteristically submissive speech with
which Katharina ends the play.

In the theatre, however, the Induction is often omitted, or swept off the
stage at the beginning, so that the theatre audience cannot see the play-audi-
ence of Sly and the servants watching the embedded play all the way through.
The experience of this serves to make most people forget about the Induction
scene. Since it is never referred to and is not deictically instantiated at all

again, it fades from memory in a process I have called *decomposition*. This is an important facet in understanding that cognitive processes in reading are dynamic. Deictic centres need constant maintenance by continuous use of the associated deictic expressions. If they are not mentioned for a while, they decompose and are replaced by another default deictic centre.

Shifting deictic centres depends, of course, on identifying the boundaries of deictic fields. The process of identification is called **edgework**. Some shifts, such as between the real world field and the literary text field, are easy to identify: the book cover and other external appearances often determine that the contents encode a different deictic storyworld of fiction. Similarly, some cues are graphologically manifest inside the text: chapter headings, blank lines or stars between sections, paragraph breaks, and so on. These are always accompanied by stylistic features which can also mark the edge of new deictic fields in their own right. Very strong examples of deictic shift cues are spatial and temporal locative expressions and new names or pronouns. For the rest of this chapter, I will explore the stylistic detail of these features in relation to *Wuthering Heights* by Emily Brontë.

Discussion

Before proceeding, you could think about and discuss some of these ideas. The following questions might help you get started:

- Looking back at the diagram of entity-roles in literature, can you think of any other functional roles that are played on either the production or reception side that are not precisely accounted for by these categories? What other kinds of reading roles might be needed, for example?
- In the pragmatics of spoken discourse, the following participant roles have been identified and differentiated within perceptual deixis:

speaker	source
recipient	target
hearer	addressee

For example, the US President gives a speech (as speaker) written by a scriptwriter (source) in front of a crowd of schoolchildren (hearers) but the speech is addressed to the school principal who invited him (addressee), and the speech is recorded by TV camera crews (recipients) though the actual aim of the event is to communicate with the national electorate (target). Can you discern any other roles that might be evident in the communicative situation? How might these categories be adapted for written literary situations?

- The entity-roles listed were largely generated by theorists thinking about narrative fiction. Do you think they apply equally to different sorts of poetry, especially non-narrative forms such as lyrical or imagistic verse? And how might the categories be adapted or radically revised for drama?

- Taking a literary text that you know well, decide on the narrative structure in terms of entity-roles, and sketch these out. Now look at the detail of the text and try to track the points at which the entity-roles are established and shift using deixis. You might discuss the differences between a text in which the roles are collapsed (like an autobiography) and one with many deictic layers (such as a dream-vision, or a modern text that plays with the idea of narrators and virtual worlds).

Cognitive poetic analysis

You can visit Haworth Parsonage where the real Emily Brontë lived, in Yorkshire not far from the setting of Ted Hughes' poem in Chapter 2. There is also Celtic connection between the ancient kingdom of Elmet and the Cornish mother and Irish father of the Brontës. But this is merely tourism, not literature. The extrafictional voice, Emily Brontë, created a complex narrative structure in *Wuthering Heights* (1847) that has been recognised as one of the main reasons behind the effective force of the novel, but the implied author of the novel seems different, to my mind, from the author implied in poems such as 'No Coward Soul is Mine', 'The Prisoner', 'Remembrance' and the stanzas that begin: 'Often rebuked, yet always back returning'. Chronologically, the novel runs from summer 1771 until New Year's Day, 1803, and it is narrated primarily by Mr. Lockwood. Though he is a character in the novel as well, he occupies only the framing level, and takes no real part in the central story.

The first part of the story proper begins when Lockwood reads Catherine Earnshaw's diary-like comments in the margins of an old Bible he finds when spending a night at Wuthering Heights. This part of the narrative pushes and pops from the deictic centres of child Catherine (within the textual deixis of the Bible notes) almost twenty years previously and Lockwood reading in the same location in the narrative present. There is a further push into a dream that Lockwood has, which preserves his perceptual deixis but introduces characters that are only accessible through him: a mad preacher and a chapel congregation. Popping back out of the dream, the narrative follows Lockwood down the moorside in the morning back to his own rented house, Thrushcross Grange.

However, at this point we perhaps need more detail in terms of embedded narration. Most of the novel is told to Lockwood, while he is subsequently laid up with a cold, by a secondary narrator, the housekeeper Nelly Dean. She has taken part in some of the narrative as a participating character, so a push to her deictic centre involves a shift where 'I' means Nelly Dean, and her viewpoint and evaluations are Lockwood's filter. The following is the passage surrounding this first major deictic shift in narrative, from Lockwood to Nelly Dean:

> 'Well, Mrs. Dean, it will be a charitable deed to tell me something of my neighbours: I feel I shall not rest, if I go to bed; so be good enough to sit and chat an hour.'

'Oh, certainly, sir! I'll just fetch a little sewing, and then I'll sit as long as you please. But you've caught cold: I saw you shivering, and you must have some gruel to drive it out.'

The worthy woman bustled off, and I crouched nearer the fire; my head felt hot, and the rest of me chill: moreover I was excited, almost to a pitch of foolishness, through my nerves and brain. This caused me to feel, not uncomfortable, but rather fearful (as I am still) of serious effects from the incidents of to-day and yesterday. She returned presently, bringing a smoking basin and a basket of work; and, having placed the former on the hob, drew in her seat, evidently pleased to find me so companionable.

Before I came to live here, she commenced – waiting no further invitations to her story – I was almost always at Wuthering Heights.

The deictic shift is preceded by Lockwood inviting Nelly to tell him all about Heathcliff. The first part is clearly deictically centred on Lockwood. It is constantly renewed with first person pronoun usage throughout, and third person reference for Nelly. Pronoun variations are constrained properly within Nelly's direct speech. Mental predicates ('my head felt hot', 'This caused me to feel') are centred on Lockwood; where there is an opportunity for Nelly's thoughts to be shown, they are filtered through his perception (she was '*evidently* pleased'). The shift is also preceded by a spatial relocation: Nelly moves to be near Lockwood (notice that the verbs 'returned' and 'bringing' are spatially centred on him too).

The shift in deixis is perceptual (to Nelly), temporal (back twenty years), relational (Nelly's values are encoded hereafter), and textual (she becomes a new teller after the paragraph space, and her perceptions then apparently structure the narrative, though in fact the implied author 'Emily Brontë' continues to insert chapter headings across Nelly's narrative – 'Brontë' retains the compositional deixis). The spatial deixis remains constant: 'here' is Thrushcross Grange; though Nelly immediately shifts this to Wuthering Heights within a locative expression.

There is something of a blend in the edgework here, as 'I', 'she' and 'her' in the final sentence excerpted above all point deictically to Nelly Dean. However, we understand the reporting clause and comment to belong to the deictic centre of Lockwood, and the surrounding text to Nelly Dean. Thereafter the story follows, deictically centred in Nelly Dean and consistent with her perceptually, temporally and spatially. Occasionally, as embedded narrator, she renews the deictic push by using textual deixis to acknowledge the narratee, Lockwood: she says, 'I was deceived completely, as you will hear'. There are, though, even further pushes into other deictic centres. The chronological first part was told to Nelly by Heathcliff when he was a boy, over several pages of direct speech, and she recounts this verbatim to Lockwood. Further on, she reads out the contents of a letter written to her by Isabella which itself contains large stretches of direct speech from other characters. The reader in the middle of this letter is four pushes into a different deictic centre.

Nelly Dean ends the main part of her narrative some thirty chapters later (chapters arranged by Emily Brontë, of course) with an account told to her by the servant Zillah. At the end of this there is a paragraph space, and then a shift initiated by textual deixis:

> Thus ended Mrs. Dean's story. Notwithstanding the doctor's prophecy, I am rapidly recovering strength; and, though it be only the second week in January, I propose getting out on horseback in a day or two, and riding over to Wuthering Heights.

Here we have the deictic shift initiated with textual deixis, referring back to the previous text. The 'I' narration suddenly shifts to a third person participant, the form of which ('Mrs. Dean') serves to encode the relational deixis that cues Lockwood as deictic centre once again. We have popped up to the framing level of the novel. Later in the year (in September 1802) Lockwood returns to Wuthering Heights, and Nelly Dean concludes the story:

> And afterwards she furnished me with the sequel of Heathcliff's history. He had a 'queer' end, as she expressed it.
>
> I was summoned to Wuthering Heights, within a fortnight of your leaving us, she said; and I obeyed joyfully, for Catherine's sake.

The shift here is again prefaced with textual deixis, including some blending of the edgework again: Nelly's phrase is first placed into speech marks while embedded in Lockwood's deictic centred text, but her speech appears without speech marks and only with a very late reporting clause ('she said') once the paragraph break has marked the shift to Nelly's deictic centre. Again, the perceptual, spatial and temporal deictics are consistent with this shift, and the relational deixis encodes her attitude ('joyfully').

The narrative reverts to Lockwood on the last page, for him to give Nelly some money for her patience in telling him the story, and to visit the churchyard and the graves of the main characters in the novel.

This narrative complexity allows two distinct themes to be developed while maintaining a realistic frame around the tempestuous events of the novel. Nelly Dean's story is a romance. It features a romantic passion, gothic grotesques, spirit visions, superstition, and elemental forces. Unless the reader is to believe she has a perfect memory, it is clear that the quality of her oral account is ornamented and embellished, dramatised or at the very least filtered through her story-teller imagination. By contrast, Lockwood's story is cool and relatively detached, and filtered through his deictic centre the novel is mainly concerned with land, property rights and the legal affiliations and ownership accorded by marriage. Heathcliff's first words to him are, 'Thrushcross Grange is my own, sir' – a property claim that is a result of his manoeuvrings in getting his sickly son married to the second Cathy. The deictic centre around which Lockwood's beliefs revolve do not encompass ghosts, for example, unless in dreams. Nelly's story is complex and dynamic, and relational deixis can be followed in the variants of her name: Nelly, Ellen, Nelly Dean, Mrs. Dean, the housekeeper. Lockwood is just 'Lockwood', or 'Mr. Lockwood' – we never discover his first name. His evaluations are ordinary and belong to the sociable and civilised world away from Wuthering Heights.

The novel sits in two halves. The first half details the Catherine/Heathcliff love-story; the second half after Catherine's death features Heathcliff's manipulation of the two families to become master of both properties. Those who read *Wuthering Heights* primarily as a romance (that is, with the Nelly Dean deictic centre prominent) tend to love the first half and find the second half dull. There have been several film and stage adaptations, for example, which simply omit the second half altogether. However, those readers (mainly literary critics) who have engaged with the Lockwood narration have focused on the political and ideological elements in the novel, with the romance as a melodramatic background. (This is a nice example of wilful professional reversal of figure and ground). Taken together, however, between Nelly's over-dramatisation and Lockwood's cool detachment, there is both reasonable credibility and first-hand authority, and a wide space for a range of readerly interpretations. The deictic shifts between different embedded narrators allow readers to track consistent threads through the novel. However, in the edgework, there are many examples where textual deixis and the compositional deixis of the implied author cut across chapter headings throughout. Thematised, these two further deictic aspects can unite the two readings.

To close this chapter, we are now in a position to be precise about the stylistic features that most usually act as deictic shift devices, when the narrative voice shifts, or the deictic centre shifts between characters' speech, perceptions or points of view. Of course, these are prototypical, and other features could be used in special contextual circumstances. The following checklist combines my deictic categories with specifications of those expressions which prototypically shift the deictic centre. I also give the typical means by which the shift is maintained (by anti-shifting devices).

- **Perceptual shift** – where poetic and literary 'voices' are introduced through *presentative structure* ('Once there was a girl called Goldilocks', 'Into the valley of death rode the six hundred') and using *noun phrases,* such as proper names. Perceptual deixis is maintained when the noun phrase is definite and in subject position, and, of course, when the perceptual 'voice' is *frequently mentioned.* So characters who are constantly named and pronominalised stay current. Any *perception and mental predicates* that are associated with the character also help to maintain that deictic centre. Perceptual shifts are often *preceded by spatial shifts* ('Meanwhile back at the farm, Peter was digging ditches').

Anti-shifting devices (that is, features which make it unlikely that a perceptual shift will occur) include *placing noun phrases in non-subject position*, for example, as direct/indirect objects or as complements. This keeps the character being referred to current in spite of the new subject. Characters can also be kept 'live' by *conjoining co-ordinate clauses to maintain co-reference* to the character, by *subject-chaining* (using pronouns to keep the current entity-role live, and by frequent mention). If potentially new deictic centres are placed into *relative clauses*, then the subordination stops it becoming the focus of a shift. Lastly, *indefinite subjects* are usually not the focus of shifts, as they are more presentative and introductory in nature, as in the examples above.

- **Spatial shift** – spatial shifts are typically enacted by *movement predicates* such as verbs of motion: 'Hannibal crossed the Alps'. *Preposed locative adverbials* also shift spatial deixis: 'Somewhere over the rainbow, skies are blue'. *Spatial adverbs* ('here', 'there') introduce and maintain the spatial centre.

  Spatial deixis is maintained, again, by *conjoining co-ordinate clauses to maintain co-reference*, as in perceptual deixis. Spatial elements embedded in *relative clauses* tend not to shift the centre: 'I looked at the ship which had travelled across the sea'. *Co-ordinate clauses* work for the same reason: 'I hear you knocking, but you can't come in'. Spatial shift is resistant to the effect of *perception verbs* on their own: a character just thinking about a different place still allows the current location to be maintained.

- **Temporal shift** – most obviously, any *tense and aspect shift and chaining* will shift the temporal centre. *Preposed locative adverbials*, such as 'In olden days … ', also act as shifters. Consistency of tense and aspect maintains the temporal deictic centre. Brief departures from the current temporal sequence do not shift the centre if they are introduced with *conjunctions*. For example: 'I am staying here. I will come when the time is right, but for now I am staying'. Here, the 'but' stops the aspectual from shifting the temporal location to the future. Embedded *past perfects* work in a similar way: 'I was there. I had been before, but now all I wanted was to relax'.

- **Relational shift** – *proper names and address forms* ('Colonel Mustard', 'Your Excellency') serve to mark out relational deictic centres, as do *evaluative and judgemental adjectives and adverbials*, which indicate a narrative or authorial voice – a sense of a socially situated person 'speaking'. Expressions of *social politeness* and *markers of modality* ('it seems to be', 'it might be', 'may', 'will,' 'would have been' and so on) also encode the attitudes and social relations of deictic centres. The maintenance of *point of view* and a character's apparent *mind-style* serve as anti-shift devices for relational deixis.

- **Textual shift** – *titles, chapter titles, epigrams, paragraphing, and other graphology* all encode textual deixis, by drawing attention to the evidence for an authorial arrangement. Similarly, *co-reference to other stretches of text by discourse anaphora* ('In the last chapter … ') and *the* *use of predicates from the lexical set of writing, printing or creation* ('I am writing to you from... ') both enact a shift in the textual deictic centre. Any *pop-shifts in perceptual deixis to author, extrafictional voice, implied author or narrator* also tend to mark textual shifts, and *generic or proverbial sentences* draw attention to themselves as textual constructs and thus also have a deictic dimension. Any text in which the extrafictional voice is prominent (as in Fielding's *Tom Jones*), when this perceptual deixis is consistent across the text, will also serve to act as an anti-shift device for textual deixis.

- **Compositional shift** – finally, the *external presentational factors* (such as the book cover, or a recontextualisation of a text by placing it in a classroom context) can serve to relocate the compositional quality of the discourse. Compositional deixis is also marked by any register selections that *index a literary convention* (such as a fourteen-line sonnet, a cast list at the head of a play, or the dedication of a novel, for example). *Consistency of usage* will maintain this composition. Shifts in register which could potentially shift the compositional deixis can be made to serve as anti-shift devices if they are framed somehow (for example, by presenting compositions as an in-text quotation or interlude). Announcements in the interval of a play, for example, are usually understood not to be part of the compositional centre of the surrounding performance.

Explorations

1   In many branches of critical theory, the emphasis given to author, text and reader has shifted around (as Abrams (1953) noticed). Ever since Wimsatt and Beardsley's (1954) essays 'The Intentional Fallacy' and 'The Affective Fallacy', critics have felt the need to justify their discussions of either authorial production and history or readerly reception and psychological affect. The argument against second-guessing writers' intentions has always seemed very sensible to me (confirmed by Roland Barthes' (1977) famous essay 'The Death of the Author'). However, since cognitive poetics lies close to psychology, the question of the status of cognitive poetic analysis in relation to these issues is again relevant. There is not the space here for me to outline my own thoughts on the matter, and you might find it interesting to read these essays and develop your own thinking.

2   If you enjoy critical theory, you might also explore the potential consequences of cognitive poetic thinking on new historicism, cultural materialism, ecological criticism, post-structuralist deconstruction, hermeneutics or reception theory. The easiest way to do this would be to take a representative essay or work in one of these areas and read it with a cognitive poetic pencil poised above your notebook.

3   One of the most prominent features that has had literary value attached to it over the last century has been the 'psychologising' of character.

Literary texts in which the characters seem 'well-rounded' rather than flat 'everyman' tokens have been praised. Some structuralist and narratological analyses have reduced character to the status of a linguistic device. To what extent does the cognitive understanding of deixis reframe our perceptions of 'character' in literary reading? (See Culpeper (2001) for interesting recent work on this).

4   There are many literary texts which use embedded narrative centres in the form of tales-within-tales, second-hand accounts, plays-within-plays, imaginary journals, diaries, memoirs, flashbacks, anticipations, dream-visions, hallucinations, or stories brought back by travellers. You could examine the global narrative structure of the following texts, for example:

- *The House of Fame* (Geoffrey Chaucer, *c*.1380)
- *Hamlet* (William Shakespeare, 1601)
- *Gulliver's Travels* (Jonathan Swift, 1726)
- *The Rime of the Ancient Mariner* (Samuel Taylor Coleridge, 1798)
- *Mansfield Park* (Jane Austen, 1814)
- *The Shape of Things to Come* (H.G. Wells, 1933)
- *The Female Man* (Joanna Russ, 1975)
- *Betrayal* (Harold Pinter, 1978)

You might also examine the local points of deictic shift, using the checklist given above (see pp. 53–5) to identify the stylistic features used. Can you determine a thematic reason or general literary motivation or effect in the stylistics of the deictic patterning?

5   *Betrayal* by Harold Pinter, is a play that tells its story in reverse chronological order. The technique of reversal has been used in novels (such as *Slaughterhouse Five* by Kurt Vonnegut, 1970, *Time's Arrow* by Martin Amis, 1991) and films (*Pulp Fiction*, directed by Quentin Tarantino, 1995; *Memento*, directed by Christopher Nolan, 2001). You could examine these or similar literary works for their narrative structure and deictic shifts, and try to use your analysis to help account for the overall effect.

Further reading and references

The schematic of entity-roles drawn at the beginning of this chapter is an amalgamation of terms mainly from Booth (1961), Iser (1974, 1978) and Chatman (1978, 1990). Alternative terms for my 'idealised reader' can be found in Riffaterre (1959, 1966), Eco (1976, 1981), and Fish (1970, 1973). Notions of the carnivalesque were developed by Bakhtin (1968).

The categories of 'origo' deixis were originally developed by Bühler (1982 [original 1934]) and subsequently set out by Lyons (1977) and Levinson (1983). Key work on deixis is collected in Jarvella and Klein (1982), Rauh (1983) and Green (1995). Applications to literature include Green (1992) and Semino (1997). Fleischman (1982, 1990) addresses the deixis of tense and aspect shifts. My comprehensive list of deictic categories in literature was first set out in Stockwell (2000b: 23–46), where I also use the notion of 'decomposition' (p.150). It should also be noted that the chapter above collates aspects of point of view, narrative voice, and deixis, which some writers would consider separate. I have argued for their continuity here.

Deictic shift theory was developed in the collection edited by Duchan, Bruder and Hewitt (1995). The parameters of the theory are set out by Segal (1995a); pops and pushes in literary texts are discussed by Galbraith (1995); edgework in narrative fiction by Segal (1995b); literary reference in Wiebe (1995); third person narratives in Bruder and Wiebe (1995); and global narrative structure in Talmy (1995). The checklist that ends my chapter derives from Zubin and Hewitt (1995), though I have rearranged their layout and extended their categories somewhat to give it a clearer literary application. For example, they schematise 'origo' deixis as 'WHO', 'WHAT', 'WHEN' and 'WHERE'. I assimilate the first two into perceptual deixis, and place the last two into temporal and spatial slots, preserving a standard terminology but, with them, dividing time and space. I have then used their principles to add the features for relational, textual and compositional deixis.

5   Cognitive grammar

Preview

One of the great advantages of cognitive poetics is that it binds together the philosophical and practical sides of literary investigation. It offers a grounding of critical theory in a philosophical position that is scientific in the modern sense: aiming for an account of natural phenomena (like reading) that represents our current best understanding while always being open to falsifiability and a better explanation. It avoids the trap of circularity by deriving analytical methods not from within literary reading but from the fields of linguistics and psychology. Most engagingly of all, it is concerned not simply with conceptual and abstract structures but with addressing the central issue of how those conceptual structures are manifest and actualised in language.

So far I have presented two of the three major patterns in cognitive science: prototypicality, and the figure/ground distinction (the third – *metaphor* – will appear in Chapters 6 and 7 and be described directly in Chapters 8 and 9). I have been concerned so far to present practical applications of the conceptual frameworks, and so I have necessarily anticipated some of the grammatical concerns of this chapter. The practical realisations of both prototypicality and figure/ground will be picked up again and developed here, in order to move towards a stylistics that is fully bound to a cognitive dimension. I will illustrate the approach with some seventeenth-century poetry.

Links with literary critical concepts

Close-reading, critical discourse analysis, interdisciplinarity, practical criticism, rhetoric, stylistics, transitivity

The main direction in the historical development of linguistics has been to generate abstract and highly theoretical models away from the actuality of language forms. These abstract structures are presented as conceptual constructs – sometimes as universals across all languages – that constrain and determine the forms in which different languages appear. However, a more functional approach to linguistics would relate form to conceptual structure more directly, and, crucially, would also pay attention to the circumstances of use as an essential part of the linguistic account. A cognitive grammar in particular must build its conceptual constructs out of language in its psychological and social circumstances of use.

Sometimes cognitive poetics has been called **cognitive stylistics** or **cognitive rhetoric**, demonstrating its close relationship with detailed linguistic analysis. In terms of linguistic theory, we are going in the opposite direction from linguistic theorising. We are interested in taking concepts from cognitive linguistics and using them to animate our readings of real literary texts, where language is actually used for a purpose. It is not surprising, then, that cognitive poetics has been embraced first in literary studies by those who have practised **stylistics**. My colleagues in stylistics, or **literary linguistics**, have been concerned with a rigorous and systematic analysis of literature. Informed primarily by developments in linguistics, more recently stylistics has embraced advances in psychology, social theory and discourse analysis, as well as the philosophy of language and critical theory.

All this means that a concern for 'literary analysis' includes the complex consideration of the connections between the particular texture of literary works, their relationship with other patterns in the literary and linguistic system, as well as effects derived in the process of literary reading. Stylistics is no mechanical engineering disassembly: it has to be sensitive to many different disciplines, and at its best it is engaged, precise, sophisticated and humane. This is sometimes quite a feat of conceptual juggling.

A cognitive turn in stylistics offers a means of drawing together many of the traditional concerns of what used to be regarded as an interdisciplinary approach to literary analysis. It offers one way of rooting stylistic exploration in embodied experience; validating some of the readerly intuitions through stylistic analysis in a theory of understanding; connecting some of the different source disciplines used in stylistic discussions. It means that the practical analysis of literary texture is placed at the forefront of study, rather than being an offshoot or consequence of it. Theoretical advances come partly out of detailed stylistic analysis, and language study is fast becoming the unified discipline at the centre of the various literary studies.

Stylistic prototypicality

In Chapter 3, I briefly outlined how the form that a proposition seems to take can be understood as a prototypical scale of actualisation: involving degrees of predication, verb-form, positiveness, mood and definiteness. This approach to grammatical realisations has been applied much more widely and radically in cognitive linguistics. A comprehensive account is beyond the scope of this book, but I will sketch out some of the most important and useful insights from cognitive grammar.

A subject in a clause can be regarded as prototypical if it is also the agent and topic. Variant forms such as passives, personifications, and so on, are noticeable departures which need to be accounted for in terms of some thematised motivation. In a similar way, the **topicality** of the subject can itself be understood as a prototype structure, along four dimensions as summarised in the diagram below. Certain arrangements of subjects in expressions seem cognitively more 'natural' than others.

In the diagram, the 'topic-worthiness' of a subject depends primarily on its **semantic role** in the event that is being expressed, and secondarily on the degree of **empathy** that people typically have with the entity, then its **definiteness**, and finally its **figure/ground** organisation as subjectively perceived.

The topicality of subject

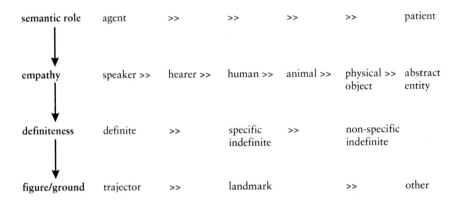

semantic role	agent	>>	>>	>>	>>	patient
empathy	speaker >>	hearer >>	human >>	animal >>	physical >> object	abstract entity
definiteness	definite	>>	specific indefinite	>>	non-specific indefinite	
figure/ground	trajector	>>	landmark		>>	other

Taking semantic role first, a subject is prototypically the **agent** in a clause, rather than functioning in the **patient** role. Choosing a patient as the subject (such as in a passive) is a marked expression that requires some special explanatory motivation: defamiliarisation, or evading active responsibility, or encoding secrecy, for example.

People typically have an empathy scale, such that the *speaker* is usually expected to be the subject of an utterance. If the subject is not a speaker, then it is expected to be the *hearer*. If not, then some other *human* should be in the subject position; if not a human, then some *animal*, and lastly a *physical object* or even an *abstract entity* can act as subject. Personifications of 'liberty' (abstract) or 'hill-stone' (physical object) represent movements along the prototype scale that need to be thematised by readers, for example.

Definiteness is more subjectively decided, depending on the reader's prior contact with the subject. **Definite** subjects ('The town', 'that man') are generally preferred to indefinites, and **specific indefinites** ('a certain Mrs Jones', 'a girl I know') are preferred to **non-specific** ones ('a girl'). Lastly, subjects are usually seen as figures or *trajectors*, then as primary *landmarks*, and then as background or *other* secondary landmarks.

Compare:

> *I* met a traveller from an antique land (subject is agent and speaker).
> *A traveller from an antique land* met me (subject is agent and 'hearer').
> *I* was met by a traveller (subject is not agent but is high 'speaker' on empathy scale).
> *A traveller* was met by me (subject is again not agent but is lower 'hearer' on the empathy scale, so this sounds odd).
> *An antique land* encountered me (physical object low on empathy scale, seems like personification).
> *A traveller* is in an antique land (this specific indefinite seems better than …).
> *Travellers* are in an antique land (a non-specific indefinite. This would more usually be expressed as 'There are travellers in an antique land').
> *An antique land* formed the face of the traveller (odd figure/ground order which might motivate a metaphorical resolution).

Certain intuited effects of deviance can be accounted for using this scale. For illustration, here is a poem by Ben Jonson, written on the death of his seven-year-old son from the plague in 1603, and published some years later.

On My First Son

Farewell, thou child of my right hand, and joy;
 My sin was too much hope of thee, lov'd boy,
Seven years thou wert lent to me, and I thee pay,
 Exacted by thy fate, on the just day.
O, could I lose all father, now. For why
 Will man lament the state he should envy?
To have so soon 'scap'd world's, and flesh's rage,
 And if no other misery, yet age?
Rest in soft peace, and, ask'd, say here doth lie
 Ben. Jonson his best piece of poetry.
For whose sake, henceforth, all his vows be such,
 As what he loves may never like too much.
                              (Ben Jonson, 1616)

Looking first at the clause structures here, there is not a single prototypically actualised sentence. In order, the poem consists of a vocative address 'thou child'; an attributive clause with 'my sin' as subject; a passive 'wert lent'; a declarative which is lost in both an exclamatory 'O' and a verb-reversal 'could I lose' that makes it look like a question; a real 'why' question; a non-finite extension of the question 'to have 'scap'd'; two imperatives 'rest' and 'say'; and a final existential clause 'vows be such' that the prepositional phrase 'for whose sake' connects as if it is an extension of the previous imperative. It is easy to thematise this avoidance of declarative forms in the loss and uncertainty evident in the subject-matter.

There are, however, other local consequences for the texture of the poem in these unprototypical clausal patterns. The lack of predication or finite verb-form in the first line means that the relations between the noun phrases are not exactly defined, allowing for some ambiguity. He bids 'farewell' both to the child, and to his joy, or to the 'child of his joy', which parallels the poem itself, also the child of his writing hand, where 'right' is for writing and for good: so the poem begins by saying goodbye to itself.

The conceit of children and poetry as creative products is of course taken up later in the text explicitly: 'Ben. Jonson his best piece of poetry'. Again there is ambiguity here, though, in that Jonson's son was also called Benjamin, and the poet is careful with the punctuation to leave the reference ambiguous between him and his son. The imperative echoes this: I assumed at first that 'Rest in peace' is addressed to the son, but then the second conjoined imperative, 'and, ask'd, say here doth lie', cannot be addressed to the dead child. Instead it can only be attached to the reader of an epitaph at the graveside, or the reader of these lines.

The second clause, 'My sin was too much hope of thee', places an abstract entity ('my sin') as subject before the intimate second person pronoun 'thee'. Notice too the possessive structure ('my sin', 'of thee') that displaces both father and son grammatically as well. The 'sin' mentioned here is hubris on the part of the poet, but the grammatical structure does not place him as agent or subject – instead the responsibility is indirect ('my') or merely by association ('too much hope'). The attributive form of the clause blends easily into the passive in the line that follows: 'Seven years thou wert lent to me'. The subject 'thou' is patient, and the missing agent is in the next line identified as the personified 'fate'. The active clause at the end of the line is compacted again to render ambiguous possibilities: 'I thee pay'. 'Thee', here, can be either direct or indirect object: I pay my poem to the son; I pay my son to fate.

The poem is full of religious cues yet is careful not to rail against God or assign any blame directly to him. Connections between 'my son', 'my sin', 'my right hand', 'all father', 'the just day', are accompanied by a careful passivised deletion of God ('wert lent to me') and a replacement with the vaguely personified 'fate'. It seems there is no comfort to be had by looking outwards.

Looking inward, the exclamation, 'O, could I lose all father, now', represents his most intimate and abandoned words, where 'father' comes to be placed as a quality, and both his semantic and syntactic skills seem almost to fail him. The following question places an abstracted generalised and indefinite subject, 'man', next to embedded personifications in the (definite) 'world's', and (indefinite) 'flesh's rage'. From being personally displaced from 'man', even the personal disappears altogether in the next subject-less clause. The displacement is complete in the last couplet, where he expresses himself in the third person. 'For whose sake' is again ambiguous between himself, his son, or his piece of poetry. Finally, from the definite direct closeness of the first line, the poem ends in a vague sense that his capacity for love itself has been devalued and lost.

Throughout the poem, the usual, natural points on the scale of agency, empathy, and definiteness are being unfixed and blurred confusingly together. The 'natural' figure and ground of the dead son being more important than the poem seem almost to be reversed by the end, or certainly at least brought into question. The deviance in this poem is not a radical or highly prominent feature, but there are just enough features that are non-prototypical to upset a reading and discomfit a reader. This is not a poem for comfort or engraving as a reassuring epitaph, but one that only just evades bitterness through its barely held restraint.

Action chains

The roles that different participants (whether people, animals or rocks) play in the cognitive model underlying a clause are based on **role archetypes**. These roles constitute the basic **thematic relationships** expressed by a clause, and can be summarised in a diagram.

zero	agent patient instrument experiencer mover	absolute	theme

The most usual roles taken by noun phrases in an utterance are listed in the second column. That is, we have a general sense of an *agent*: an acting participant who wilfully causes things to move, in a whole range of situations that are generalisable. Conversely, the participant that receives the energy of a predicate is the *patient*. The patient is changed in some identifiable and attributive way. A participant which is used by the agent is the **instrument**. A participant which is the location for a mental perception, such as thought, emotion, viewing or even saying, is an **experiencer**. A participant which physically moves to another location is a **mover**.

Where the participant merely exists but does not actually do anything ('His face was red', 'She was there'), no energy has been transmitted and its semantic role is **zero**. Since all participants begin fundamentally with existence and attributes, all roles are also zero by default.

Sometimes a participant is unchanged in a predication (the objects in 'I love Paris', 'I have a copy of the book') and it can then be called an **absolute**.

Lastly, events can be presented as if they occur autonomously ('The glass broke', 'The tree fell over') – here the participant is a **theme**, where the relationship to agent, patient, experiencer or mover is verbally expressed as action, change of state, mental experience or motion. Cognitively, themes subsume all the other categories in that roles such as agent, patient and so on are often understood as being the likely roles if the clause were to be expressed differently.

In the last two paragraphs I used a metaphor of energy-transmission for the process of a predication. In cognitive linguistics, predications are seen in this way as **action chains**. In an active clause, the agent acts as the **head** of an action chain, which moves through several stages perhaps including an instrument to arrive at the **tail** of the action chain with the patient. The role in subject position is usually seen as the trajector figure, and other participants in the action chain are primary or secondary landmarks. Of course, there can be other elements in a clause that are non-participatory. For example,

Alice made the bed

has an agent ('Alice') and a patient ('the bed'). However, in

Alice is under the bed

'Alice' occupies a zero role, and here 'the bed' is not a participant: it is simply a part of the background **setting**. An action chain that represents a predication, then, consists of a trajector role at the head of the chain, and one or more landmark roles along the chain to the tail, and the action chain itself can be seen as being placed in a setting or background.

How does this relate to linguistic features? The processes and roles are cognitively part of **domains** which can be realised in a variety of ways. It is a principle of cognitive linguistics that there is no necessary one-to-one link between a linguistic form and its cognitive domain. However, I can begin to summarise the discussion so far in a way that can be used for stylistic analysis. In the following diagram, nominals are linguistically realised as noun phrases. Relationals can be stative or processual, in a variety of types as indicated.

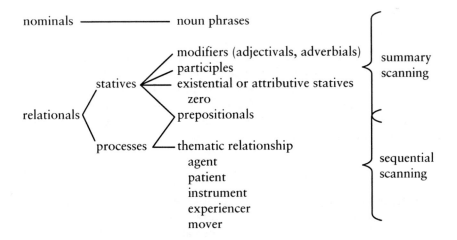

The new concept here is the notion of how the cognitive input is scanned. **Summary scanning** is typically what happens when nominals are processed: attributes are collected into a single coherent gestalt that constitutes an element. The *sun* in 'Look at the sun' or 'It's a sunny day' is a static feature that is summarily scanned. Contrast this with the *sun* in 'The sun shone down' or 'The sun crossed the sky in a blaze of light'. Here, there is **sequential scanning** which is typically what happens when an event or configuration has to be tracked. The difference has been likened to examining a still photograph and watching a film.

Crudely, static entities (like nominals and stative modifiers, participles and stative verbs like 'are', 'sits', 'stands') are summarily scanned as objects, while active processes involving dynamic changes in configuration are sequentially scanned. The diagram shows an overlap when it comes to prepositional phrases (which also should remind us that cognitive grammar is not about labelling parts of language but is about outlining reading processes that are applied to linguistic elements). A prepositional phrase can act as a static part of the setting, or as a participant in the action chain. Compare, for example:

> There is a bridge across the river
> (non-participatory 'river', summarily scanned)
>
> He waded across the river
> (patient 'river', sequentially scanned in the action chain)
>
> He crossed the river
> (patient 'river' again, as part of a sequentially scanned process)

We can thus distinguish different cognitive impacts between nominals and relationals, between stative processes and active processes, and between the different semantic roles played by participants in those processes, viewed against their non-participating settings.

Discussion

The theoretical consequences of accepting a cognitive approach to grammar are significant for linguistics, but what about the impact on how we conceive of the *literary* act of communication? Before proceeding to some examples of analysis, you might want to consider or discuss some of these difficult problems. The first two points are different facets of the same question; the third point is a means of exploring the issue.

- Taking cognitive grammar seriously involves an understanding of linguistic form in terms of what that form is doing in the mind. Purely formalist literary criticism – such as pure close-reading, New Criticism, or structuralist analyses – are outlawed by this imperative. Stylistics also used to be criticised for being too formalist. Can you imagine a fully contextualised stylistics that has to take account not simply of the words on the page but also of the reader's cognitive processes in realising the literary text? Both cognitive and cultural models of current and background knowledge, linguistic and literary competence, personal experience, memories, wishes and imagination would all need to be included. What would be excluded from a literary reading in this approach?

- There is no direct link between linguistic form and the categories of cognitive grammar since each slot can be seen as being prototypically related to all the others. Furthermore, the figure and ground distinction can be **construed** in many different ways by readers. This would seem to suggest that the 'rules' of cognitive grammar are different from linguistic rules as they are traditionally understood, in that they do not absolutely constrain linguistic expressions. If you treat the prototypical models produced in cognitive grammar as producing a sort of 'most natural' reading, where does this leave the status of other, interesting readings?
- Using some of the terms from cognitive grammar, take a literary text and analyse the participant roles that are played out. How is the literary world built up? How are the elements in the world (the setting) related to the participants? How does the cognitive grammar encode narratorial attitudes to the characters by presenting them in particular archetypal roles?

Cognitive poetic analysis

Here is a poem whose action chains are a major foregrounded aspect of its patterning.

Easter wings

Lord, who createdst man in wealth and store,
    Though foolishly he lost the same,
        Decaying more and more,
            Till he became
                Most poore:
                With thee
            O let me rise
        As larks, harmoniously,
    And sing this day thy victories:
Then shall the fall further the flight in me.

My tender age in sorrow did beginne:
    And still with sicknesses and shame
        Thou didst so punish sinne,
            That I became
                Most thinne.
                With thee
            Let me combine,
        And feel this day thy victorie:
    For, if I imp my wing on thine,
Affliction shall advance the flight in me.

(George Herbert, 1633)

The first noticeable thing about the poem is, of course, that its graphological arrangement represents in a very direct way the subject in the title. Turning the book sideways to read it you will also notice that the lines are made shorter and longer not simply by arbitrary chopping of two syllables out of the line-lengths but by a carefully deployed grammatical arrangement as well. Each stanza consists of a similar action-chain pattern, the contexts of which are explicitly named in the poem:

Stanza 1   creation,   decaying,   rising,   singing, and the last line;

Stanza 2   beginning,   thinning,   combining,   feeling,   and the last two lines.

While there are many other aspects to the poem, I want to focus on the participant roles and patterns in these action chains. I have set the stanza themes out like this so that the parallelism is most apparent.

The first pair of action chains represent a dynamic predication of a process beginning: 'Lord, who createdst man' and 'My tender age … did beginne'. Unsurprisingly, God is the active agent here who initiates the poem, with 'man' the patient receiver of the act of creation. In the second stanza, however, 'my tender age' is still the patient in the process, even though it is in subject position. In fact this comes close to appearing as an autonomous process, leaving 'my tender age' simply in a theme role. The individual is further displaced by being represented grammatically within a possessive expression (the receiver in a process of containment), and 'my tender age' is ambiguously either his individual life or his general times.

The participant who is 'decaying' in the first stanza is the third person 'he', 'man', referring to the generalised mass of humanity. The thinning participant in the second stanza is 'I'. In both cases, they play passive roles as themes in the process, a process which semantically diminishes them in both cases (and is paralleled by the shortening lines). The verb 'became' in both cases points to a process in which both participants are transformed – though they are trajectors, they shrink in prominence into the action chain.

At this point in both stanzas, the directionality (another figure/ground relationship) of both action chains reverses: 'With thee O let me rise as larks' and 'With thee let me combine'. Instead of trajectors in action chains that shrink inward and downward, the trajectors here rise and expand. An imperative is addressed to God, though cast in the permission rather than command form ('Let me'), with 'me' apparently as patient; but the semantics of the whole action chain perhaps suggests that 'me' is instead a mover here, rising and combining.

There is a difference, of course, between the predications. The first introduces an analogy with larks rising, drawing in domain knowledge of birdsong at dawn, and perhaps (and certainly for the contemporary reader) alluding to Christ's rise in the resurrection. Analogy draws elements from two domains together, but there are still implicitly two separate domains. In the second chain, the process is one of identity ('combine') and the poem has moved on to the end of the day, after the completion of 'thy victorie'. In the next pair of chains, the speaker is experiencer: 'sing this day', 'feel this day'. Again, though, there are differences in directionality if you imagine the action chain scheme. In the first stanza, the experiencer sings out 'thy victories'; in the second, the experiencer feels 'thy victorie' inwardly. The plural victories have been combined into a single victory, just as the poem moves from generalised 'man' to the redemption of the individual 'I'.

I have left the closing lines of each stanza to the end, because they express different action chains from the rest of the poem. Both the grounded processes ('further' and 'advance') are placed in the future using the modal 'shall'. Both are part of condition-fulfilment syntax: 'let me rise ... then shall ... ' and 'if I imp ... affliction shall ... '. And 'shall' modalises definiteness rather than uncertainty. At first these processes seem synonymous. However, a close examination of the participant roles involved reveals precise differences.

First, it helps if we recognise the differences in time reference. In the first stanza, 'the fall' refers back in time both to the symbolic fall detailed in the poem and to the biblical expulsion of Adam and Eve from the Garden of Eden. In the second stanza, the time reference is from near-present to future, beginning with the conditional 'if I imp my wing on thine'. The currency of this is not just grammatical but cultural: the process refers to the practice of grafting feathers onto the damaged wing of a falcon to enable it to fly again or faster.

In the first stanza, 'the fall' is a mover and 'flight' is the patient which is moved. The first is trajector and the second is the landmark in the action process. Given the rest of this stanza, I would read the prepositional phrase 'in me' as a stative preposition; in other words, as part of the setting. I am arguing that 'in me' in the first stanza is summarily scanned, and the speaker is almost entirely inactive and non-participatory throughout. The agentive elements have been 'Lord' and 'fall'; the only verb that looks as if it might profile an agentive speaker ('sing') is in fact subordinate to the polite imperative, 'let me', in which God is the agent again. For me, the stanza begins with the undistinguished mass of humanity and it ends with the primacy of a process and with personified abstractions as participants ('fall' and 'flight'), with the individual pushed into the background. This reading of 'in me' as a stative is supported by the fact that the only other uses of 'in' before and after it are also unambiguously statives that ground the setting: 'in wealth and store' and 'in sorrow' are background settings for creation and the beginning of life respectively. 'Further' in this context seems to move the abstract 'flight' only as far as the next stanza.

However, the final line of the second stanza presents a different pattern that profiles the speaker as a participant and reaches out into the future (in which the afterlife is symbolised by the end of the day, the rising flight, and the spreading out of the line at the end of the poem). 'Affliction', again, is the mover in this process, and 'flight' again is patient. However, I think that this time the prepositional 'in me' is most likely to be sequentially scanned as part of the process rather than as a stative. This means that 'me' right at the end becomes a participating *instrument* of the process. This construal is partly because of the proximity of 'I' in the penultimate line of the second stanza, which raises the speaker explicitly to prominence in the action chain, compared with the omission of the pronoun in the penultimate line of the first stanza. Also, 'me' as the very last word of the entire poem is more prominent than as the last word of the first stanza. Most crucially, though, the inclusion of 'then' in the conditional of the first stanza serves to restrict the location of the action chain profiled by 'further' to a specific point. By contrast, the omission of 'then' in the conditional of the second stanza (made more pointed and prominent by all the other parallelisms across the two stanzas) serves to give 'advance' an ongoing, continuous sense, or a sort of everlasting action chain.

Throughout the poem, God is the final cause, agent either implicitly as the trajector participant in the action chain or also explicitly in the text. 'Man' and the poetic voice both begin either as patients or merely as elements in the setting, but by the end the speaker is allowed to become an instrument of God's action. A final difference between the action chains encapsulates the progression: 'further' creates for me an image of an action chain in which a trajector moves *along* an existing path. This is an image contained within the domain of life. However, I construe 'advance' as a movement *out of* the ground into the foreground. Prominence is achieved by combining with God rather than being merely a passive or echoing recipient as in the first stanza. The final image is one of moving out of the constraints of life in a flight to redemption.

Explorations

1   An interesting comparison with Langacker's cognitive grammar, as set out in this chapter, is Halliday's systemic-functional linguistics. Halliday sees three **metafunctions** in language: the interpersonal, the textual, and the ideational. Forming part of the last of these, the following is a summary of transitivity relations. Though Halliday comes out of a different tradition, he has recently affirmed that his approach is cognitively sympathetic, and though it does not have an explicit connection with mental representations, it seems to me a usable grammar without contradicting cognitive principles. You could compare it with the categories in Langacker's scheme. (For each, I have found two examples from John Donne).

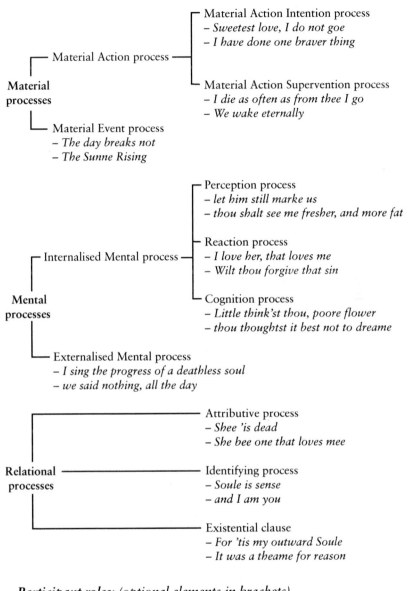

Material processes

Material Action process
- Material Action Intention process
  - *Sweetest love, I do not goe*
  - *I have done one braver thing*
- Material Action Supervention process
  - *I die as often as from thee I go*
  - *We wake eternally*

Material Event process
- *The day breaks not*
- *The Sunne Rising*

Mental processes

Internalised Mental process
- Perception process
  - *let him still marke us*
  - *thou shalt see me fresher, and more fat*
- Reaction process
  - *I love her, that loves me*
  - *Wilt thou forgive that sin*
- Cognition process
  - *Little think'st thou, poore flower*
  - *thou thoughtst it best not to dreame*

Externalised Mental process
- *I sing the progress of a deathless soul*
- *we said nothing, all the day*

Relational processes

Attributive process
- *Shee 'is dead*
- *She bee one that loves mee*

Identifying process
- *Soule is sense*
- *and I am you*

Existential clause
- *For 'tis my outward Soule*
- *It was a theame for reason*

Participant roles: *(optional elements in brackets)*

- Material processes:
  actor   *(goal)*
- Mental processes:
  internalised
    senser   *(phenomenon)*
  externalised
    sayer   *(target)*

- Relational processes:
  attributive
  > *carrier*   *attribute*
  identifying
  > *identifier*   *(identified)*
  existential
  > *dummy subject*   *'it/there'*
- Circumstantial elements (usually adverbials and prepositionals):
  > *extent and location* where, how long?
  > *manner*   how?
  > *cause*   why?
  > *accompaniment*   with what?
  > *matter*   what about?
  > *role*   what as?

Where does cognitive grammar and systemic-functional linguistics overlap?
Which do you find most useful or convincing?

2   Here is the opening of John Donne's poem 'The Extasie':

> Where, like a pillow on a bed,
> A Pregnant banke swel'd up, to rest
> The violets reclining head,
> Sat we two, one anothers best;
> Our hands were firmly cimented
> With a fast balme, which thence did spring,
> Our eye-beames twisted, and did thred
> Our eyes, upon one double string,
> So to'entergraft our hands, as yet
> Was all the meanes to make us one,
> And pictures in our eyes to get
> Was all our propagation.
> As 'twixt two equall Armies, Fate
> Suspends uncertaine victorie,
> Our soules, (which to advance their state,
> Were gone out,) hung 'twixt her, and mee.
> And whil'st our soules negotiate there,
> Wee like sepulchrall statues lay,
> All day, the same our postures were,
> And wee said nothing, all the day.
> (John Donne, pub. 1633)

On first glance, this extract represents the two lovers in their constituent parts, but the 'extasie' is later described as a feeling which 'interinanimates two soules'. Can you use either Langacker's scheme or Halliday's scheme to track the action chains/processes and the participant roles here? You might want to continue your analysis with the rest of the poem, or with other Donne love poems from *Songs and Sonets*.

3   The precise specification of types of action and participant roles is especially pertinent in literary texts which deal with responsibility for actions. Find the murder scenes in some detective, crime or thriller fiction, and use a grammatical analysis to track how blame is assigned or withheld. Essentially, you are answering the question: who does what to whom (with what and how)?

4   Consider how the cultural model of subjectivity might have changed over time. For example, the prototypical scale of empathy seems to have special reconfigurations in the case of traditional fairy tales or magical tales which feature talking animals, rocks, spirits and gods. You might examine some medieval texts which feature 'everyman' tokens or 'characters' who are obviously personifications of sins, virtues, vices and other qualities. Morality plays (such as *Everyman, Mankind,* John Skelton's *Magnyfycence,* and others) are good sources for this, but you might also apply the same perspective to William Langland's *Piers Plowman* (late fourteenth century) or John Bunyan's *The Pilgrim's Progress* (1684). Look particularly at how different participants are introduced, interact through their actions, and are given attributes.

5   You could look in detail at very short literary texts, such as haiku, epitaphs or epigrams (I have Donne's two-line epigrams in mind, though you could also look at those of Ben Jonson, or later writers). Focus on the concentrated action chain, and decide on how you construe the figure and ground roles of trajector, primary and secondary landmarks, and setting.

Further reading and references

Most of the theoretical content of this chapter is compiled from Langacker (1987, 1991). These volumes set out a comprehensive framework in cognitive grammar. I have especially focused on Part II of the second volume, dealing with clause structure (Langacker 1991: 193–413), and particularly the chapter on 'Transitivity and Grammatical Relations' (Langacker 1991: 282–329). The scale of topicality in subjectivity is outlined in Langacker (1991: 305–29); role archetypes in Langacker (1991: 282–91); domains in Langacker (1987: 147–82); scanning in Langacker (1987: 141–6). See also Langacker (1990). Ungerer and Schmid (1996) give a clear outline with some suggested simplifications to Langacker.

Other approaches to grammar that share some similar concerns include Fillmore (1975, 1976, 1977, 1985), and Talmy (1978, 1988). Taylor (1995) explores the application of prototypes to linguistic categories.

The systemic-functional linguistic scheme for transitivity was adapted from Berry (1977) and Halliday (1985). Analyses which use this approach have come to be called **critical linguistics** or **critical discourse analysis**

(CDA). For studies which use this approach and combine cognitive and social factors, see Fowler (1996), Fairclough (1995), Caldas-Coulthard and Coulthard (1996), and for an attempt to see common ground between CDA and cognitive linguistics, see Stockwell (2001).

6   Scripts and schemas

Preview

Why do people read literature? Why do people write literature? These questions have been cogitated by philosophers, literary critics, writers, publishers, booksellers, and readers for as long as literature has existed. As we have already seen in examples in previous chapters, often literary texts are about themselves as texts: as much about writing and reading as they are about the apparent subject-matter. Different motivations for reading have been suggested, ranging from an appreciation of realism to a value placed on escapism. You hear people praising a book because it reflects something to them of their own lives, has a character they can identify with, or is written out of real experience and therefore seems to be authentic in a way that is admirable and engaging. Alternatively you hear people praising a book because of its depth of imagination, the richness or exotic nature of the characterisation, or the intricate plotting or surrealism or absurdity of the events.

Both of these opinions, and all points between, rely on a view of the literary experience that presents a world, a rich setting beyond the words on the page. The text interacts with the reader's mental faculties, memories, emotions and beliefs to produce a sum that is richer than the parts: the text is actualised, the reader is vivified, by a good book.

In order to understand what is going on here, we need to be able to understand how exactly texts interact with readerly experience. We need to address the difficult question of *context* in relation to literary texts and reading, and we need to develop a principled idea of context that does not simply ascribe particular readings to some vague sense of 'background knowledge'.

As a first step in this direction, one of the earliest applications of an approach from cognitive science to literature was **schema theory**. This was originally developed as a means of providing computer programs in artificial intelligence research with a contextual 'knowledge' that would enable them to process language. Several different frameworks have been proposed over the years, with different terminology and with slightly different aims, but I will gather them together here under the general term 'schema theory'. Since there are many examples of schema theoretical applications to the literature of the last two centuries, and schema poetics does not depend primarily on stylistic form, I will present an analysis of literature from the Anglo-Saxon period.

Links with literary critical concepts

Context, contextualisation, defamiliarisation, experience, fictionality, historicism, history, imagination, literariness, literary worlds, readerliness, realism

Many of the shifts in critical theory and 'crises' in literary theorising revolve around the thorny question of how much textuality, how much readerliness, and how much history should be brought into literary critical discussions. One of the advantages of formalist approaches to literature is that analysis is easily visible and cited evidence is apparent and demonstrable on the surface of a text. Of course, absolute formalism has to explain how meanings can be generated without readerly or other contextual input. What is satisfying at the level of pure description is not very satisfactory as a general account of literary understanding.

By contrast, approaches that have focused on readers reading have been accused of being psychological studies rather than literary study as such. Either they emphasise individual idiosyncrasy, or they treat groups of readers as sources of 'data' rather than interpretations. At the other extreme, critical approaches grounded in historical contexts can be seen as being more interested in history than the literature itself, treating a literary text as no more than an archaeological artefact, and engaging in a sort of slapdash poorman's history, where claims can be made about the past while evading the disciplinary rigour and evidence required in genuine historical study.

All of these solutions represent different views of what counts as relevant and appropriate context. In fact, none of them is either fully contextualised or entirely decontextualised. Furthermore, they address in different ways and mainly implicitly the real questions, which are not whether context is important but how is it important and how is it used. Given the vast amount of historical context that is potentially available, and the hugeness of the imagined experience of the author and the contemporary society, and given the massive encyclopedic knowledge carried around in the heads of readers, how can we decide which bits of context are used and which are not, in a principled way? That is the ground of schema poetics.

Conceptual dependency

The main obstacle to artificial intelligence is the fact that language exhibits **conceptual dependency**. That is, the selection of words in a sentence, and the meanings derived from sentences, depend not on a dictionary-like denotation of these strings of words but on the sets of ideas and other associations that the words suggest in the minds of speakers and hearers. Often, both speaker and hearer are familiar with the situation that is being discussed, and therefore every single facet will not need to be enumerated for the situation to be understood. Similarly, human eyes looking at a set of visual patterns will link elements together or see shapes and features that are derived from previously encountered experiences. In the visual field, the context brought by viewers to disparate objects is called a *frame*. In the linguistic field, the conceptual structure drawn from memory to assist in understanding utterances is a schema that was first called a **script**.

For example, I live in Britain and have a 'going to the pub' script which I will need when I finish this chapter later on today. Until it occurred to me to use this as an example just now, the 'going to the pub' script was not at the forefront of my mind. Later on, I will go not to the pub down the road but to a pub in the countryside not far from here, where I have never been before. However, I know that when I get there I will know exactly what to expect and what to do. My pub script has elements that I expect to see (a bar, a person behind the bar, tables, beer pumps, bottles, glasses, and so on). Besides these objects, my pub script includes procedures that I can use in order to get a drink. I know that I have to go and stand at the bar. I know what form of words to use and what the other person will say. I know how to reply to the various questions I am asked. I understand how to pay for the beer there and then, and I know where I am allowed to sit, the sorts of behaviour that are appropriate, and so on.

Of course I was not born with this knowledge: my pub script has been learned from experience. Neither is it a static script: I have expanded it and refined it through experience of a range of different sorts of pubs – pubs that are also restaurants, pubs that have adopted the continental European practice of having waiting staff, pubs that have only bottled beers, pubs that shade into bars, cafés, nightclubs, social clubs, working men's clubs, Labour clubs. And I have had to apply my pub script adaptively to a range of situations – in beer tents, at private parties, at barbecues, buying a beer on an aeroplane, on a boat on the Danube, in a bar in Tokyo, in a late-night drinking den in Liverpool, at a Basque festival by catching cider in a glass from an enormous vat with a pinhole in the side, and so on. All of these are examples of different **tracks** through the pub script.

It should be apparent from these examples that a script is a socioculturally defined mental protocol for negotiating a situation. Miscues in script application can explain the confusion caused to the French family waiting in an English pub to be served at their table, or expecting to pay as they leave rather than there and then, or my confusion when I seemed to have paid for an empty glass at the Basque festival.

Scripts such as the pub script are **situational** scripts. We use these to negotiate commonly experienced events such as being in a restaurant, taking the bus, or weeding the garden. Additionally, we have scripts that are **personal**, such as what to do and say in order to be a complaining passenger, a husband or wife, or how to talk to someone you have never met before. Lastly, we have **instrumental** scripts such as how to light a barbecue, how to switch on the computer, how to read, and so on.

Knowing which script to draw upon in a particular situation depends on **headers** that instantiate the script. In terms of written discourse, headers can be of four types:

- **precondition headers** – these are references that act as a precondition for the application of a script ('Peter fancied a beer').
- **instrumental headers** – references to actions that are a means toward the realisation of the script ('Peter walked down to the pub').
- **locale headers** – references to the setting in which the script usually applies ('Peter stood at the bar').
- **internal conceptualisation headers** – references to an *action* or role from the script ('Peter ordered a beer').

Of course, some of these elements can also display prototype effects, such that 'Peter fancied a beer. He walked down to the Ferry Inn' is more likely to instantiate the pub script than 'Peter fancied a packet of peanuts. He sat at an outside table'. It also seems to be the case that at least two headers are required for a script to be activated: 'Peter fancied a beer. He got one out of the fridge and carried on typing' represents a **fleeting script**.

A script consists of **slots** that are assumed to pertain in a situation unless we are explicitly told otherwise: **props; participants; entry conditions; results;** and **sequence of events**.

In any particular script, these slots are filled with specific items (respectively, beer glasses, a barman, walking into a pub, getting a drink, ordering and being served, for example). This can explain why 'but' in the following sentence seems natural: 'Peter walked into the pub, but the place was deserted'. Compare this with the oddity of, 'Peter walked into the pub, but there were people in there, and beer pumps and glasses'. The application of schema theory can thus contribute to our understanding of textual **coherence**.

Scripts develop out of **plans**, which are generalised conceptual procedures such as 'socialising' or 'getting a drink'. When a plan becomes routine in experience, it becomes a script. Plans and scripts arise out of higher level **goals**, which are very general aims and objectives carried by individuals, such as satisfaction goals, achievement goals, preservation goals, and so on. Plans and goals are the conceptual tools we use to negotiate new situations.

It should be pointed out that scripts, plans, goals and their contents are not fixed structures but are assembled in the course of discourse processing. Their configuration is dynamic and depends both on the stylistic input and the particular experiential base of the reader.

Literary schemas

Schemas have also been used to explain bundles of information and features at every level of linguistic organisation, from the meanings perceived in individual words to the readings of entire texts. Literary genres, fictional episodes, imagined characters in narrated situations can all be understood as part of schematised knowledge negotiation. One of the key factors in the appeal of schema theory is that it sees these knowledge structures as dynamic and experientially developing. In general, there are three ways in which a schema can evolve:

- **accretion** – the addition of new facts to the schema
- **tuning** – the modification of facts or relations within the schema
- **restructuring** – the creation of new schemas

For example, for readers who have only a passing familiarity with science fiction, the SF schema typically has slots such as: spaceships, rayguns, robots (props); scientists, explorers, aliens (participants); extraterrestrial settings or time or space travel (entry conditions); apocalypse, or its cunning avoidance (results); and space battles or laser shoot-outs (sequence of events). As people read more SF, their schemas accrete extra features, such as the time-dilation effects of faster-than-light intergalactic travel, or 'warp' engines, or positronic brains, and so on. In the 1960s, there was a perceptible shift in science fiction from outer space to 'inner space', and a concern for psychological, biological and social science fiction, that represented a tuning of the SF schema for many readers. New sub-genres within SF later appeared, such as 'cyberpunk' or 'feminist SF' – for some critics this involved tuning their schemas further, for others it represented a thorough restructuring of the schema.

Schema theory has been used to revisit the issue of literariness and literary language. It is argued that most everyday discourse is **schema preserving**, in that it confirms existing schemas. Where the confirmation is stereotypical, as in much advertising discourse, this is **schema reinforcing**. Sometimes surprising elements or sequences in the conceptual content of the text can potentially offer a **schema disruption**, a challenge to the reader's existing knowledge structure. Schema disruptions can be resolved either by **schema adding** (the equivalent of accretion above), or by a radical **schema refreshment** – a schema change that is the equivalent of tuning, above, or the notion in literature not so much of defamiliarisation as 'refamiliarisation'. Clearly, this is not a definition of literariness as a whole, but a definition of 'good' literature, or literature which is felt to have an impact or effect. The types of schema management can be summarised as follows:

- **knowledge restructuring** – the creation of new schemas based on old templates.
- **schema preservation** – where incoming facts fit existing schematic knowledge and have been encountered previously.
- **schema reinforcement** – where incoming facts are new but strengthen and confirm schematic knowledge.
- **schema accretion** – where new facts are added to an existing schema, enlarging its scope and explanatory range.

- **schema disruption** – where conceptual deviance offers a potential challenge.
- **schema refreshment** – where a schema is revised and its membership elements and relations are recast (tuning, defamiliarisation in literature).

This view of schema theory in a literary context points to three different fields in which schemas operate: **world schemas, text schemas,** and **language schemas.** World schemas cover those schemas considered so far that are to do with content; text schemas represent our expectations of the way that world schemas appear to us in terms of their sequencing and structural organisation; language schemas contain our idea of the appropriate forms of linguistic patterning and style in which we expect a subject to appear. Taking the last two together, disruptions in our expectations of textual structure or stylistic structure constitute **discourse deviation,** which offers the possibility for schema refreshment.

However, if we are going to isolate the literary context in this way, why not short-circuit the argument and simply raise the possibility of a 'literature' schema that comprises these deviations? One branch of schema theory suggests exactly this. A literary schema would not be an ordinary schema but a higher-level conceptual structure that organises our ways of reading when we are in the literary context. It is thus a **constitutive schema,** rather like a plan or a goal in terms of early schema theory. Any ordinary schema can appear in a literary context, but once there it is treated in a different way as a result of literary reading. It is this reading angle that 're-registers' the original schema and processes it in terms of literary factors.

A literary schema for fiction, for example, is based on **alternativity** when compared with the organising principles of our other world schemas (more on worlds in Chapters 7 and 10). Measuring the divergence from our everyday expectations of text schemas and language schemas in literature is a matter of narratological and stylistic analysis. The degree of deviation from our sense of reality in world schematic structure can be measured on a scale of **informativity,** on the basis of three orders of informativity:

- **first-order informativity** – normal, unremarkable things are schema preserving or reinforcing.
- **second-order informativity** – unusual or less likely things encountered in literary worlds develop schematic knowledge by accretion.
- **third-order informativity** – impossible or highly unlikely things represent a challenge to schema knowledge as schema disruption. This can result in schema refreshment or radical knowledge restructuring if the challenge necessitates a wholesale paradigm shift, a change in worldview.

Second- and third-order occurrences are assimilated into existing knowledge by **downgrading,** which is a motivation search through schema knowledge for a resolution: an attempt at schema preservation in the first instance. Downgrading can be either **backwards** into the memory of the previous text, or **forwards** in anticipating what will happen. For example, at the beginning of Franz Kafka's *The Trial* (1925), Joseph K. is arrested without having done anything wrong. This anomaly (second-order, I would suggest) cannot be downgraded backwards as it occurs in the first sentence of the novel. The reader's only option is to read on for an explanation in an attempt to have the anomaly downgraded forwards. Of course, no downgrading ever appears, and the anomaly has eventually to be downgraded **outwards** by recognising that the alternative world of a literary schema (Kafka-esque metaphysical absurdism) is in operation.

More radically, Greg Egan's short story 'The Infinite Assassin' begins:

> One thing never changes: when some mutant junkie on S starts shuffling reality, it's always me they send into the whirlpool to put things right.
>
> (Egan 1996: 1)

There are various disruptions of language schema here: what is 'S', 'the whirlpool', and 'shuffling reality'? In the world schema, who is 'me' and why is he being sent 'to put things right'? These second-order anomalies are quickly joined by third-order elements, as the story outlines people, cars, buildings and even people's clothes, hair and faces all shifting and changing, appearing and disappearing in front of the narrator's eyes. Only by the end of the story can I downgrade all this by discovering that 'S' is a drug in which hallucinations generate breaks between alternate parallel universes, and the narrator is an employee of 'The Company' with an infinite number of parallel personalities. In every parallel universe, he has to kill the drug-dreamer in order to regularise every local universe again. Clearly, new physical properties of the world schema are required here, but this is not allowed to present a radical shift in worldview as soon as the reader realises that the story is constituted by a science fiction track within the literature schema.

Discussion

Before proceeding, you might like to discuss the application of schema theory in the context of literary reading. Here are some possible questions to think about and discuss:

- There is a problem of regression underlying schema theory: that is, where do schemas ultimately come from? Schank and Abelson (1977) posit plans and goals as increasingly abstract motivations, but it should be pointed out that their model was intended for *computer programming* not human psychology. In applying it to human minds, we are faced with questions such as: Where do babies get their schemas? Could there be a schema for schema construction that generates all other knowledge? What are the psychological mechanisms by which unfamiliar experiences are assigned to different schemas?

- There is a more practical methodological problem when schema theory is applied to literary reading. It is not easy (indeed sometimes it seems quite arbitrary) to reach a *principled* decision as to which level of schema is being used in a particular situation. Do I have a pub schema, or is it really just a track through my more general restaurant/bar schema? Or is this in turn simply a specific part of my transaction schema? Alternatively, might I not have separate schemas for country pubs, town pubs, Irish pubs, gastro-pubs, or theme pubs? When I read or see *Macbeth*, do I have a Shakespearean play schema, or a court politics schema in operation? Or in fact, do I accrete a *Macbeth* schema, and can every literary text be said to generate its own specific schema?

- What do you think of the distinction between schema reinforcement and schema refreshment? Does it offer a convincing means of understanding 'literariness' as opposed to closely related modes such as advertising, travel writing, religious sermons or parables?

- Schema poetics is essentially an approach to the *conceptual* organisation of literature and readers' minds. Other than the consequences of different language schemas in operation, it should then be possible to sketch schematic readings of translated works without any problems (unless there are large cultural issues at the level of world schema, of course). However, the headers and slots within schemas and the tracks through schemas can also be discussed in terms of their *stylistic* and *narratological* features. How far do you think schema theory can be assimilated with stylistics? You might consider two parallel translations of a text in order to help you come to a conclusion.

Cognitive poetic analysis

Here is the opening of the 156-line poem which is usually called 'The Dream of the Rood' ('rood' meaning 'cross'), written down in the ninth or tenth century. In the translation, I have tried to preserve the sound of the vocabulary as closely as possible, though Anglo-Saxon grammar allows great flexibility which makes it difficult to keep the word-order exact:

Hwæt, ic swefna cyst secgan wylle,	Listen, and I will say the best of visions
hwæt mē gemǣtte tō midre nihte,	which came to me in the mid-night
syðþan reordberend reste wunedon.	while chatterers lay in bed.
Þūhte mē þæt ic gesāwe syllicre trēow	I thought that I saw a wondrous tree
on lyft lǣdan lēohte bewunden,	held high aloft, wound round with light,
bēama beorhtost. Eall þæt bēacen wæs	the brightest of beams. All that beacon was
begoten mid golde; gimmas stōdon	arrayed in gold; gems stood
fægere æt foldan scēatum, swycle þǣr fife wǣron	fair at the earth's corners, and there were five too

uppe on þām eaxlgespanne. Behēoldon	upon the axle-span. Beheld by legions
þær engeldryhta feala	of the lord's angels,
fægere þurh forðgesceaft; ne wæs	fair through all creation; this truly was
ðær hūru fracodes gealga,	not a criminal's gallows,
ac hine þær behēoldon hālige gāstas,	but it was beheld by holy ghosts,
men ofer moldan, and eall þēos mǣre	men over the land, and by all this
gesceaft.	glorious creation.

Unless you are very familiar with Anglo-Saxon (or 'Old English'), you are likely to find this poem bewildering, firstly because any language schema you possess is unlikely to offer you more than a bare understanding of the language of the poem. Even with my gloss to help you see the roots of words such as 'will', 'night', 'tree' and 'ghosts', your language schema probably does not include other words such as 'scēatum' or 'syllicre', grammatical word-endings, and some odd symbols (þ and ð, both versions of the sound 'th', and æ; and the vowel lengthening marks over ā and ē, for example).

Any text schematic knowledge you possess (again, unless you have studied this literature) is likely also to be insufficient. If you can read the text correctly out loud, you might notice the heavy alliteration across each line and perhaps also notice that each line falls into two halves, but would you recognise this pattern as the characteristic feature of Anglo-Saxon literature? You might even be tempted to read all sorts of stylistically significant meanings into the strange word-ordering, unless you know about Anglo-Saxon inflectional grammar and simply ascribe the grammatical flexibility to the demands of half-line alliteration. Would you recognise this patterning as a consequence of a 'literary' tradition that was primarily oral and memorised, and only committed to writing late in the period? Would you recognise some of the phrases from the poem from what might be a popular earlier shorter poem, or realise that these echoed some runic phrases carved onto a stone cross at Ruthwell in the Scottish borders around the year 700? Would you think that the poet had cleverly reworked some popular material into a full and complex narrative and surrealistic world, embedded in layers of dream-vision and mystical revelation? Perhaps only if you were an Anglo-Saxon listener.

This leads us to the first issue in schema poetics: whose schema is to be used? We cannot talk of 'the schema of the poem', since schemas belong to people not texts. I will offer a schematic reading that, inevitably, is my own modern one, but I will return in the Explorations at the end to the question of recreating a contemporary schematic reading of the poem.

An exploration of the world schema dimension might get us some way initially. The poem is structured into the sort of narrative embedding that is familiar to modern readers (not very dissimilar to that of *Wuthering Heights*, for example). The speaker is compelled to describe a dream in which they see a vision of a fantastically bright and decorated tree. It becomes clear in the description that this is the cross on which Christ died, with the speaker giving an account of his own sense of fear, sinfulness and guilt. Then the cross speaks directly through the narrating speaker, describing how it was torn from its roots from the forest's edge and forced by enemies to hoist up criminals. This central part of the poem, over 94 lines, is spoken in the first person by the cross. It describes how it was used as an instrument of God when Christ climbed up onto it, and it shares the wounds and pain of the humiliation. Then:

Feala ic on þām beorge gebiden hæbbe	Again and again on that hill I lived through
wrāðra wyrda: geseah ic weruda God þearle þenian; þȳstro hæfdon	cruel events: I saw the God of warriors terribly racked; darkness had
bewrigen mid wolcnum Wealdendes hrǣw;	wreathed with clouds the Lord's corpse;
scīrne scīman sceadu forðēode,	sheer radiance overcome by shadow,
wann under wolcnum. Wēop eal gesceaft,	dark under clouds. All creation wept,
cwiðdon cyninges fyll: Crīst wæs on rōde.	lamenting a king's fall: Christ was on the cross.

These most famous lines express the most forceful alliteration in the poem. The cross goes on to describe how men came to carry the body away and lament the death; Christ was placed into the tomb and the cross was buried in a pit. Christ's resurrection is not described directly at first, but in terms of the cross being dug up and adorned with gold and silver. The cross ends by rejoicing in the fact that it was chosen for the task and it enjoins the dreamer to repeat the vision to others. The narrative then pops up a level back to the dreamer who emphasises the salvation available to those who rely on the symbol of the cross. The poem ends with a worshipful prayer:

Se Sunu wæs sigorfæst on þām sīðfate,	The Son was victorious from that journey,
mihtig and spēdig, þā hē mid manigeo cōm,	mighty and successful, when he came with many,
gāsta weorode, on Godes rīce,	a company of souls, to the kingdom of God,
Anwealda ælmihtig, englum tō blisse	the almighty Ruler, to the bliss of the angels
and eallum ðām hālgum þām þe on heofonum ǣr	and all the saints that in heaven till then
wunedon on wuldre, þā heora Wealdend cwōm,	had lived in glory, when their Ruler came,
ælmihtig God, þǣr his ēðel wæs.	almighty God, there where his home was.

First, there is the third-order anomaly of a speaking tree to be reconciled with world schematic knowledge. Downgrading backwards, the anomaly is part of a dream account. Downgrading outwards, the literary rhetorical figure of 'personification' is familiar enough for it to be easily recognised, but this action immediately cues up a literary schema for the analysis of the poem (as well as the cues provided by the layout and language). It seems to me that the blend of conventional dream schema and conventional literary schema allows a twofold angle to be maintained throughout the poem. This pattern of complementary dimensions is the major strategy perceived in my interpretation, as I will illustrate below.

The most obvious schematic knowledge required is the schema of Christ's death (properly a narrative script, familiar from 'scripture'), and the schema of the central tenets of Christian faith. It is not until the ninth line, however, that an explicit header ('engeldryhta feala') might invoke these schemas. This is an internal conceptualisation header, but the religious cues which quickly follow it ('forðgesceaft' and 'hālige gāstas') might make the reader re-evaluate the dream-vision opening as a precondition header for a spiritual revelation.

However, what follows is not a simple re-telling of the passion of Christ, a schema reinforcement by simple repetition. The story is recounted with a radical shift in point of view from that of the synoptic gospels. Placing the cross as both instrument and witness offers a potential schema disruption that at least holds the possibility of a defamiliarised if not variant interpretation of the crucial event in Christianity. (If sustained, this might even be seen as the grounds of a heresy). How this disruption and higher-order informativity is resolved is the rhetorical brilliance of the poem.

It seems to me that giving the tree a first-person voice in the text evidently encourages a schematic reading that equates the tree with the idea of a human individual. The individual tree, unremarkable in the forest, is chosen to be an instrument of God's plan: like Christ on the eve of the crucifixion, it describes how it did not want to be placed in this role, but accepts its fate stoically. As Jesus is God made man within the Christian schema, so the tree is vivified and made flesh, given a voice, consciousness, wilfulness and freewill. It is both chosen and given a choice.

The humanised aspects of the cross are what generate most of the vivid images in the poem, and this further serves to create a strong identification between the dying man and the instrument of his death. At the crucifixion, it is the cross, rather than the body of Jesus, that experiences the wounds ('þurhdrifan hī mē mid deorcan næglum; on mē syndon þā dolg gesīene, / opene inwidhlemmas – they drove through me with dark nails; in me still the wounds are seen, / open evil gashes'). The personification allows an identity to be created between seeing something and being an active part of it. There is a combination of both instrumentality and witnessing throughout the poem.

It is interesting to compare the points at which the schema of Christ's passion and the poem's narrative diverge. A prominent consequence of the shift in viewpoint to the cross is in the agency and wilfulness of actions. The cross, an instrument, is passive throughout: enemies cut it down, hauled it on their shoulders, set it on a hill, and many enemies secured it there. However, these enemies are not active when it comes to Jesus: he 'efstan elne micle, þæt hē mē wolde on gestīgan – he hasten[ed] with great courage, that he wanted to climb up on me'. The enemies' actions are mediated through the cross: it was raised up, and it raised up the Lord of heaven. The usual roles of active and passive from the gospel schema are refreshed here, primarily as a consequence of the shift in viewpoint.

Overall in the cross' speech, then, there are reversals judged against schema expectations along the dimensions of active and passive, participating and observing, instrument and witness, inanimacy and a manifestation of human faculties, wilfulness and acceptance. These blends of binaries are paralleled in the various slots of the schema: a prop (the cross) becomes a participant alongside Jesus, and his enemies, friends and angels, and yet the cross remains an accepting recipient of all the other participants' actions. Its only action is its account, its witness to its experience, yet it is narratologically the central participant in the poem. An identity is created in the core of the poem that equates witnessing and evangelising with Christian duty and its redemptive consequence.

The final third of the poem is often regarded as a sort of 'tacked on' Christian litany of faith. The cross pops out from its biblical experience to address the dreamer directly twice, beginning both lines 78 and 95 with, 'hæleð mīn se lēofa' (my beloved man), in order to emphasise that its act of witness is now enjoined on the dreamer too. A conventional statement of judgement day and redemption follows. The vivid humanised imagery is replaced by abstract terms, long rambling sentences, and a close repetition of the Christian creed of heavenly salvation. However, this conventionality is important in a discussion of the poem's schema poetics. Given the highly unconventional schema disruption which has preceded this point, schema preservation by this sort of catechism rehearsal appears more like a reassuring schema reinforcement. There is, though, a final rhetorical shift that the poem allows which makes it more than just a restatement of Christian ideology.

The narratological pop back to the level of the dreamer effects a shift back to a real personal and human viewpoint, and we are given individual hints of this person. He is probably an old man, alone:

Nāh ic rīcra feala	I do not have many powerful
frēonda on feoldan, ac hīe forð heonon	friends on earth, but onwards from here they
gewiton of worulde drēamum	have departed this world of dreams.

And he prays for his death in order to join them in heaven, where the Lord's people are seated at a feast. He prays that the Lord will be a friend to him, and ends with the passage quoted previously (p.84), closing the triumphant return of Christ and the angel armies from the harrowing of hell with a simple and domestic homecoming: 'þær his ēðel wæs'.

At the end, then, we get a shift of the act of witness to the dreamer, now awoken and telling the poem to the listening audience. His vicarious dream participation in the story of the cross has compelled him to become a witness like the cross, and that act is the poem itself. The personal details emphasise his human reality in our world, and the homely details further reinforce a schema of familiarity and domestic warmth. However, all this reality is in fact a 'world of dreams'. It is heaven, redemption and salvation that are real and true. Though this is a schema reinforcement, it is one which asserts the truth of mysticism and spirituality. It manages it not by the usual downgrading of unreal elements into a familiar resolving schema, but by an **upgrading** of the familiar world into an anomalous and mystical dream state, over which the abstractions of the vision of salvation are the incomprehensible reality.

The potential schema disruption in the first part of the poem is resolved not by a schema refreshment but by a powerful act of schema reinforcement. Unusually, this is negotiated by a radical point-of-view shift, accompanied by other aspects of schematic and discourse deviance as set out above, and an act of conceptual upgrading in order to participate in the Christian schema that is the necessary consequence of the poem. The abstractions are not simply made concrete (such as through personification), but are presented with a sensitivity to individual consciousness: the poem directs the listener to listen and see and feel and call to mind familiar homely comforts. The overall effect is to map transcendental concepts into the schema of the individual's personal sense and life: a reinforcement of the Christian schema in the strongest and most personally relevant terms.

Explorations

1 Schema poetics is a good way of accounting for the fact that different readers produce different interpretations of the same text. You could use schema theory to track the readings made in two published critical studies of a literary text. You could also examine the rhetorical means by which each critic claims that their reading is the more convincing, appropriate or just.

2 You might explore whether the notion of *genre* is represented by schemas. Taking a genre that you know very well, compare your own schematic understanding of its typical slots with someone who is not so familiar with the genre. You can use this to account for differences in your interpretations and evaluations of texts within the genre.

3 In a play, the staging presents a world that can be very rich in schema headers. The audience has to take account not only of the schema cues offered by the set, but must also keep a projected track of the knowledge schemas carried by each character, and finally try to assimilate all of this into the literary schema which they imagine best represents either the author or director or both. You might try to draw this out of a particular performance (it will be easier if you have a video of the play). On a more theoretical level, you might consider what is the schema theory status of

a theatre audience. Individuals might respond differently to the same play, but is there any sense of a group or collective consciousness: an audience schema?

4   Schematised differences in literary presumptions, allusions, genres and other socio-political audience expectations can be used to account for historical variations in readings. Do you think it is possible to reconstruct the schema of the contemporary readership or audience of the original text?

5   Take a story in which something very unexpected happens. Spy thrillers, crime fiction and science fiction are good places to find this. Can you account for the sense of surprise and the effect of the 'twist' in schema poetic terms? How does the narrative set the reader up for the surprise?

6   A criticism that has been levelled at schema theory is that in a dyadic (two-person) exchange, it only accounts for the behaviour and expectations of one of the participants. In a pub schema, for example, it cannot predict which one of many different possible appropriate things the barman might say. Since, in the literary context, authorial intention is inaccessible, this might not be such a problem for schema poetics, where the focus is on the reader. However, schema theory in general has addressed this question by emphasising the dynamic nature of reading as a negotiation through a mental space (see next chapter). Applying this to literary reading, it might be necessary to follow the process of schema accretion in stages through a text-reading, rather than focusing on one moment. You could try this by tracking the schema instantiation offered by the beginning of a novel, and then follow its development at key points in the narrative.

Further reading and references

The original psychological model of schema theory was proposed by Bartlett (1932) and developed for artificial intelligence by Schank and Abelson (1977) and Schank (1982a, 1982b, 1984, 1986). Alternative terms for 'scripts', which I have gathered as *schemas*, include the terms 'frame' (Minsky 1975, 1986; Tannen 1984; and Fillmore 1985) and 'scenario' (Sanford and Garrod 1981). For a critique, see Edwards (1997).

What I have called *schema poetics*, the use of schema theory in literary discussion, is accessible through the work of Rumelhart (1975, 1980, 1984; Rumelhart and Norman 1978; see also Thorndyke 1977, and Thorndyke and Yekovich 1980). Schema reinforcement and refreshment, and arguments about literariness, come from Cook (1994; see also 1989, 1992). I have assimilated Rumelhart's and Cook's terms, as suggested by Semino (1997: 159).

Semino (1997) also demonstrates a schema poetic analysis of modern poetry. Culpeper (2001) applies schema theory to drama and characterisation. Tsur (1992: 207–43) applies schemas to poetry. Cockcroft (2002) connects schema theory and classical rhetoric. Other examples of schema poetics include Freundlieb (1982), Mandler (1984), Gladsky (1992), and Müske

(1990). The orders of informativity and the idea of literature as a constitutive schema are from de Beaugrande (1980 and 1987 respectively). Abelson (1987), Lehnert and Vine (1987), Meutsch and Viehoff (1989), Miall (1988, 1989) and Spiro (1980, 1982; Spiro, Bruce and Brewer 1980) have all discussed schema poetics.

7   Discourse worlds and mental spaces

Preview

One of the main obstacles to a rigorous linguistic analysis of literature has been the problem of context. Any approach to a literary text that insists on pure formalism, restricting itself to syntax and semantics and the words themselves on the page, is doomed to failure. The sorts of conclusions that a narrow structuralist linguistic analysis can reach are in general of little interest to the literary critic. The 'meaning' of a literary work can be found in the minds of readers, configured there partly from readerly processes and individual experiences, and only partly from the cues offered by the elements of the text object. Even if 'meaning' or interpretation is not the primary area of interest, the craft of the text cannot simply be understood by formal decontextualised analysis either. More recently, language study informed by pragmatics and cognitive linguistics has offered systematic and principled ways of discussing these matters.

In this chapter, I will outline two of the main approaches to the idea of the contextual 'worlds' that are brought to mind by texts. From pragmatics and the philosophy of language, I outline *possible worlds theory*, and its narratological and literary application – since this application fundamentally changes the nature of the theory, I refer to it as a model of *discourse worlds*. Then, from cognitive linguistics, I outline one of the most prominent discourse world proposals: *mental space* theory, and its possibilities for literary analysis. In order to demonstrate the range of these approaches, I present a discussion of the worlds generated by science-fictional literature.

Links with literary critical concepts

*Allegory, beliefs, character, context, contextualisation,
fiction, imagination, literary worlds, readerliness, realism,
setting, universality*

Perhaps the prototypical form of literature is fiction. So central is fictionality to the notion of literature that many studies of literary theory focus on imagination and alternativity without recalling that much literature is religious, lyrical, autobiographical, or political, or describes real journeys, satirises real people, or recounts real events. Nevertheless, it has become a principal feature of value for literature that it is *universal*. In general, literature which is too particularistic, too closely tied to its social, historical or political roots, has tended not to be valued except by specialised literary scholars. By contrast, literature which seems amenable to modern reinterpretations, or which does not require a gloss or extensive footnotes, tends to be reprinted and popularly read today.

Associated with the value of universality is the notion that good literature, though dis-joined from its original context, nevertheless carries within it the means of reconstructing a rich context. The 'world' which literature evokes is praised for its richness, texture, believability and plausibility. In fiction, these dimensions of the literary work are to be found in the lyrical, descriptive passages, in the characterisation, in the poetic imagery and word-choices that fit the imagined setting. In fiction, a rich resolving context is specified for the reader. In non-fiction (typically lyric poetry and love poetry), universality is attained by non-specificity. Ambiguity, vagueness, or values that are felt to be eternal human qualities and emotions are the ground for the reader to create a context by mapping their own human experience onto the framework offered by the poem.

Either way, the richness of the perceived context is judged to be important. Yet until recently there has not been a principled means of understanding exactly how readers construct and engage with the context arising from reading a literary work. Cognitive poetics offers just such a means of understanding.

It seems psychologically unlikely that we have developed different cognitive strategies for dealing with fictional worlds and non-fictional worlds. In the sections that follow, therefore, the process of literary context creation is understood as being essentially the same process as the means by which we understand the context, background and setting of all discourse. Our ability to talk about literary and fictional characters, places and events as if they were real, our ability to imagine new situations in which they might live, our ability to write sequels and stage dramatisations, all arise from our general ability to create rich contextual worlds from very limited and under-specified strings of language in texts. In Chapters 10 and 11, I return to these abilities with rich-world theories. In the rest of this chapter, though, I first present the basic cognitive ability in context creation and manipulation.

Possible worlds and discourse worlds

As a means of calculating the truth-value of a sentence, philosophers of language developed the notion of **possible worlds**. You might think that a sentence like 'The Allies defeated the Axis in the Second World War' is obviously true. However, it is only true in our **actual world**. The actual world is only one of a multitude of possible worlds which could provide a context for the sentence, and some of these possible worlds would alter the truth-value of that sentence. For example, in the Philip K. Dick novel *The Man in* *the High Castle* (and numerous other science-fiction stories), an imaginary world is presented in which Japan and Germany defeated the US and Britain. Within the possible world of that novel, the sentence above is false.

Only a very few sentences are 'obviously' true: those which present analytic truths or universal assertions that are necessarily true by definition ('The bald man has no hair', '2 + 2 = 4'). In possible worlds theory, no context could make these sentences false while preserving the same sense of the words: a world in which they were false is an **impossible world**. Of course, you could say that the sentence 'The bald man has hair' could be true if he were wearing a wig in our actual world, but this is cheating since you are using the word 'hair' in a different sense. Similarly, it might be possible to imagine a different universe with cosmological rules so different that in its mathematics 2+2 does make 5 (as imagined by Olaf Stapledon (1937) in *Star Maker* and Greg Egan (1998) in *Diaspora*), but these imaginary places can only be gestured at rather than described or comprehended: they remain impossible.

In order for a statement to be part of a possible world, the world that it belongs to must be **non-contradictory**. For example, it cannot be true in a possible world that 'Alien intelligence exists' and at the same time 'Alien intelligence does not exist'. A world that could contain both these statements as true would be an impossible world. Equally, statements within a possible world must not break the rule of the **excluded middle**. In a possible world, if one of these statements is true, then its opposite must be false; there is no middle ground that could be occupied by a third statement.

A possible world (even the actual possible world) is not the same as the rich everyday world we experience around us. A possible world is a philo-sophical notion, constituted by a set of propositions that describe the **state of affairs** in which a sentence can exist. It is a formal logical set, not a cognitive array of knowledge. This means that possible worlds theory has little to say about the worlds of literary reading. However, the approach can be adapted so that we can speak of **discourse worlds** that can be understood as dynamic readerly interactions with possible worlds: possible worlds with a narratological and cognitive dimension.

It will have become clear from the discussion of deixis in Chapter 4 that the cognitive perspective alters our understanding of notions such as refer-ence, truth and falsity, since these concepts must be understood in relation not to an objective reality but in relation to a mediating mental representa-tion. For example, philosophers have grappled with the logical status of a variety of propositions that are non-actualised in our world: lies, metaphors, symbols and fiction. In order to preserve a purely logical view of these, special circumstances have been suggested, such as proposing that state-ments made within fictional worlds can have fictional truth or falsity. So it is 'true' to say that Hamlet is Prince of Denmark, and 'false' to claim he is a CIA agent. However, where does this leave more complex statements, such as the truth-value of a psychoanalytical interpretation of Hamlet's unconscious mind?

It has further been proposed that fictional entities are simply incomplete, since they are semantically and textually underdetermined. Statements about them can be judged fictionally true or false only as far as the textual evidence allows reasonable judgement to be made. We can even talk of the relatively differing degrees of completion of fictional beings, in comparing fiction and 'faction', or history with its reconstructions and dramatisations. Of course, by now we have come a long way from the logical proofs of possible worlds theory, and the fragmentation of the theory into special circumstances is hardly satisfactory.

By extension, a discourse world is the imaginary world which is conjured up by a reading of a text, and which is used to understand and keep track of events and elements in that world. It is a principle of cognitive poetics that the same cognitive mechanisms apply to literary reading as to all other inter-action, and so we can understand a discourse world as the mediating domain for reality as well as projected fictions. In order to be able to do this, we must be able to negotiate **trans-world identity** – that is, we must have a mapping facility between worlds, as follows.

Usually we identify a particular persona with a particular world. Hamlet meets George Bush is the stuff of satire. Each of the text entities presented in Chapter 4 (real author, implied author, narrator, character, and so on) are framed deictically by the world level they inhabit. These are worlds embed-ded within each other, and we also have embedded worlds whenever anyone has a flashback, a flashforward, imagines something, plans something, or considers an unrealised possibility. In each of these cases, we have to keep track of the character in the current discourse world, as well as the idea of the same character who is younger (flashback), older (flashforward), or an alter-native version of themselves. These other versions are **counterparts** within the fictional discourse world.

Counterparts can also exist between different fictional discourse worlds and between them and the actual world. 'London' in Dickens is a counter-part of the actual London. In this case, the counterparts have different prop-erties, though they have a trans-world identity. The counterpart relations can become quite complex, as in the chain of identities in 'The Dream of the Rood' between the speaking poet, the narrator/dreamer in his bed at midnight, the figure of the dreamer within the dream vision, the changed dreamer after he wakes, and the anticipated redeemed soul of the dreamer on Judgement Day.

Each character, of course, also has a virtual discourse world inside their fictional heads, and the reader often needs to keep track of these belief systems as well. There are several types of alternativity that are character-centred in this way:

- **epistemic worlds** – knowledge worlds; what the characters in the fic-tional world believe to be true about their world.
- **speculative extensions** – things the characters anticipate about their world, or other hypotheses they hold.

- **intention worlds** – what characters plan to do to deliberately change their world.
- **wish worlds** – what characters wish or imagine might be different about their world.
- **obligation worlds** – different versions of the world filtered through the characters' sense of moral values.
- **fantasy worlds** – the worlds of characters' dreams, visions, imaginations or fictions that they compose themselves.

Literary texts often work by exploiting disjunctions between character-knowledge and the wider knowledge offered to the reader, with the reader having to keep track of both systems and compare them. Some texts push this to its limits. Brian Aldiss' (1987) *Cracken at Critical* is a science-fiction novel in which the Axis won the Second World War, featuring a character in that other 1995 reading an illegal 'maybe-myth' novel set in 1945 which imagines the US winning the war. However, the alternative history within the alternative history is not our actual 1945 history, but yet another version of 1945, closer to ours than his, but one in which Churchill was assassinated by communists and Norwich is the capital of Nazi-occupied Britain.

Even fictions which seem absolutely realist are still examples of discourse worlds. The simple test of alternativity from our actual discourse world is to ask whether the fiction is part of that world: usually no one in a television soap opera watches that soap; no one in *Star Trek* ever mentions the fact that there used to be a famous series called *Star Trek*; none of the academics in David Lodge's campus novels have ever heard of Professor David Lodge. The 'closeness' of alternate discourse worlds to the actual discourse world is a matter of **accessibility** to its conditions. These can be measured along a set of dimensions:

- **accessibility of objects**
  - properties: whether the objects in the alternate world have the same properties as actual objects.
  - inventory: whether the alternate world has all the same objects as the actual world, fewer objects, or additional objects.
- **accessibility of time**
  - whether the alternate world exists in the same present, and has the same history as the actual world.
- **accessibility of nature**
  - whether the natural laws of the alternate discourse world match the natural physical laws of the actual world, its logical and mathematical properties.
- **accessibility of language**
  - whether the alternate world and the actual world share the same language, the same principles of language, the same cognitive patterns, and whether the inventory of words in the alternate world matches exactly the inventory of words in the actual world.

Finally, a **principle of minimal departure** operates as a cognitive mechanism of efficiency in understanding alternate discourse worlds. Unless the text tells us otherwise, we assume an identity with the actual world. Gravity still works, China exists, there was a Norman Conquest of England in 1066, and unless we are directed otherwise, these and all our other actual world assumptions are put into operation by default.

Mental spaces

In order to extend the basic usefulness of possible worlds, one form of discourse world theory has been proposed that is explicitly cognitive in its orientation. This involves understanding the cognitive tracking of entities, relations and processes as a **mental space**. Mental space theory offers a unified and consistent means of understanding reference, co-reference, and the comprehension of stories and descriptions whether they are currently real, historical, imagined, hypothesised or happening remotely. There are thus four main types of mental space:

- **time spaces** – current space or displacement into past or future, typically indicated by temporal adverbials, tense and aspect.
- **space spaces** – geographical spaces, typically indicated by locative adverbials, and verbs of movement.
- **domain spaces** – an area of activity, such as work, games, scientific experiment, and so on.
- **hypothetical spaces** – conditional situations, hypothetical and unrealised possibilities, suggestions for plans and speculation.

The spatial metaphor underlying mental space theory seems apt when you consider that these spaces are often built with a spatially metaphorical preposition: 'in 2001', 'on Mars', 'in physics', 'in the event of attack'.

To understand and negotiate reality, we build a **reality space** with mental representations of everything we perceive. Any operation on that set of knowledge creates a **projected space**, whenever we make a predication, description, imagine a counterfactual, anticipate or recall. The same process applies equally to **fictional spaces**, which we build to follow an ongoing narrative. Minimally, the process can be seen to operate in simple sentence predications. 'Perhaps there is intelligent life on other worlds' involves both a hypothetical and a spatial projection from Earthly reality. In a **base space**, our familiar cognitive representation of life on Earth is an *idealised cognitive model* (ICM – see Chapter 3) possessing entities and a familiar structure, with intelligent life(a) on planet Earth(b). The hypothesis builder 'perhaps' creates a new projected space that is similarly structured:

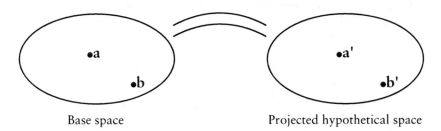

Base space   Projected hypothetical space

Alien life (a') on an alien world (b') is perceived as being similar to our reality. This new mental space is now available for reference, so subsequent sentences are comprehensible, such as 'they' and the definite developmental presumptions in: 'They will not yet have reached the level of space-flight.'

A mental space is constructed with **space builders**. Locatives ('in', 'at'), adverbials ('actually', 'really') and conditionals ('if', 'when') open a new space or shift focus to a new part of an existing space. Spaces are structured by names and descriptions, tense, mood and other aspectuals, by presuppositions, and by **trans-spatial operators**. These are the copulative verbs in English such as 'be', 'become' and 'remain'. They link elements in different spaces.

Mental space theory develops the possible worlds notion of counterparts to explain how reference to the counterpart in a target space can be made by using the name or identifier for the counterpart in the base space (this is called the **access principle**). So in saying, 'I walked around Surrey looking for the places where the Martians landed in *The War of the Worlds*', 'the places' acts as a **trigger** in the base space that has a counterpart in the fictional target space which is built by the locative 'in'.

Though mental space theory is mainly focused on the discussion of simple sentences as above, there have been some developments into exploring the **discourse management of spaces**. The **base** is the starting point for a space construction. The **focus** is the space which is then internally structured in the process of discourse comprehension, and the **viewpoint** is the space from which other spaces are accessed. For example:

'Peter can't fly.   He believes   he can fly,   but he's wrong'
    BASE   VIEWPOINT   FOCUS   BASE

Extended narratives have also been discussed in mental space theory, through the useful notion of conceptual **blending**. This involves a mapping between two spaces, and common general nodes and relationships across the spaces are abstracted into a **generic space**. Specific features which emerge from this mapping then form a new space, the **blend**. Conceptual blends are the mechanism by which we can hold the properties of two spaces together, such as in metaphorical or allegorical thinking, scientific or political analogy, comparisons and imaginary domains involving characters from disparate areas (like Hamlet and George Bush).

Consider, as an example, the famous exchange between Lady Astor and Winston Churchill: Astor said, 'If you were my husband, I would give you poison', and Churchill is supposed to have replied, 'Madam, if you were my wife I would drink it'. First, there is a **cross-space mapping** involving the partial mapping of counterparts in two spaces. In this case, the real space Churchill and Astor are projected into a new hypothetical space. Certain properties of the base space are carried over, and these commonalities form a common *generic space* containing Churchill and Astor, and also the real space traits that they are male and female, adults, named 'Churchill' and 'Astor', and hate each other. However, out of this new space an **emergent structure** develops that is neither the base space nor the new projected space, nor is it limited to the few elements of commonality in the generic space. Instead, we have a fourth, **blended space** in which Churchill and Astor, though in one sense the same as their counterparts in reality, are also married to each other while simultaneously hating each other. Elements from both base and new space have been combined. In the verbal exchange, this blend is then 'run' through its logic: Churchill would drink the poison in the blended space.

The stages can be summarised as follows:

- *cross-space mapping* – the partial mapping of counterparts in two spaces
- *generic space* – a reflection of the abstracted common elements and structure
- *blend* – a fourth 'blended' space, combining the other spaces
  - emergent structure
    - **composition**   new relations become apparent in the blend
    - **completion**   frame knowledge fits the blend to wider knowledge
    - **elaboration**   'running the blend' through its emergent logic.

Discussion

Before proceeding to an application of the notion of discourse worlds in literature, you might consider some of the following:

- Chilton (1985, 1986, 1988) discusses a similar sort of pattern as mental space mapping and blending in the domain of politics (he calls the mapping a **morphism**):

  > A morphism exists when you can prove or calculate something by mapping one set of things into another, doing the proof or calculation in another domain, and then mapping back to the problematic domain you were first interested in.
  >
  > (Chilton 1988: 63)

As an example, Chilton cites Hook's (1983) study of the media in Japan, at a period of Japanese sensitivity to the visits of US naval ships which might have been carrying nuclear weapons. This sensitivity was metaphorically presented as an allergy. The basic terms of the familiar base domain are *patient, allergen, doctor*. These map onto the targets *people, nuclear weapons, government*. The predicate relations between these nodes produce a complex expression which is mapped between the domains: *a patient over-reacts to the allergen, so a doctor injects a small dose, and the patient no longer reacts*. The process is mapped thus: *people overreact to nuclear weapons, so the government introduces them gradually, and the people no longer react* (Chilton 1986: 9). When this elaboration was worked through, the process resulted in real policy implications, structured by the metaphorical blend, asserting nuclear weapons are harmless to normal people.

Can you apply the same sort of mental space blending analysis to other examples of government or political rhetoric?

• Both possible worlds theory and even its discourse worlds developments such as mental space theory tend to use single sentences or simple narrative passages for examples. Can you imagine ways in which these approaches to fictionality could be extended to encompass whole texts and the rich worlds of literary discourse? Some answers in this direction are provided in Chapters 9, 10 and 11, but try to develop your own thinking before turning to them.

• Taking twenty literary texts from as many different genres as you can find, try to put them along a scale of closeness or remoteness to the actual world, using the dimensions of world accessibility set out in this chapter. Do the groupings of certain genres along the scale tell you anything about the relationships between certain genres?

Cognitive poetic analysis

Almost no literary work maintains a unity of cognitive space: it would have to include no breaks of narrative sequence, no shifts in time or location, no plans, wishes or memories, and no characters with views different from each other or the reader! The structure of discourse worlds provides much of the texture of a text, and offers much of the attraction of reading literature. The shifts between worlds and the trans-world identities of counterparts transform a simple love-story and family history into *Wuthering Heights*. The space-builders and other mechanisms of fictional space and projected character-worlds can be tracked through realist novels, but in this section I am going to examine some science-fictional texts, where the divergence between worlds is most radical.

Thomas More's *Utopia*, written in Latin in 1515, can be seen as an example of proto-science fiction. It embeds the description of the island of Utopia in a complex narratological framework, beginning with a letter from Thomas More to his friend Peter Giles, in which he describes being told by the Portuguese explorer Raphael Hythloday about his adventures. In the first part, Hythloday describes the abuses of property and the corrupt state of modern Europe. The second part is a description of the ideal island of Utopia, its geography and political economy. An Appendix reproduces four verses in the Utopian language, and the book ends with a note from the printer apologising for not having any letters of the Utopian alphabet available, but promising to obtain some for the next impression.

'Thomas More' is thus a counterpart across the four principle spaces of the book. In the historical actual world of 1515, he is the real author. In the alternate 1515 in which Utopian poetry and printing are real, he is the implied author. In the world of the description of actual Europe which represents the epistemic world-view of the fictional Raphael Hythloday, and in the fictional Hythloday's account of the fictional place Utopia, More is the narratee. The text is presented with a claim to the verisimilitude of the whole, and the effect of shifting down into these embedded related narrative worlds is that the fictionality is engaged step-by-step rather than abruptly.

The description of Utopia (a pun on the Latin *eutopia* and *outopia* – good place and no place) is given realistically as the epistemic world of Hythloday. Its geography is described with measurements and dimensions in miles, and with a very precise account of its layout; this is followed by the detail of its commonwealth. However, the alternativity of Utopia begins immediately to undercut this apparent realism. The dimensions of Utopia – a crescent shape in which the horns of the crescent are 11 miles apart, 200 miles wide at its broadest centre, and with an external length of 500 miles – are geometrically impossible. There are 54 cities, none of which are less than 24 miles apart, which cannot be accommodated within the island, and the main river is called the Anyder, which is not far from the Greek 'an-hydōr' (no water). For Utopia to exist as a possible world, it would have to possess different natural and physical laws.

Utopia is barely possible along other dimensions. Its chronology (it is 1760 years since its foundation) places it out of step with Christian chronology (it is 1515). There is a similarity in the inventory of objects between the actual European world and Utopia (horses, marriage, agriculture, houses, wells and so on) but the way these objects are perceived and used varies between the worlds, and the device of the Portuguese narrator serves to highlight the nature of the alternativity. Both worlds are constantly and explicitly compared. Lastly, there is an inaccessibility of language. The Appendix presents four lines (26 words) of Utopian poetry, which is 'rudely englished' into eight lines (67 words), and the printer claims that Utopian is stranger than Egyptian, Cyprian and Scythian. All of these world disjunctions point to the impossibility of Utopia, and encourage a reading of the book not as a travelogue but as a satire and manifesto.

The technique of realistic presentation of near impossibility realised in

Utopia is a major feature of alternate worlds in science fiction. *The Difference Engine* by William Gibson and Bruce Sterling (1990) is set in 1855; however, this is not our actual 1855 but an alternate Victorian London in which Babbage's computing engine has been perfected and these machines accelerate the Industrial Revolution. The inventory of objects in the world of the novel corresponds with actual world counterparts, but they are drawn from a range of actualities from our actual history. So counterparts in the actual nineteenth century such as coal fires, horse-drawn carriages, Ada Byron, Disraeli, Karl Marx and Manhattan sit alongside objects which have more recent counterparts: cinema, international air-flight, an internet database, military uniform camouflage. However, the fictional world objects are explicitly differentiated from our historical actuality: Ada Byron is a computer scientist, Disraeli a sleazy hack journalist, and Karl Marx leads the communist state of Manhattan. Furthermore, the novel itself functions as an extended blended space in which the elaboration of the plot is a 'running of the blend' from the initial premise of the alternative history.

A different angle on this is provided by Neal Stephenson's (1995) *The Diamond Age*, which is set in a future in which advanced capitalism and nano-technology have created a global society of ideological enclaves across nation-states. The focus of the novel is on the neo-Victorians, who adapt the technology towards an ideal of British nineteenth century life. They speak a mannered style of eloquent drawing-room Victorian English. Sub-titled '*or A Young Lady's Illustrated Primer*', the text is written in the style of a Victorian novel, combined with technological neologisms and some modern idioms. Large parts of the book are given over to the 'Primer', a book-within-a-book which is an interactive text designed to teach a young girl the principles of computing and genetics. Here, the disjunctions between worlds at the levels of objects, chronology and language are rendered into a blend between the reader's historical knowledge and their science-fictional knowledge.

Once the extended blend has been established (largely through the style of the language in the novel), the cognitive mechanism of *completion* draws in this readerly knowledge to create a very rich and densely imagined fictional world. The experience of reading the text, like much science fiction, involves a quite rapid and easy acceptance of the workings of nano-technology and the social structure to the point at which the rich social texture is the naturalised background. (I have called science-fictional narratives which accomplish this **architexts**). The technique of placing long passages from the Primer within the novel also serves to create another blended space which teaches the reader about the framing world alongside the little girl in the story.

We can examine this further in *Frankenstein Unbound* by Brian Aldiss (1973). Most of the novel features an extended blended space that mixes objects from worlds with different truth-value statuses. Fictional presidential advisor Joe Bodenland is the victim of space–time fractures that send him back from 2020 to 1816. There he meets the actual Mary Shelley, Percy Shelley, Byron and their doctor, Polidori. However, he also meets the fictional Victor

Frankenstein and the monster from Mary's novel. Aldiss' text is mainly the recorded journal of Bodenland, so it is written in modern casual English, but the other characters speak 'in character', and the novel itself is set out like Mary Shelley's *Frankenstein* in letters and with embedded narrators. The cross-space mappings involved here, which the reader must perform in order to make any sense of the novel, are very complex. The frame knowledge required for completion would ideally include historical knowledge, literary knowledge and competence in dealing with both gothic and science-fictional texts. The novel uses this chaotic blend to explore the relationship between literary art and industrial technology and its moral consequences.

Lastly, Jack Womack's (2000) *Going Going Gone* seems to be set in 1968 New York. However, it gradually emerges that what appears to be the actual world seems to be a different 1968 from our actual historical one. The narrator's language is a hip jargon that is not quite 'Sixties'. Here is the opening:

> Soon as I spiked I turned my eyes inside. Setting old snakehead on cruise control always pleases, no matter how quick the trip. I looked out the window for a minute or an hour or so, listening to stoplights click off blue, orange, blue.
>
> (Womack 2000: 1)

There are details here that are not quite true, but the cleverness in setting the novel in 1968 is that it is initially difficult for a modern reader (perhaps especially a non-American one) to decide for certain that this is not genuine. Determining the degree of accessibility becomes part of the process of resolving the setting for the novel.

However, at the same time, the protagonist, Walter, through whose epistemic world the novel is focused, starts hearing voices and seeing ghosts, and increasingly strange things happen to him. At the same time, more and more details emerge to suggest the setting is clearly not our actual 1968: the Kennedys are a mob family, President Nixon was assassinated by Oswald in 1963 New Orleans, there was a holocaust of African–Americans sometime in the early twentieth century, and all Black-originating music is banned. Though the novel thus preserves the principle of minimal departure (in that these departures are mentioned) they are not foregrounded but are asides in the narrative setting.

The ghosts turn out to be from yet another alternative New York, more chronologically advanced than ours, that is in the process of collapsing into Walter's world. Walter is taken to the other New York, this one flooded and moved north, filled with black people, superspeed elevators, and 'visual radio' (television), which he doesn't have in his world. The novel ends with these two epistemic worlds physically falling into each other, a sort of science-fictional literalisation of blending that creates not just a new mental space but a new universe in the novel. The emergent world is a morally better place than either of the two which composed it. The final chapter, 'In a New World', lists sketched biographies of random characters, detailing how their personalities and lives are different in the new blend. Some people, such as John F. Kennedy and Elvis Presley, simply never existed at all.

Explorations

1   One way of exploring the parameters of possibility, in terms of non-contradiction and the excluded middle, is by using a **semiotic square**. Take a term (such as 'black') and write it at the corner of a square. In the opposite corner, write its contradiction ('not black'). In an adjacent corner, write its contrary ('white'), and in the remaining corner write the contradiction of the contrary ('not white'). Thinking about the relationships between these terms can help to determine more than just the parameters of the possible world in which they occur; if you start with more complex terms, the exercise can reveal value-systems and other interesting relationships when you consider the implications and possible meanings of each word. Try starting with: *literature, science fiction, mind, democracy, prototype, possible, true, false, reading, interpretation, cognitive poetics*. For more complexity, try sentences in the square: *The king was pregnant* (from Ursula Le Guin), *This is not an apple* (from the painting by René Magritte), and for a real mindwarp, *This statement is false*.

2   Take a lyric poem that describes a landscape or moment (Wordsworth is good for this), and draw out the mechanisms of the discourse world that is being created. You might compare the detail of your own projected discourse world with those of other readers after reading the same poem. Try to determine which parts of your schematic knowledge have been used in different ways to produce differences in your views; which parts of the text allow different readings; and which parts of the text constrain all your readings into being similar.

3   Many novels (especially modern thrillers) proceed by alternating between scenes, so that two parallel stories are presented alternately, and tied together as the narrative progresses. Use mental space theory to track the elements of these different domains, and try to account for the effects when they are brought together. For example, in the science fiction short stories 'By His Bootstraps' and 'All You Zombies' by Robert Heinlein (1959a, 1959b), time-paradoxes create many characters who in the end all turn out to be the same person at different points in the time-loop: counterparts rather than separate characters. Tracking such deliberately misleading 'errors' in mental space construction can help to explain tales with a twist.

Further reading and references

The philosophy and logic of possible worlds theory can be found in Bradley and Swartz (1979), Rescher (1975), Rorty (1982) and Putnam (1990). Lewis

(1973, 1986) is accessible (in the sense of being readable). This is possible worlds theory proper. It becomes discourse world theory when it is applied to literature: see Searle (1975), Walton (1978), Maitre (1983), Ronen (1994), Dolezel (1976, 1988, 1989), Semino (1997) and the collection edited by Allen (1989) for examples of literary applications. The typology of worlds and their accessibility relations are taken and adapted from Ryan (1991a, 1991b). For an explicitly cognitive psychological angle, see Gerrig (1993).

The theory of mental spaces was developed by Fauconnier (1994). The principle of conceptual blends within mental spaces is from Fauconnier (1997: 149–86). See also Fauconnier and Turner (1996), Turner and Fauconnier (1999), and the collection edited by Goldberg (1996). For applications, see the collection edited by Fauconnier and Sweetser (1996).

Chilton's (1985, 1986, 1988) work is an interesting attempt to synthesise cognitive linguistics and critical discourse analysis; see also Stockwell (2001) for my suggestions along these lines. For more science-fictional applications of worlds theory, see Stockwell (2000a), Suvin (1990) and Ryder (1998).

8   Conceptual metaphor

Preview

Metaphor has been seen as the use of one expression to refer to a different concept in a way which is still regarded as meaningful, and metaphor has most prototypically been associated with poetic and literary usage. However, much work in cognitive science has demonstrated that metaphor is a basic pattern in the way the human mind works. Understanding the role of metaphorical patterning in cognitive processes has driven cognitive psychology and cognitive linguistics to radical new insights in the study of the mind. In previous chapters of this book, many of the processes which underlie patterns such as figure and ground, deictic projection, cognitive grammar, schema management and mental space mapping are fundamentally metaphorical. Cognitive science is responsible for placing metaphor at the centre of language and thought in general. However, for cognitive poetics, these general insights can be returned to the literary sphere in order to understand more clearly how metaphor works in literature.

It is important, first of all, to make a fundamental distinction between linguistic expressions of metaphor and their underlying conceptual content. There is an unfortunate terminology clash here. Traditionally, 'That man is a shark' would be seen as a **metaphor** whereas 'That man is like a shark' would be seen as a **simile**: a distinction based only on surface realisation. However, the same **conceptual metaphor** underlies both forms: THE MAN IS A SHARK (conceptual metaphors are always written in small capitals like this). The distinction is useful because the conceptual metaphor THE MAN IS A SHARK can underlie several possible surface expressions of the metaphor: 'that man is a shark', 'shark-man', 'he was in a feeding frenzy', 'he's always got to keep moving forward', 'he's sharking', and so on.

In this chapter, I deal briefly with stylistic realisations of metaphoric mappings, then discuss conceptual metaphor, and offer an analysis of imagery in surrealist writing.

Links with literary critical concepts

Allegory , imagery, interpretation, metaphor, metonymy, poetics, rhetoric, simile, symbol, tone

Metaphor study has been a major feature of literary study since ancient rhetoric. There are many dozens of different approaches to metaphor, designed to answer questions such as (but not limited by) the following.

Is metaphor ornamental or essential for meaning? Aristotle takes a **dualist** view in seeing metaphor as an ornament to the sense: poetic imagery is simply a pleasing artistic attraction. Coleridge, on the other hand, takes the **monist** view of the 'untranslateableness' of metaphor: every expression is unique and metaphor constitutes the world. At stake is the very definition of 'metaphor', which must encompass cases such as: 'the man is a wolf', 'Juliet is the sun', 'you are the apple of my eye', 'there is an explosion of geraniums in the ballroom of the hotel', 'I'm spitting feathers', 'no man is an island', 'he blew his top', 'he poured himself home', 'the wine-dark sea', and many other constructions. A theory of metaphor must describe the conceptual differences between metaphor, simile, analogy, and metonymy. Do metaphors constrain the way we understand the world? Is metaphor a linguistic or psychological phenomenon? What is the relationship between metaphor and idioms? Can interpretations of metaphors be predicted, or measured theoretically? What are the different possible ways in which a conceptual metaphor can be expressed? Given two 'sides' to a metaphor, how does one side change by being affected by the other? How are metaphors interpreted in literary reading, and how are the themes and worlds of literature metaphorical?

What is clear is that metaphor is not an object: metaphors are only metaphors if they are perceived as such. Given this readerliness, cognitive poetics must describe how the potential spaces for interpretation offered by metaphors are negotiated. It must explain existing possible interpretations, and, more crucially, it should provide a means of determining central, peripheral and eccentric readings of literature.

Metaphor as mapping

Most definitions of metaphor involve an understanding of two or more conceptual domains. Traditional literary criticism has differentiated **tenor** (the familiar element) and **vehicle** (the new element which is described in terms of the old familiar element). Stylistically, new elements tend to occur first, as in 'Juliet (vehicle) is the sun (tenor)'. The common properties between the two elements (here, warmth, beauty, life-affirming) constitute the **ground** of the metaphor.

Since cognitive linguistics is interested in the conceptual level primarily, these elements are seen as **source** and **target** cognitive models: the expression conveys the conceptual metaphor JULIET (target) IS THE SUN (source). You might see straight away that this approach is easily assimilated with the mental space feature of blending (see Chapter 7). The base space and focus space share common properties, which can be abstracted as the generic space (equivalent to the traditional term 'ground' here). The blended space represents the new emergent understanding. Cognitive linguistics models the process of metaphor as a **mapping** of properties between the two spaces or domains.

Of course, this is an easy example, since both source and target cognitive models are stylistically realised. I call examples like this **visible** metaphors. In *Romeo and Juliet*, the co-text is:

> But soft! What light through yonder window breaks?
> It is the east, and Juliet is the sun.

In the first line here, the whole question-sentence could be read purely literally. However, in the light of the next line, it can also have a metaphorical resolution. 'Light' and the verb-construction 'breaks' present sources from which the target vehicle JULIET can be referenced. This is an **invisible** metaphor, since one of the cognitive models involved is not realised stylistically; the metaphor is made visible in the second line. The readerly process of resolving a metaphorical reading here is called **vehicle-construction**.

It matters quite a lot for literary interpretation whether the metaphor is visible or invisible, since the latter requires greater creative input on the part of the reader. Where there is greater potential for creative interpretation, of course, there is also greater potential for ambiguity. Which particular properties of the ground are specified can also be a stylistic matter: consider 'Juliet brings everything to life', 'Juliet makes the plants grow', 'flowers bend to Juliet's face', 'sunny Juliet' or 'heliotropic Romeo'. The stylistic detail can foreground different parts of the source domain, so that the target domain is understood in different ways in different forms of expression. The connotations and associations, the resonances and textures of the metaphor, and perhaps even the denotational meaning itself can vary the structure of the mapping, which traits in the cognitive model are mapped, and how the target model then comes to be structured.

Ranging from potentially most visible to most invisible, the stylistic possibilities for metaphoric realisation are as follows (with examples for THE BRAIN IS A CITY).

Simile, analogy and **extended metaphor**	'The brain is like a city. Its oldest parts are surrounded by developments in its later evolution'
Copula constructions	'The brain is a city' 'It was rush-hour in my mind'
Apposition and other **parallelisms**	'The brain, that teeming city ... ' 'Into my mind, into my mental cityscape ... '
Partitive and **genitive expressions**	'Paris is the city of my mind' 'In the streets and on the corners of my mind'

Premodification	'The urban brain'
	'A thinking city'
Compounds and **lexical blends**	'Mind-scape'
	'Metromind'
Grammatical metaphor	'The city considered the problem'
	'The city sleeps'
Sentence metaphor	'This is the nerve-centre of the body'
(including **negation**)	'The brain is not a city; it is a nation'
Fiction and **allegory**	(a narrative in which psychoanalytical archetypes are figured as city landmarks and inhabitants).

Understanding metaphor as a mapping between cognitive models involves structuring or restructuring the target domain using concepts transferred from the base or source domain. All of the possible patterns of figurative language set out above express different local variations in the same underlying mapping. Unless a relationship of identity is being claimed ('The name of the sun in an alien system is Juliet'), both the **attributes** and the predicate **relations** within the base domain can be mapped.

Mappings can be analysed in terms of several characteristics.

Internal characteristics:

- **clarity** – is it clear which features are mapped? (1:1 is ideal)
- **richness** – how many predicate relations are carried?
- **systematicity** – are the imported predicates part of a perceived coherent system?
- **abstractness** – what level of generality or detail is mapped?

External characteristics:

- **scope** – how wide is it? Can the base be mapped to many targets (WAR has been mapped with LOVE, TALKING, ARGUMENT, RACING, BUSINESS, GAMES and others)?
- **validity** – are the imported elements accurately placed?

Clearly, these are all matters of judgement, and people often disagree over the appositeness or applicability of a particular metaphor.

We can use the framework to distinguish **expressive** and **explanatory** metaphors. Expressive (often poetic) metaphors tend to have low clarity but a high degree of richness, whereas explanatory (often scientific) metaphors tend not to be very rich but are very clear. Some explanatory metaphors are so strong that they come to be seen as the 'natural' and correct way of understanding the target domain. In effect, they structure our understanding as **constitutive** metaphors. Scientific theories which become paradigms offer examples of such strong metaphors.

Conceptual metaphor

There has been a great deal of work in cognitive linguistics concerned with the sorts of metaphorical mappings that occur throughout everyday, non-literary discourse. Upon investigation, it appears that many ordinary expressions and ways of representing the world rely on metaphorical mappings, even when most of us do not realise the fact. Furthermore, these metaphorical patterns are so strong and widespread that we can even understand our philosophical view of life itself as being founded not on an objective world but on a set of metaphorical representations. Of course, claiming that this assertion was true rather than just another metaphorical representation would be another example of 'objectivism', so cognitive linguists prefer to see this way of conceiving reality as an 'experiential myth'. It is **experiential** because it is set against the 'objectivist myth': both are equally representational, but the experiential basis of cognitive science offers an understanding of language and thought that is grounded in human experience. The rest of this section will explain this with examples.

Many everyday expressions seem to share underlying conceptual structures that in turn are shared by groups of people. For example, in English, a **conceptual metaphor** GOOD IS UP (conceptual metaphors are written like this) seems to underlie many expressions, such as:

He was *over the moon* about it
I feel *on top of the world*
She's really *gone up in the world*
I'm finally *getting on top of my workload*
I was *high*
His popularity *went through the roof*

The converse, BAD IS DOWN, is essentially part of the same conceptual metaphor, underlying:

He was really *down in the dumps*
Public opinion has *plummeted*
I feel so *low*
He's a *down*-and-out
I don't know whether he'll ever manage to *pick himself up again*
This is really *the pits*

Sources for such conceptual metaphors tend to be grounded in everyday experience, and source domains tend to be basic-level categories (see Chapter 3). This is consistent with the cognitive science view which claims that human psychological processes all derive at some fundamental level from the embodied human condition. Basic-level categories tend to be the level at which we most readily interact with the world.

Many metaphorical expressions derive directly from embodied extensions. You need only to think of the many metaphorical uses of 'head': *head-waiter, head of state, head of the school, head of the table, head of a queue, head of a flower, bed-head, head of the pass, head of water, head on a pint of beer, tape-heads*, and morphological and grammatical developments such as *head in the right direction, on the right heading, head them off, header of a page, header of a schema*, and even *moving ahead, ahead only, trouble ahead* and many others. Recalling the image schemas in Chapter 2, there are very many apparently literal items in everyday language which derive from metaphorical mappings. Many of them (such as the spatial metaphors in prepositions like 'in', 'under' and 'through') go beyond what are conventionally thought of as 'dead' metaphors.

Some conventionalised conceptual metaphors are so powerful and pervasive that they generate many expressions and become the 'naturalised' way of recognising and communicating the world. One of the most studied is ANGER IS HEAT, which has two closely associated conceptual metaphors: ANGER IS HOT FLUID IN A CONTAINER and ANGER IS FIRE. These are related to physiological sensations, and are expressed in forms such as: *you make my blood boil, she was brimming with anger, he blew his top, I was fuming, I saw red, I was red with anger, he's a hothead, you get all hot and bothered, blow off steam, get it out of your system, he's got a short fuse, they're bottling it up, he's repressed, then it all came out*, and many others.

Other powerful conceptual metaphors that have received study include:

LIFE IS A JOURNEY	FORTUNES ARE BALANCES
COMMUNICATION IS A CONDUIT	GOOD IS UP
ANGER IS A DANGEROUS ANIMAL	TRAFFIC IS A RIVER
ARGUMENT IS A JOURNEY	DEATH IS DEPARTURE
LOVE IS WAR	IDEAS ARE PLANTS
LOVE IS A GAME	IDEAS ARE OBJECTS
ARGUMENT IS WAR	LIFE IS A STAGEPLAY
COMMUNICATION IS SENDING	LIFE IS A DAY
THEORIES ARE BUILDINGS	LIFE IS A YEAR
TIME IS MONEY	LUST IS HUNGER
UNDERSTANDING IS SEEING	AMBITION IS HUNGER
WORDS ARE COINS	WAR IS A GAME
WAR IS A FAIRY TALE	WAR IS AN ILLNESS

Of course, cognitive models overlap with each other in the manner of proto-types, and several of these conceptual metaphors become combined. Some apparent mappings, such as **metonymies** like 'give me a hand', 'Washington was angered', 'seen the latest Woody Allen' are mappings between categories within a single cognitive model (BODY, USA, WOODY ALLEN FILM) rather than across models.

Each side of a metaphorical mapping is a cognitive model. In resolving a metaphor, the structure and some of the attributes of the source model are mapped onto the target. A principle of **invariance** suggests that the mapping is mainly in one direction: that is, the metaphor resolution cannot work in reverse, so that the cognitive model structure of the target cannot in turn restructure the source model. In general this seems to be the case, though it seems that in this particular detail literary discourse works differently. Some very striking or defamiliarising metaphors (as in some literature, but not exclusively so) seem to be so strong that they make the reader re-think the source model in the light of its mapping with the target. I will give some examples later of surrealist imagery that has the potential to effect this **interanimation**.

So far in this chapter, I have discussed local examples of specific metaphors in their stylistic expression, and the conceptual metaphors that underlie collective groups of expressions. The account has largely been restricted to sentence-level features. However, when certain conceptual metaphors occur repeatedly throughout a text, often at pivotal moments and often in the form of thematically significant extended metaphors, these can be termed **megametaphors**.

Megametaphor is a conceptual feature that runs throughout a text and can contribute to the reader's sense of the general meaning or 'gist' of a work and its significance. Specific realisations of the numerous metaphors that occur in the text and that accumulate into the sense of a megametaphor are, by contrast, **micrometaphors**. For example, there are many hundreds of specific metaphors in Shakespeare's *Richard II*, but there is a thematically significant recurrence of metaphors which map the rise of Bolingbroke and the fall of Richard using the cognitive model of BALANCE. This includes metaphors of rise and fall, up and down, gravity and lightness, heat and cold, equivalent movement, substitution of position, and others. It is closely associated with linked metaphors concerning moral worth, power, the political and personal, legitimacy and respect. The mapping POLITICAL FORTUNE IS BALANCE is thus not just a conceptual metaphor but is a thematically-significant megametaphor in my reading as well.

Discussion

Before continuing to some examples of metaphorical analysis, you might like to consider the following issues, or play the metaphor game to help you think:

- From the list of words given overleaf, randomly select items to fit into the following constructions (you might have to add plurals, articles or morphemes such as '-ish' or '-ly' to make the sentence grammatical):

    A is B
    A is not B
    A is like B
    A is the B of C
    There is A in the B of C
    There is A in every B
    A–B

Words:

chair	*truth*	*love*
oil	*television*	*rose*
music	*wine*	*hand*
patience	*shoe*	*bottle*
ice	*book*	*stars*
electricity	*dog*	*rain*
night	*time*	*life*
water	*death*	*journey*
tree	*garden*	*house*
river	*child*	*coat*

What does the metaphor mean?

Which elements of the conceptual models are mapped?

What is the effect of reversing any of the elements in the sentence?

Does the metaphor create a new idea or is there just a poetic effect?

Are all the sentences metaphorical, or can some be read literally?

Which metaphors are 'better' than others? How can you decide this systematically?

- One of the big questions which has been debated in cognitive linguistics is the issue of what is the principle by which some elements of the cognitive model are mapped but not others. For example, nuclear fusion, astronomical distance and solar flares are not usually mapped onto JULIET. Can you imagine principled ways in which a constraint could be built into the theory that accounts for the selection of relevant, appropriate or most likely mappings? (Chapter 10 offers one approach in answer to this).

- Take a relatively short text (a poem or short story, simply for manageability) and sketch out the micrometaphors and their underlying conceptual metaphors. Do any of these appear to you as thematic megametaphors?

Cognitive poetic analysis

Some of the most creative and striking metaphorical expressions are to be found in surrealist texts. Surrealism was a multi-media communist movement that was strongest in the 1920s and 1930s. Partly as a response to the Great War, it appeared in continental Europe primarily as a verbal art form which rapidly spread to graphic art, sculpture, theatre and performance. In many ways it had a Romantic view of the organic and imaginative basis of language, which also has continuities with the assumptions of cognitive poetics, though surrealist writers described their activities and motivations in the psychoanalytical and literary critical language of their day.

One motivation behind the striking imagery, discourse deviance and apparent textual incoherence of surrealist writing was the political imperative to dismantle what the surrealists saw as the bourgeois values of capitalism, realism and rationality that had worked their grim logic through the war. Surrealist writing aimed to access the unconscious mind, by creating as far as possible a disjunction between intentionality and writing, between words and coherent representational meaning. The graphic technique of collage – collecting disparate objects and assembling them as an artwork – was designed to erase any rational choices made by an author. In verbal art, the surrealist 'image' was the equivalent, most directly constructed in striking expressions such as:

> there is an explosion of geraniums in the ballroom of the hotel
> there is an extremely unpleasant odour of decaying meat
> arising from the depetalled flower growing out of her ear
> her arms are like pieces of sandpaper
> or wings of leprous birds in taxis
> ('And the Seventh Dream is the Dream of Isis', David Gascoyne)

In the first line of this extract, since any cognitive model of geraniums is unlikely to include an explosive feature, it is most likely that 'explosion' is read metaphorically as a poetic representation of the impact of the colour of the flowers. Indeed, I have just realised that the word 'impact' with which I just described the effect is another expression of the same conceptual metaphor SEEING IS BEING HIT. Describing the image as 'striking' is yet another realisation.

This metaphorical resolution of the line, however, does not seem satisfactory in the context of the next few lines. Incoherence is introduced by the cognitive models which are next mentioned (the odour of MEAT, her EAR, her ARMS, SANDPAPER, BIRDS and TAXIS), none of which are semantically connected with geraniums or hotels (except perhaps TAXIS with the latter). Only the cognitive model evoked by 'flower' is relevant, and the specification in the model by 'depetalled' matches my modelled knowledge. However, this phrase is presented as a specification of a new cognitive representation which is a MALODOROUS STALK GROWING FROM HER EAR. To say the least, this is more difficult to resolve as an expression of a conventional conceptual metaphor. The comparison between her arms and sandpaper maps the feature of 'rough texture' onto her skin (which is a conventional enough analogy), but the comparison is placed on the same analogous level as the mapping with the 'wings of leprous birds in taxis'. By this point my cognitive knowledge is defeated. Furthermore, the co-referent of 'her' is unspecified, and remains so throughout the rest of the poem.

Reading these lines as potential metaphorical mappings is impossible if the world in which they are set is the familiar real world in which our store of cognitive models is set. However, recalling surrealist ideology, the framing world can be imagined as the metaphorical level in general. Framing the text as having unconscious or irrational status allows the strange images to be read literally. Put the other way round, reading the discourse deviance literally – taking the surrealist image seriously – causes the framing world to be regarded irrationally. It is the literal reading of surrealist images that allows access to the unconscious.

On this reading, I can re-read the first line non-metaphorically as a specification of the GERANIUMS model – one which is restructured from my familiar understanding in that these flowers are now explosive. The literal picture which comes to mind from the first line is now an image of incendiary petals scattered deep across the floor of a devastated hotel ballroom. (To be honest, ever since I came across this line a few years ago, I think of geraniums this way).

A similar reading can be applied to the following opening of a collectively written 'chainpoem', this line contributed by Charles Henri Ford:

> With the forks of flowers I eat the meat of morning

Here, two embedded metaphors appear within what might be a sentence metaphor. However, the vehicle-construction of the sentence metaphor remains difficult because of the invisibility of whatever the target vehicle is. 'Forks of flowers' could be simply a specification of the shape of FLOWERS, and the 'meat of morning' could conceivably be a mapping that concretises MORNING as a fulsome time. In this resolution, the sentence metaphor could map to some target meaning like 'I am living this day to the full capacity of my senses'. The alliteration in the line adds to the sense that these could be conventional idioms. Like the Gascoyne example above, though, the remaining lines of the chainpoem written blindly by different poets do not cohere with the first line. Again, the whole framing world of the poem must be made surreal, and the images read as literal descriptions. It is then like the direct presentation of a surrealist painting.

Instead of mapping between cognitive models, my reading accounts for the discomfort of surrealism by understanding it as an enforced restructuring of existing familiar source domains. How permanent or persistent that restructuring is depends on your immersion in surrealist art. Over the course of several lines or several poems, the effect can be disorientating:

> The worlds are breaking in my head
> Blown by the brainless wind
> That comes from afar
> Swollen with dusk and dust
> And hysterical rain
> ('Yves Tanguy', David Gascoyne)

Here, the common literary conceptual metaphor generally called 'personification' is pushed to its extreme. 'The brainless wind' is a metaphor by negation in the same way as John Donne's 'No man is an island': both are literally true but outrageously so, and the motivation behind this statement of the obvious must be resolved by a metaphorical reading. 'Hysterical rain' also offers a personifying metaphor. However, the first line places the personification within a real experiencing head. Again, a literal reading creates the same sorts of images as those painted by Yves Tanguy.

Sometimes the cognitive model is restructured on the basis of existing prototypical features already within it:

> In the waking night
> The forests have stopped growing
> The shells are listening [...]
> Once flown
> The feathered hour will not return
> And I shall have gone away
> ('The Cage', David Gascoyne)

There are features of conventional cognitive models here: NIGHT is associated with sleep and thus waking, trees grow in FORESTS, we listen to the sea in SHELLS which also look like ears, and we say that TIME flies. However, all these are distorted: it is the night which wakes; the forest growth is stopped; shells listen to us instead of the other way round; and time does not just metaphorically fly but now has literal feathers and has flown away from us.

A similar pattern is apparent in:

> blue bugs in liquid silk
> talk with correlation particularly like
> two women in white bandages
> ('Untitled', Philip O'Connor)

Here, there is a rapid evocation of several embedded cognitive mappings (bugs which are blue are in silk which is liquid, and they are given the ability to speak, and the way they speak is analogous to two women with the attributes of being bandaged). The surrealist technique of literalisation of the apparently metaphorical is here effected by the explicit claim to specification of the cognitive model in the word 'particularly'. The mismatch between this claim to specificity and the chaos of the embedding of concepts accounts for the surreality and discomfort.

Occasionally surrealist writing simply presents straight contradiction, as a radical challenge whereby two contradictory features are specified within the same cognitive structure:

> slowly the ponderous doors of lead imponderous
> pushed by a wedging force unthinking opened
> ('Sleep', Bravig Imbs)

Or an extreme of richness is offered, with a corresponding trade-off in low clarity:

> My wife with the hair of a wood fire
> With the thoughts of heat lightning

With the waist of an hourglass
With the waist of an otter in the teeth of a tiger
  ('Freedom of Love', André Breton, translated by Edouard Roditi)

Complex mappings like these aim at the surrealist objective of multiplying meaning out of existence. The full effect can only really be seen by reproducing a complete poem:

In the stump of the old tree, where the heart has rotted out,
there is a hole the length of a man's arm, and a dank pool at the
bottom of it where the rain gathers, and the old leaves turn into
lacy skeletons. But do not put your hand down to see, because

in the stumps of old trees, where the hearts have rotted out,
there are holes the length of a man's arm, and dank pools at the
bottom where the rain gathers and old leaves turn to lace, and the
beak of a dead bird gapes like a trap. But do not put your
hand down to see, because

in the stumps of old trees with rotten hearts, where the rain
gathers and the laced leaves and the dead bird like a trap, there
are holes the length of a man's arm, and in every crevice of the
rotten wood grow weasel's eyes like molluscs, their lids open
and shut with the tide. But do not put your hand down to see, because

in the stumps of old trees where the rain gathers and the
trapped leaves and the beak, and the laced weasel's eyes, there are
holes the length of a man's arm, and at the bottom a sodden bible
written in the language of rooks. But do not put your hand down
to see, because

in the stumps of old trees where the hearts have rotted out
there are holes the length of a man's arm where the weasels are
trapped and the letters of the rook language are laced on the
sodden leaves, and at the bottom there is a man's arm. But do
not put your hand down to see, because

in the stumps of old trees where the hearts have rotted out
there are deep holes and dank pools where the rain gathers, and
if you ever put your hand down to see, you can wipe it in the
sharp grass till it bleeds, but you'll never want to eat with
it again.

                                        (Hugh Sykes Davies)

The poem begins by evoking a cognitive model which initially simply presents a familiar gloomy woodland scene. There are some common descriptive metaphors (heart of a tree, skeletal leaves) and a conventional analogy of measurement (the length of a man's arm). If you begin the poem super-sensitive to metaphorical possibilities (which could be the case by this point in the chapter), you might generalise a conceptual metaphor, TREE STUMP IS A DECOMPOSING BODY, but I don't recall I generated this on my first reading.

The second stanza is more or less a repetition, except for a crucial difference: many of the nouns are pluralised. The detail of the dead bird's beak and its simile are added. The metaphor is made more stylistically invisible, from a premodification ('lacy skeletons') to an explicit grammatical metaphor ('old leaves turn to lace') that is barely a metaphor at all.

The third stanza removes some of the definite articles. The effect of pluralisation and indefiniteness is to generalise the description so that the entire cognitive model now seems to stand as a fictional metaphor for something else which remains invisible and uncomfortably resistant to resolution. This discomfort seems to me to have resonances which make me read other parts of the stanza in a more sinister light. The rain gathers and the old leaves turn to lace as part of natural processes in the second stanza, but in the third 'the rain gathers' wilfully and the leaves have been 'laced' (agency, like the source domain, omitted). Weasel's eyes grow disembodied, and what starts as a simile ('like molluscs') shifts in the next line so that the entire OCEAN cognitive model is evoked, and 'the tide' is no longer a simile but real. The pattern continues in the fourth stanza, with the elements blending into each other's conceptual space. The dead bird has now slipped into the concept of the rook language. (It should be noted that in some editions of the poem, this stanza is omitted).

By the fifth stanza, the weasel's eyes have become trapped weasels and someone (omitted agent in the passive, again) has laced the rook language on the leaves. Again, what has thus far been an analogy for measurement slips into the real domain: 'at the bottom there is a man's arm'. The association with weasel's eyes and dead eyelids suddenly gives a new twisted meaning to the repeated last lines of each stanza. Perhaps the man's arm belonged to someone who 'put [their] hand down to see', and the conventional metaphor UNDERSTANDING IS SEEING ends up surreally literalised as a hand with weasely eyes?

The final stanza completes the landscape of paranoia, by finally setting up an 'if ... then' clause as if to provide a resolution, but then leaving the explanatory mapping vague and unspecified. The poem completes its objective of enacting and fulfilling readerly paranoia by twisting, step by step, the reader's cognitive model of the scene from an unpleasant metaphor to a sinister reality. This is the world as it really is, *surréalisme* better translated as 'super-realism'.

Explorations

1   What are the two main conceptual metaphors in the following passage, and how do their respective mappings offer an expressive, explanatory or constitutive model?

A long time ago, man would listen in amazement to the sound of regular beats in his chest, never suspecting what they were. He was unable to identify himself with so alien and unfamiliar an object as the body. The body was a cage, and inside that cage was something which looked, listened, feared, thought, and marvelled; that something, that remainder left unaccounted for, was the soul.

Today, of course, the body is no longer unfamiliar: we know that the beating in our chest is the heart and that the nose is the nozzle of a hose sticking out of the body to take oxygen to the lungs. The face is nothing but an instrument panel registering all the body mechanisms: digestion, sight, hearing, respiration, thought.

(*The Unbearable Lightness of Being*, Milan Kundera,1984)

2   The following speech is by the dying John of Gaunt from *Richard II*. In general it contains two major metaphoric mappings: over the first nine lines, several sentence metaphors have BOLINGBROKE'S REBELLION as their (invisible) target; the rest of the speech has ENGLAND as the target, which is eventually made visible about halfway through. In both cases, an accumulation of source models make this speech very *rich* but lacking in *clarity*.

Track the detail of the mappings, and consider if specific features to be mapped are stylistically indicated. Which features of the source models are not mapped? How does the style build the characterisation of Gaunt here? You might also read the passage in the light of other micrometaphors in the play to see if any general patterns of conceptual metaphor emerge.

> *Gaunt:* Methinks I am a prophet new inspir'd,
> And thus expiring do foretell of him:
> His rash fierce blaze of riot cannot last,
> For violent fires soon burn out themselves;
> Small showers last long, but sudden storms are short;
> He tires betimes that spurs too fast betimes;
> With eager feeding food doth choke the feeder:
> Light vanity, insatiate cormorant,
> Consuming means, soon preys upon itself.
> This royal throne of kings, this scepter'd isle,
> This earth of majesty, this seat of Mars,
> This other Eden, demi-paradise,
> This fortress built by Nature for herself
> Against infection and the hand of war,
> This happy breed of men, this little world,
> This precious stone set in the silver sea,
> Which serves it in the office of a wall,
> Or as a moat defensive to a house,
> Against the envy of less happier lands,
> This blessed plot, this earth, this realm, this England,

This nurse, this teeming womb of royal kings,
Fear'd by their breed and famous by their birth,
Renowned for their deeds as far from home,
For Christian service and true chivalry,
As is the sepulchre in stubborn Jewry
Of the world's ransom, blessed Mary's Son:
This land of such dear souls, this dear, dear land,
Dear for her reputation through the world,
Is now leas'd out, – I die pronouncing it, –
Like to a tenement, or pelting farm:
England, bound in with the triumphant sea,
Whose rocky shore beats back the envious siege
Of watery Neptune, is now bound in with shame,
With inky blots, and rotten parchment bonds:
That England, that was wont to conquer others,
Hath made a shameful conquest of itself.
Ah! would the scandal vanish with my life,
How happy then were my ensuing death.
           (*Richard II*, II.i, 31–68)

Further reading and references

There is limited rigorous work on the surface expressions of metaphor. Brooke-Rose (1958) is an early study, updated in Stockwell (2000a: 169–98); see also Stockwell (1992 and 1994) for the 'visibility' of metaphor. The categories of metaphor realisation are adapted from Goatly (1997). Cameron and Low (1999) is a collection of applied metaphor studies.

Literary work on metaphor includes Richards (1924), Ricoeur (1977) and Black (1962, 1990). The characteristics of mappings are from Gentner (1982). The work on conceptual metaphor is huge. Key texts include Lakoff and Johnson (1980, 1999), Paprotte and Dirven (1985), Kövecses (1986, 1988, 1990), Kittay (1987), Johnson (1987), Turner (1987, 1991), Lakoff (1987), Lakoff and Turner (1989), Ortony (1993), and a clear summary exposition in Ungerer and Schmid (1996: 114–54).

Invariance is introduced by Lakoff (1990) and Turner (1990); see Stockwell (1999) for a critique. The question is further discussed by Forceville (1995a, 1995b, 1996). Megametaphors are in Werth (1994, 1999). Other cognitive poetic work which treats surrealism includes Gibbs (1994: 258–64), Lakoff and Turner (1989) and Stockwell (2000b). For the cognitive poetics of Shakespeare, see Freeman (1996). On the use of conceptual metaphor in politics, see Stockwell (1990), Wilson (1990), Lakoff (1992) and Fairclough (1995).

9 Literature as parable

Preview

The frameworks and models of cognitive poetics that have been outlined in this book should all be considered to be dynamic. In order to explain cognitive models, image schemas, mappings and so on, it has been convenient so far to treat them as snapshots, as static models with an implicit **dynamic** aspect. However, it is now time to put that word to work directly.

Many of the approaches within cognitive poetics have been developed within other disciplines such as linguistics, psychology, computer design and programming, and anthropology, and then adapted for the literary context. As cognitive poetics emerges as a discipline in its own right, of course, it will develop its own frameworks and useful terms that are particular to literary concerns. Furthermore, and in keeping with the principle that there is a continuum of cognition across literary and everyday language, as the field matures insights attained in literary exploration can contribute to and illuminate general aspects of human communication and thought. In this chapter, I illustrate the extent to which cognitive poetics is already achieving this.

So far, too, I have traced those cognitive approaches which offer detailed understanding of literature. Most literary criticism, however, is concerned not with literary craft and microstructure but with general intuitions and whole-text meanings. In this chapter, together with Chapters 10 and 11, I outline how cognitive poetics can address these issues in a properly principled and systematic way. This chapter ends with a discussion using Middle English literature.

Links with literary critical concepts

Allegory, archetypes, escapism, fabula, fiction, imagination, interpretation, intertextuality, involvement, meaning, message, narrative, plot, relevance, significance, story, symbol, theme, topic

The field of **narratology** within literary study has a long history, and narrative (especially narrative fiction) is regarded as one of the central modes of literary production. A common distinction has been drawn between the literary narrative artifice (the **plot**, or *sjuzhet*, or *discours*) and the 'raw' sequence of events that might in reality have been (or might seem to have been) the originating happening (the **story**, or *fabula*, or *histoire*). These distinctions depend on a fundamental difference being drawn between a story which is the perceptible original, and a representation of that undisturbed and pure reality as a narrative. If, however, we take a dynamic view of cognition – which informs our ideas about scripts, schemas, image-schemas, conceptual metaphors, keeping track of deixis, and so on – we have to admit that any pre-representational reality might exist but is literally unthinkable. Many narratological theorists have reached the same view by various different means.

It seems to be the case that anything thinkable is only manifest to us as part of a tiny story, a narrative in which even static objects are cognised not in isolation but in a dynamic relationship with other items and processes within the prototypical structure of their associated cognitive models. In other words, narratives are one of the fundamental aspects of understanding. Furthermore, we do not have access to a pre-cognitive reality, since the act of cognition itself involves a representation, and this involves selection, omissions, weighting of foreground and background, evaluations of relevance and significance, and personal salience and interest. All of these are also made more complex by the individual's social situation, and their own personal goals.

While this complexity is the territory for different readings and literary debates which you might think are irreconcilably subjective, it is also the ground which cognitive poetics has most successfully mapped out. Cognitive science begins from the same premise, that our embodied cognition creates, from reality, characteristic and explorable patterns that appear in language. Since language is the only access we have to that reality, we might as well talk about the 'myths' which we use as instruments to represent our worlds. Since cognitive science has developed systematic approaches to these issues, cognitive poetics is now in a position to offer an explanation for intersubjective readings, and also a means of exploring literary readings in a principled way. We can start to account for the traditional literary critical concerns for readerly meaning, perceived significance and discernible literary themes through cognitive poetic analysis.

Meaning and macrostructure

At the post-apocalyptic end of Ray Bradbury's *Fahrenheit 451*, the fireman Montag, whose job it had been to incinerate all books, joins a rural community who are preserving human knowledge by memorising every word of valued literary texts and thus in effect becoming those books. However, for those of us living where books are legal, and since human memory is faulty, and we view certain aspects of a text as being more important to us than others, for the most part we do not carry around entire memorised books in our heads. Instead, we preserve a representation of those texts, comprising the *gist* of the meaning, some generalised sense of the poetic texture and structure of the work, and a sense of the book's significance in our society and culture, together with a sense of what the literary work means for us.

These representations form the raw material of literary criticism and discussion. However, such representations are the outcome of a process of reading and social negotiation; in order to explore the nature and relative values of these representations, cognitive poetics is also interested in how these outcomes are formed. An early approach within the field of cognition and literary study proposed the principle of **macrostructures** as part of the reading process. A macrostructure is a hierarchical representation of interrelated propositions, which together represent the gist of a literary work for a particular reader.

Starting with the **textbase** (the word-for-word processing over the course of a reading), a reader begins to construct a macrostructure even before completing the whole text. First, a **microstructure** of all of the propositions encountered through a reading are assembled into *facts* about what is happening in the text. Then, all the facts (which can be seen as local states of affairs in the world of the text) are assembled into a generalised macrostructure using the following cognitive strategies. These are termed **macrorules:**

- **citation** – a sort of 'zero-rule' generates direct recall of specific text, able to be quoted or closely paraphrased, often a memorable poetic phrase or a key statement of theme or significance;
- **local deletion** – facts which seem to be only relevant locally, such as details of scenery descriptions, are not selected for the macrostructure;
- **global deletion** – some facts which survive local deletion turn out not to be relevant across the whole text, and so are disregarded towards the end of the text-reading;
- **generalisation** – facts which suggest logical consequences, or inferences which can be derived purely from the facts presented in the text, are generalised into propositions which capture a general statement about the text world;
- **construction** – facts which are generalisations in the additional light of sociocultural knowledge (from schemas) are built into the macrostructure.

Although only the last of these principles – construction – explicitly mentions schematic knowledge, all of the macrorules feature some element of readerly decision-making. Different readers bring different knowledge and different personal goals to a reading, and this is why the same textbase can produce a range of macrostructural representations, or different 'readings'.

There are two crucial advantages in this approach. First, the idea of macrorule strategies allows us to identify where and how different readings arise, and rather than simply accepting them as matters of random individual variation, we can begin to explore the precise social and personal saliences involved. Second, across groups of readers in a specified sociocultural situation, we can begin to distinguish prototypical and common readings from eccentric ones. This also encourages us towards a greater specification of the evidence in the textbase that is claimed to generate different readings.

Parable and projection

The framework of macrorules set out above illustrates that the relationship between the accumulation of propositions in a literary text and the reader's sense of its general meaning cannot simply be regarded as a single direct, metaphor-like mapping. Claiming that *Wuthering Heights* is a love story is not simply a matter of a conceptual metaphor such as WUTHERING HEIGHTS IS A LOVE STORY taking precedence over WUTHERING HEIGHTS IS A FABLE OF PROPERTY RIGHTS or WUTHERING HEIGHTS IS AN EXERCISE IN PERSONAL MEMORY or WUTHERING HEIGHTS IS ABOUT THE TRIUMPH OF LITERACY or CHARACTERS IN WUTHERING HEIGHTS ARE DRAMATISED ELEMENTAL FORCES, or any other possible readings of the novel. The apparent source domains offered here are too vague or ill-specified to count as likely cognitive models for mapping. The questions 'What is it about?' and 'What does it mean?' and 'What does it mean for you?' are different questions, complicated by different emphases placed on personal and social and cultural schematic knowledge. So we cannot simply regard the literary text (even a schematic representation of it) as being a target domain and its 'meaning' as being a source domain in a conceptual mapping.

In Chapter 8, fiction and allegory were placed as the most stylistically generalised of metaphoric mappings, but we must now be careful to treat fiction and allegory differently. In allegory, where certain elements in the structure tend to have a fairly clear significance or meaning, we certainly can say that the macrostructure is a metonymy of the microstructure (one is a specification of the cognitive model of the other), and we can also describe the macrostructure and its 'impact' or 'meaning' as being in a metaphorical relationship. The relationship between fiction and its meaning is more complex and less direct. This complexity increases when we consider that literature is composed not exclusively of fiction, but also of personal meditations, travelogues, autobiography, historical dramatisation, and expressions of political opposition, love, hatred and malicious satire.

In cognitive poetics, the relationship between the microstructure of the text and its meaningfulness is captured in general by the notion of **parable**. This is a recognition that stories are at the heart of cognitive understanding. For example, if we reconsider the presentation of image schemas and figure and ground in Chapter 2, we can see that the cognitive models involved are composed of a sequence, a movement of an element (the trajector) in relation to its ground (the landmark). Even in those image schemas where we are presented with a resting state (such as involving the prepositions 'in', 'under', 'on top of'), we reconstruct the dynamic movement leading up to the static position in order to recognise the phrase as an example of a familiar and conventional image schema. In short, image schemas are little stories of a very general and widely applicable sort.

There are, of course, many different possible combinations of mappings between any image schema and the potential range of its linguistic expressions. The actual detail of the story can be complex. When we are dealing with the multiple elements comprising an entire fictional narrative, the complexity of the mapping is compounded. Taking the literary work as the target cognitive model, we can, however, distinguish two main types of location for mappings from the source. The macrostructural account given above provides us with these. A newly encountered literary work can be generalised and constructed into a socially and culturally shared reading. Alternatively, the target literary macrostructure can be generalised and constructed into the reader's own personal values and experience. Where the latter sort of readings take precedence, readers tend to keep their ideas for their own reflection, unless they express them as personal tastes or personal recommendations to friends. In the published scholarly and journalistic fields, however, it is the first sort of mapping which is dominant. Students' essays often blend the personal and the sociocultural, either because they are only just learning the disciplinary patterns, or because they want to present what is primarily a personal account but recognise that decent grades depend on making an accommodation towards the collective disciplinary standard.

Either way, what is being **projected** from the story is a parable: a newly tructured cognitive model that is the reader's representation of the meaningfulness of the literary work. The notion of a parable (or a **parabolic projection**) recognises that the cognitive model of the literary work is primarily derived from the text-reading, but has a structure in which key features are picked out and foregrounded as being highly salient for the reader, or for the reading community as determined in the reader's mind.

So, for example, usually **actors** are differentiated from **objects**, since the reader projects their own embodied experience of wilfulness, consciousness and ability to act onto text-entities that are labelled with human names or predications usually associated with self-hood: speech and thought, emotion and perception, and active material verb forms. Differentiating actors and objects is a key schematic pattern that is overlaid onto the world of the text in constructing the parable. Similarly actors and objects are differentiated from **events** in the parable representation, as image schematic actional knowledge is used to structure the parable.

However, I have been emphasising that parable is not simply a straight metaphorical mapping between the narrative and its meaning. Parable is a projection of story in the sense of extending it as well as straightforwardly representing it, and other input comes from trans-world identities and mappings from other cognitive domains, including the reader's model of the world, as well. For example, any given narrative will usually contain several mentions of a particular character, and their entry in the cognitive model will be indexed by their name, by a pronoun, by tracking their focalisation, and so on. If the narrative extends over time, different mentions of the character will be attached to different states of affairs in the cognitive model – or to different versions of the cognitive model itself. Furthermore, hypothetical or conditional situations might be expressed in which the character is involved. As in possible worlds theory (see Chapter 7), these indexed actors are regarded as many **counterparts** of one character. In the parabolic model, the character might have a counterpart that allows the reader to imagine what that character would do in the real world. Or, even more loosely, the reader might identify with the character, setting up a readerly counterpart of the character that blends in the parabolic space.

Sometimes characters in the text can be regarded as emblematic in the parable. That is, some of their characteristics are seen as generically significant beyond the specifics of their world. Similarly, the whole narrative can become an **emblem**. In this sense (which is different from the direct metaphorical linkages in allegory, for example), a specific narrative is read as having elements which are generic in similar conceptual domains. *Robinson Crusoe* becomes an emblem of isolation and abandonment; *Anthem for Doomed Youth* stands as an emblem for war poetry; *Romeo and Juliet* is emblematic of tragic thwarted love. Such emblems can be metaphorically mapped back onto specific narratives again: *Romeo and Juliet* onto street gangs in New York (*West Side Story*), or lovers on different sides in Belfast (*Cal*), for example.

Because of the complexity of inputs, **blending** is central to the notion of parable. As explained in Chapter 7, various input spaces (such as the parts of a narrative text, the reader's experience, sociocultural knowledge, or literary allusions) are mapped to form a generic space, and combined into a blended space. When occurring within parable, the blend is run through its emergent structure, and the conceptual content of the blend takes on a life of its own. So new relations become apparent in the blend (composition), without recourse back to the input spaces. Readerly schematic knowledge connects aspects in the blend to wider concerns (completion), and the blend contributes to the whole parable in its ongoing elaboration.

Blending can be applied, for example, to the way that **intertextuality** operates in literary works. Sometimes a text relies heavily on another single identifiable text, such as through direct citation in Huxley's *Brave New World* (the title is a quotation from *The Tempest*) or through the transposition of plot into a different world as in the SF film *Forbidden Planet* (a loose version of *The Tempest*) or in the sequence of poems by Sylvia Plath called *Ariel* (a character in *The Tempest*). Sometimes the intertextuality recreates and extends the same world, as with sequels by the same author (Isaac Asimov's *Foundation* trilogy), sequels by other authors (Greg Bear's *Foundation of Chaos* and Gregory Benford's *Foundation's Fear* are set in Asimov's universe), or sequels that undermine the ideology of the original (Margaret Mitchell's *Gone With the Wind* was recently re-imagined as *The Wind Done Gone*, written from the viewpoint of the black slave characters in the old South). Literary texts lift characters, plots, settings and themes out of their original environments and place them into new blended spaces where an emergent structure develops independently. Aldiss' *Frankenstein Unbound* blends future, historical, literary and real characters, settings, plot and the epistolary novel form.

In all these blends, there is also the potential for interanimation (see Chapter 8). At this parabolic level, the emergent structure of the blend allows new insights to appear and a new understanding of the elements of the input spaces. Blended space in parable allows us to apply inferences, arguments, concepts and emotions back into the input space in order to alter our original cognitive models. Aldiss' novel changed the way I saw Shelley's *Frankenstein* (an input space), my image of Percy and Mary Shelley and Byron (another input space) and how I thought of the development of science fiction (a further input space). Alice Randall's *The Wind Done Gone* was regarded by Margaret Mitchell's estate not simply as a literary parody but as a challenge to a set of values they held, and its British publication was challenged in the courts.

Finally, as my use of all these examples here in this textbook illustrates, blends can be inputs to further blends, where emergent structure can again potentially offer modifications of the original cognitive models. This is the mechanism by which, through parable, literature alters our perspective, knowledge, and way of thinking.

Discussion

Before reading on, you might like to consider or discuss some of the implications of these ideas.

• The notion of macrostructures can illuminate the concept of genre. To demonstrate this, try to rewrite the following narratives from memory: *the New Testament of the Bible, your life, this year, the history of the English language, Hamlet, The Wizard of Oz, the structure of your studies, a recipe for rhubarb crumble.* However, you should 'regenerate' them, not in their original generic pattern but as one of the following: *a gothic novel, a cookery recipe, a travel article, an advert in a women's magazine, a tabloid newspaper article, a car manual, a satirical radio script, a football commentary.* What knowledge and what sorts of knowledge do you need to do this? Consider the stages by which the original is transformed into your version. For an example of the serious literary effect of this, see J.G. Ballard's (1970: 108–9) 'The Assassination of John Fitzgerald Kennedy Considered as a Downhill Motor Race'.
• Consider how the notion and mechanism of parable could be tested empirically on groups of readers.
• Take two detailed readings of the same textbase (such as by two literary critics, or two students' essays) and schematically compare the parabolic models represented in each piece of writing. Using your understanding of parable and blending, can you begin to tease out the factors which have determined the similarities and differences in the readings?

Cognitive poetic analysis

In some respects there are more similarities between cognitive poetics and the medieval view of language and thought, compared with the 'objectivist' myths expressed by post-seventeenth century scientific rationalism. For example, in the Middle Ages, a logic of *homology* (identity beyond analogy) between nature and language was widespread. Since creation was consistent, natural resemblances were thought to be reflected in linguistic resemblances, and so literary co-incidences of sound and sense had a thematic significance beyond mere craft, making an impact in the world of the reader (this had its culmination in the conceits and puns of the metaphysical poets, see Chapter 5). The most proper mode of being for language was disputation and conflict (contrast this with the post-Enlightenment idea of fixing and defining the objects in language), and the point of speaking or reading was to establish a variety of modes of understanding, not in order to arrive at a conclusion but as an experiential training in the process of thought. After all, only God had the right to truthful conclusion, and to claim truth for a proposition was a claim to divine parity, a heresy called hubris.

In the fourteenth century poem usually entitled *Sir Gawain and the Green Knight*, these ideas can be illustrated through some of the cognitive poetic concepts introduced in this and previous chapters. The story of the poem is divided into four parts or 'Fitts', beginning at King Arthur's court on New Year's Day. A strange green knight challenges the court to a test of *trawþe*, the knightly virtue of honesty and fidelity. Only Sir Gawain accepts, and begins the game as asked by chopping off the knight's head; but his body picks it up and replaces it, and makes Gawain promise to find him a year later for the return blow. The second Fitt jumps a year as Gawain sets off from Camelot to journey through the winter landscape to find the green knight. He is welcomed into a castle by a lord and lady, and they persuade him to stay until the end of December when he will be taken to the Green Chapel to meet the knight. Gawain accepts the lord's challenge to exchange any gains he might achieve in those three days. In the third Fitt, the lord goes out hunting and Gawain remains in the castle where he faces temptation from the lady. He faithfully exchanges the lord's prizes for the kisses he has gained from the lady, but on the third day he keeps secret a green belt she gave him, telling him it would protect him from the green knight. In the final Fitt, he reaches the Green Chapel and faces the knight, who takes three blows at his neck, slightly injuring him only on the last blow. The knight explains the significance of the *trawþe* test in this outcome, and Gawain returns penitent and chastened to Arthur's court.

One of the main structuring conceptual metaphors running through the poem relies on the source domain GAME. In the poem, LIFE IS A GAME, with its sub-divisions, THE QUEST IS A GAME, HUNTING IS A GAME, LOVE IS A GAME, and REDEMPTION IS A GAME. These conceptual metaphors underlie the four main actions in the narrative. The two rounds of the beheading challenge frame the entire poem; the lord's hunt is a game; the lady's temptation is a game; and Gawain and the lord exchange their winnings from these games.

Part of the conceptual model of GAMES involves the recognition and adherence to rules. All four games are initiated by the Green Knight (in the castle in his disguise as the lord), but the rules are different. Hunting is a highly codified game; the beheading game is also well-defined, though more unusual and not as conventional as hunting. However, the exchange of winnings does not have explicit rules, and Gawain seems to make them up as he goes along, though it is clear that something is expected. The temptation game with the lady has no agreed rules at all: its rules are its ongoing content, which Gawain must learn. The aim of this game is simply to learn its rules. Underlying all the conceptual metaphors of GAME in the poem, though, is the image schema of BALANCE and its main aspect, EXCHANGE.

In the poem, material items are exchanged: a boar's head and a deer for kisses, a fox which Gawain should have exchanged for the green belt, an axe-blow for an axe-blow, a pentangle for the green belt, and others. Clearly these are local emblems, which we can map onto a generic space: the boar's head is a tactless reminder of Gawain's upcoming fate, kisses are temptations, the axe-blows are tests of *trawþe*, the green belt represents Gawain clinging to a pagan talisman, perhaps. Of course, in order to apply a working BALANCE image schema to these, we have to reconstruct all these material, actional and abstract things as equivalents in weight. We have to accept the rules of exchange just as Gawain should. There is an emergent structure once you accept this. For example, the lady's kisses are exchanged for noble creatures, a boar and a deer. However, Gawain is offered a fox, conventionally vermin, on the day he should have exchanged the green belt. Here, the blend logic suggests the green belt is verminous and useless. Like the fox, Gawain is also figured as a thief.

Furthermore, Gawain takes the green belt as his protection in place of the pentangle. In the poem, the pentangle has already been assigned a heavily emblematic importance, both literally and metaphorically. It combines the values of Christianity (another input domain) and courtly chivalry, 'Hit is a synge that Salamon set sumquyle in bytoknyng of trawþe' (it is a symbol that Solomon once devised as a token of fidelity).

The pentangle is a closed pattern of five lines and five points, encompassing linearity and circularity at an abstract generic level. The poem describes the pentangle as being emblematic of the 'fyve wyttes' (senses) and 'fyve fyngres' (fingers), both spiritual and secular strengths. Then it also makes it an emblem of the religious virtues: the 'fyve woundes that Cryst kaght on the croys' and the 'fyve joyes'. The five secular virtues of 'fraunchyse', 'felawschip', 'cortayse', 'clanness' and 'pité' (tolerance, fellowship, courtesy, purity and compassion) are also symbolised in the pentangle.

All of these mappings are made explicitly in the poem. Gawain sets out under the protection of the pentangle (it is painted on his shield), expecting to use his senses and his hands to meet the challenge. However, once arrived at the castle, he is the passive recipient of the lord's and lady's games. None of his knightly training prepares him for the new rules which he has to learn. In medieval theology, virtue was something achieved by abstinence and asceticism, gained by giving something away, and Gawain learns that lesson in the four games. Again, a balance is reached between body and spirit, religious and secular values, in combining *virtus* (strength) and *pietas* (piety, or holiness, closer to the modern word 'virtue' in fact).

The patterning and symbolism throughout the poem encourage a reader to regard the genre as a fairy-tale, like a moral fable. It seems that Gawain sees things like this too, in accepting a magical talisman to protect himself. However, it becomes clear by the end that Gawain is actually in a romance, and should have been more true to his spiritual and chivalric values. In retrospect, aspects of the cognitive model of romance can easily be mapped onto the narrative: it begins and ends in court; the events take place during the inverted time of holidays; Gawain journeys through Advent, the time of penitential preparation; the Green Knight is an obvious chivalric blend, hugely tall with a slender waist, holding a holly branch and an axe; and the narrative lasts as romance convention dictates exactly a year and a day.

Like the multiple scope of the GAME metaphor, the poem also blends other complementary concepts, such as TIME. In the poem and like the pentangle, time is sometimes linear and sometimes cyclical. Allied to conceptual metaphors such as LIFE IS A JOURNEY (enacted again by Gawain in his quest), the poem presents both TIME IS A LINE and TIME IS A CIRCLE. The narrative is a year and a day over 101 stanzas, as if turning full circle and beginning a new sequence, framed by Christmas and the beheading game. A consequence of the cyclical view is that Gawain's fate is already determined, and he will return to where he started with deeper experience and wisdom. Gawain thinks he is in a realistic linear quest, though, a consequence of which is that he thinks he has choice and freewill. His human choices (who would not accept a protective green belt over a dead fox?) turn out to be the wrong ones, since he is playing a symbolic not a real game. In trying to control what he should simply accept, he commits hubris, and is punished appropriately and with exact balance at the end. The poem manages to combine the two contradictory models of time and perception, and the potential clash can be thematised as the mechanism by which Gawain – and the reader – learns the value of *trawþe*.

Some of these literary manoeuvres can also be discerned in other medieval texts. In Thomas Malory's fifteenth century *Le Morte d'Arthur*, for example, throughout most of the tales of the knights of Camelot, a set of values and an emblematic currency emerges. Tournaments and adversaries tend to come in threes, evil knights wear black and virtuous knights wear white, success in battle is an emblematic measure of personal goodness, and so on. However, in *The Tale of the Sankgreal* (the holy grail), many of these values are overturned, subverted or just arbitrarily altered. Near the beginning of the tale, Sir Galahad and Sir Melyas come upon an inscription on a cross which offers peaceful passage by the right and an opportunity for a test of prowess on the left. Melyas takes the adventure and is almost killed by a stranger knight. When Galahad carries him back to an abbey, a monk emerges to heal Sir Melyas and to inform him directly that he was wounded because he had not made a confession. So far, so conventional. But then the monk goes on to give him a list of items that the different elements in his adventure signified, a list so complicated and spiritually exacting that Sir Melyas could not possibly have anticipated their meaning.

This happens again and again throughout the tale, with hermits, recluses and good men appearing from nowhere to provide the keys to events and the meanings of people and their clothes, all completely impossible to anticipate, and culminating in the tale of Sir Bors. Here, the knight is met in a dream by a black bird and a white bird, and later by a holy man, and later by a fair lady, and a dry tree and white lilies. Applying the usual conventions, he supports and fights for the white, holy and fair, and is almost killed. An abbot explains that the colours symbolised 'ipocresye', the lady was a devil, and throughout he had made the wrong choices.

Like Gawain in his own poem, the knights in Malory's grail quest have their established cognitive models undermined by new experiences (and of course the reader parallels this confusion). Again, the text acts in the teaching sense of parable, in training the readers (and the knights) to shift their thinking up into the spiritual level, while at the same time dramatising the fact that true enlightenment is transcendental and not attainable on Earth. Only the impossibly pure Galahad, who instinctively and miraculously makes all the right decisions, is allowed to touch the grail, and is rewarded with a holy and painless death. Having attained this level of spiritual understanding, there is nowhere left for the reader to go, and Malory's book draws to a close with the affair of Lancelot and Guinevere and the ensuing fall of Camelot.

In the late fifteenth century *Morall Fabillis*, Robert Henryson retells many of Aesop's animal fables, but applies a similar parabolic twist for the reader. Each fable ends with an explicit moral, which can be seen as a specification of meaning in the parable. Often the moral is conventional: the town mouse and the country mouse fable suggests you should be satisfied with small possessions. However, sometimes the moral is the shocking opposite of what is expected: the cock who leaves a stone in dung should be regarded as being as wise as the two mice, but is chastised because the stone represents 'perfite prudence and cunning'. For the reader, as for him, there was no clue that this was a possibility. Here, the revelatory moral forces a restructuring of the cognitive blend that we have built to account for the story in which we have assigned speech, consciousness and moral values to a cock. We are forced to restructure the input and perhaps thematise our error as either sudden divine enlightenment or as a chastening recognition that we are in fact no better than stupid animals.

In 'The Taill of the Foxe, that begylit the Wolf, in the schadow of the Mone', the complexities of the fable seem highly allegorical. A farmer saves his main livestock by sacrificing his hens to the wolf, rather than leaving them for the fox. The moral asserts that the wolf is a wicked man, the fox is the devil, and the farmer is a godly man. However, then it goes on to assert that the woods and cheese in the tale are worldly riches and covetousness, and the farmer's hens are good works. At this point, it seems as if every single element has to be allegorised to the point of ridiculousness. One way of thematising this over-precise mapping (over-precise against the conventions set up by the other fables) is perhaps to see the moral as satirising the whole idea of allegorical exegesis. The farmer's possession of the hens saves him from the fox and the wolf. (Read that back in your blend allegorically). However, if you push the allegory further, the farmer has used his good deeds through the wicked man to buy off the devil! Although this is a perfectly feasible restructuring effect from the parable to the input, it is so much at odds with any input from Christian ethics that we must blend a new space that renders this as satire.

Explorations

1   Using your knowledge of cognitive metaphor from Chapter 8, investigate the main conceptual structures across a single long text (an entire play, a novel or a long poem). Then sketch out the role this conceptual scaffolding plays in the global construction of the literary work as parable.

2   Parable is a projection of story and is necessarily narrative in its conceptual organisation. It seems most obviously applicable to literary narratives. However, the notion is presented by Turner (1996) as an illustration of how all language and thought (not just literary works) are based on parable. It ought, then, to be a relatively easy matter to apply the notion of parable to examples of literary texts that are on the surface non-narrative. Try this, for example, with the modes mentioned at the beginning of the discussion of parable above: personal meditations, travelogues, autobiography, historical dramatisation, and expressions of political opposition, love, hatred and malicious satire.

3   To a large extent, parable encompasses many of the ideas presented so far in this book, especially conceptual metaphor, schemas and mental spaces. A large question still remains: what is the precise mechanism or principle by which certain elements in a cognitive model are mapped and others are left behind? The idea of parable answers this by using the mental space theory constraints on blending, and suggests that the avoidance of conceptual clashes in the emergent structure of the blend is the key to a coherent reading. Can you try this out on some literary texts to see if you find it satisfactory?

4   Take as a case study a literary work which has had a major social, political or personal impact. How does the notion of parable illuminate the processes involved? Examples which spring to my mind include:

News from Nowhere, William Morris
Nausea, Jean-Paul Sartre
1984, George Orwell
The Catcher in the Rye, J.D. Salinger
Catch-22, Joseph Heller
On the Road, Jack Kerouac
Howl, Allen Ginsberg
Fear of Flying, Erica Jong
The Colour Purple, Alice Walker
The Women's Room, Marilyn French
The Satanic Verses, Salman Rushdie

Further reading and references

The narratological work referred to at the beginning of this chapter can be found in Booth (1961), Chatman (1978), Genette (1980), Prince (1982), Bal (1985), and is surveyed by Toolan (2001).

The work on macrostructures was primarily developed by van Dijk (1977, 1980). The set of macrorules set out in this chapter is adapted from van Dijk and Kintsch (1983) and de Beaugrande (1987).

Most of the content of this chapter on parable is taken from Turner (1996). The central concept of blends is restated for the literary context in Turner (1996: 57–115), from Fauconnier (1994) and Turner (1987). See also Fauconnier (1997, 1998), Fauconnier and Turner (1996) and Turner and Fauconnier (1995, 1999).

10 Text worlds

Preview

Several frameworks within cognitive poetics have been concerned with the global end of reading, where the world of the literary work attaches to the world of the reader. Various schema theories, as outlined in Chapter 6, use this aspect of cognition to shed light on the meaningfulness of specific utterances. Similarly, theories emerging from possible worlds theory (see Chapter 7) have been interested in the logical and mental representation of worlds as a mechanism for accounting for fictional reference and the imagined or alternative worlds in literature. These approaches are focused in their scope on the notion of a world as a representation system for resolving issues of reference and semantics.

The cognitive poetic notion of parable (Chapter 9) moves beyond these approaches, extending the potential of mental spaces through blending, in order to discuss in more holistic terms the relationships readers build up with literary texts. In this chapter, I outline an approach to reading which offers a rich world as a means of understanding the negotiation of literary works. Various different world-based models of reading have proposed different solutions to the large question of how the reader's vast background knowledge is specified for application in any particular context of reading. What constraints operate that determine those aspects of knowledge which are required at any given moment of reading? In this chapter, I set out a model suggesting that those constraints are provided by the text itself, and I illustrate the discussion with a variety of texts.

Links with literary critical concepts

Background knowledge, character, context, gist, interpretation, phenomenology, readerliness, theme

In the philosophical tradition known as *phenomenology*, a distinction has been made between objects which exist in the world in their own right (**autonomous** objects) and objects which only come into being when engaged by an observing consciousness (**heteronomous** objects). The former have a material and objective existence that can be verified and discussed: examples of autonomous items include objects such as a parliament building, a house for the government executive, ballot boxes, voting slips. Out of these there is a heteronomous object called 'democracy', which is a holistic and inter-subjectively agreed object that is partly composed of the first few items. Books are autonomous objects, but literature is a heteronomous object.

In terms of presenting a scientific account of literature, then, we have two complementary focus-points that must be maintained. First, there is the unchanging materiality of the words on the page, to which must be added the material texture of the book, the layout, the font style and size, the cover details, the physical sensation of the paper, the dry sandy smell of the book, the crisp sound of the pages as they are turned, and so on. Some of these material textures are already entangled with the conscious participation of the reader, which is the second focus of our account, which also includes the knowledge, experiences, memories, feelings and emotions that the reader brings to a reading of the book.

The autonomic aspects of the text have been the ground of traditional linguistic analysis, where the text-as-object has been described within the frameworks of the linguistic system. More recent stylistic approaches to literature have emphasised the dynamic and readerly aspects of texts, and have become cognitive poetic in orientation by encompassing ideas from cognitive science. In order to be fully cognitive poetic, however, the analysis of literary works must push the two focus-points together so that the engagement of the reader is not an 'add-on' feature but is an inherent part of the analytical theory from the beginning. Only then is the literary work properly treated heteronomously. The cognitive poetic notion of parable is one means of moving towards this. In this chapter, another possible approach – text world theory – is outlined as a means of achieving a holistic view of the literary work.

Text worlds and participants

In text world theory, a **world** is a much richer and cognitively complex affair than in possible worlds theory or its equivalent in mental space theory. A world is a language event involving at least two **participants,** and is the rich and densely textured real-life representation of the combination of text and context. At the highest level is the **discourse world**, prototypically involving face-to-face **discourse participants,** such as two speakers in a conversation, or a letter-writer and receiver, or an author and reader. The language event that is the discourse world is the immediate situation, including the text, surrounding and including the discourse participants.

Factors in the discourse world include the *perceptions* of the immediate situation, and the *beliefs, knowledge, memories, hopes, dreams, intentions* and *imaginations* of the discourse participants. However, in order to prevent this mass of information being unmanageable in the framework, text world theory asserts that only that information which forms a *necessary* context, rather than all possible contexts, is used. The means of usage is through the notion of the **common ground** (CG), which is not all knowledge but the totality of information that the discourse participants have agreed to accept as relevant for their discourse. This notion of agreement is a function of language rather than an assumption of ideological consensus (in other words, even people having an argument use the notion of common ground in order to engage in the argument).

Elements of context are **incremented** into the common ground in the course of discourse processing. The common ground itself shifts during the process, as new ideas are introduced and old concepts are discarded as no longer relevant, or fade away by no longer being mentioned. The composition of the common ground is not mystical, telepathic or so complicated it cannot be tracked: behind the notion of necessary context is its **text-drivenness**. In order to decide which elements of the discourse participants' knowledge are relevant in the discourse world, the text itself provides linguistic and inferential information that narrows the search down to one or a very few specific domains of knowledge.

Text world theory is innovative, then, firstly in providing a specification of how contextual knowledge is actually managed economically; secondly, in placing text and context inseparably together as part of a cognitive process; and thirdly, because it is founded not on the analysis of sentences but on entire texts and the worlds that they create in the minds of readers.

The cognitive mechanism that is the means of understanding is the **text world**. Discourse participants use the text to construct the text world, which consists of **world-building elements** and **function-advancing propositions**. World-building elements constitute the background against which the foreground events of the text will take place. They include an orientation in time and place, and they create characters and other objects that furnish the text world available for reference. Function-advancing propositions propel the narrative or dynamic within the text world forward. They constitute the states, actions, events and processes, and any arguments or predications made in relation to the objects and characters in the text world.

Of the world-builders, **time** (t) is recoverable from the tense and aspect system of verbs, temporal adverbs and adverbial clauses. The place or **location** (l) is recoverable from locative adverbs and adverbial clauses, and noun phrases specifying a place. **Characters** (c) and **objects** (o) are recoverable from noun phrases (including proper names) and pronominals.

In the function-advancers, several different patterns are possible, such as:

Text type	Predicate type	Function	Speech act
Narrative	Action, event	Plot-advancing	Report, recount
Descriptive:			
scene	State	Scene-advancing	Describe scene
person	State, attribute	Person-advancing	Describe character
routine	Habitual	Routine-advancing	Describe routine
Discursive	Relational	Argument-advancing	Postulate, conclude ...
Instructive	Imperative	Goal-advancing	Request, command ...
and so on.			

At a basic level, we can distinguish two sorts of function-advancers (analogous to Halliday's distinction between *material processes* and *relational/mental processes*: see Chapter 5). Some function-advancers express predications that are attributive, relational or descriptive, and others represent actions or events.

This is most easily explained by analysing a simple text:

> Very soon after they had left Ramandu's country they began to feel that they had already sailed beyond the world. All was different. For one thing they all found that they were needing less sleep. One did not want to go to bed nor to eat much, nor even to talk except in low voices. Another thing was the light. There was too much of it. The sun when it came up each morning looked twice, if not three times, its usual size. And every morning (which gave Lucy the strangest feeling of all) the huge white birds, singing their song with human voices in a language no one knew, streamed overhead and vanished astern on their way to their breakfast at Aslan's Table. A little later they came flying back and vanished into the east.
>
> (*The Voyage of the Dawn Treader*, C.S. Lewis)

This passage, near the end of the novel, can be divided into its separate text world elements.

World-builders:

Time	soon after they had left Ramandu's country.
Location	near the edge of the world in the east (built from the previous chapter).
Characters	'they' (Edmund, Lucy, Drinian, Caspian and the crew, from previous chapter).
Objects	the ship 'Dawn Treader' (from previous chapter) and its component parts, sails, bed, astern; also sun, birds, Aslan's Table.

Function-advancing propositions:
they → had left Ramandu's country
they → began to feel they → had sailed beyond the world
they → found they → needed less sleep
one → did not want to go to bed, etc.
light → too much
sun → came up
returning birds → gave Lucy a feeling
birds → streamed overhead
birds → came flying back
birds → vanished

In a diagram of this text world, we can differentiate attributional or relational predications (horizontal arrows) from material actions or events (vertical arrows).

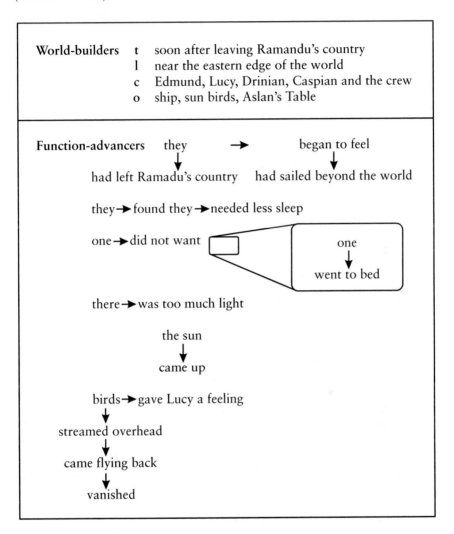

The text world that is built and running here is more than these simple predications, since all of these elements have been enriched by our ongoing knowledge of the previous text and inferences that we make about the ship and the characters and the birds. Lucy is a person with a life and experiences and beliefs that we have been tracking through the novel (as well as in previous novels such as *The Lion, The Witch and the Wardrobe*, if we have read that too). When I read these books as a child, they were fantastic adventure stories of the land of Narnia and Aslan the lion. After I became aware of some literary criticism of the books, I now read them as Christian allegory, and my text world of the passage above would increment religious inferences from the morning ritual of white birds (emblematic of the holy ghost) flying to Aslan's Table (an altar) and back to the east (the traditional orientation of Christian churches). This gives me a motivation for Lucy's emerging religious sensibility ('the strangest feeling of all').

The passage is straightforward apart from the point at which there seems to be an embedded predication ('one did not want to go to bed'), which I have placed in a rounded rectangular projection. This cues up a **sub-world,** as outlined in the section below.

Sub-worlds

There are three layers within text world theory: the discourse world, the text world, and the sub-world. All of these levels are equivalent in terms of structure (with world-builders and function-advancers), and they are all capable of containing the same rich deictic and referential detail. Sub-worlds represent a variation in the texture of the world in focus, without the sense of leaving the current text world. So, for example, a *flashback* in a narrative constitutes an embedded sub-world, and the main text world focus is regained as soon as the flashback is concluded. The beliefs and views held by characters within the text world can also constitute sub-worlds.

There are three types of sub-world:

• **Deictic sub-worlds** include flashbacks, as well as flashforwards, and any other departure from the current situation, such as the world within direct speech, or any view onto another scene (a character watching a play, talking on the telephone, watching television, and so on). Shifts into deictic sub-worlds involve a variation in one or more world-building elements, most usually shifts in time and location. The world expressed within direct speech is a sub-world, since it is distinct from the surrounding discourse, and will often involve shifts from third to first and second person, a proximal-remote reversal, and other features deictically recentred on the speaker within the narrative. Reported speech, by contrast, does not in itself invoke a sub-world, since it fits within the current text world as part of the narrative voice. Compare the direct speech, 'Yesterday when we were there he said, "I'll come back here tomorrow"', with the reported speech, 'He said that he would return there today'. In the latter form, we do not enter into the sub-world of the direct speech, but remain in the narrator's here-and-now.

• **Attitudinal sub-worlds** include alternations due to the desire, belief or purpose (constituting **desire worlds, belief worlds** and **purpose worlds,** respectively) of participants or characters. Attitudinal sub-worlds based on desire are cued up by predicates such as 'wish', 'hope', 'dream', 'want', and similar others. In the passage from *The Voyage of the Dawn Treader* above, the sub-world invoked by the sentence 'One did not want to go to bed' is an attitudinal sub-world. It takes us out of the current text world to a sub-world in which the attitude of the characters (generalised as 'one') towards an action is expressed. Belief worlds are typically introduced by predicates such as 'believe', 'know' and 'think', where these relate to beliefs. Purpose worlds relate to the stated intentions of participants or characters, regardless of whether the action is actually carried out. Examples would include promises, threats, commands, offers and requests.

- **Epistemic sub-worlds** are the means by which text world theory handles the dimension of possibility and probability. Hypothetical worlds are introduced by participants or characters using predicates such as 'would', 'will' and 'should', and conditional constructions of the prototypical form 'if ... then ... '. The content of these epistemic sub-worlds (as with deictic and attitudinal types) can contain shifts in time, location, character and objects, and a whole new richly textured world of possibility can be evoked. For example, here is the opening of a story:

> It has been a quiet week in Lake Wobegon. It was cloudy and rainy and pretty chilly, and in a town that's plain to begin with, when it gets wet and cold you lose most of the charm you didn't have in the first place. Some storytellers would take one look at a little town on a cold wet fall day and tell you about a family on a vacation trip through the Midwest who wonder why this town seems so deserted and get out of their car and there on Maple Street, coming at them with a pitchfork, is a gigantic man with no eyes and chunks of his face falling off and big clods of brown dirt stuck to his bib overalls, but I am a storyteller who, for better or worse, is bound by facts, so I simply observe that nobody was out walking because it was raining, a steady discouraging rain. But there were strange cars driving through.
>
> (*Leaving Home: A Collection of Lake Wobegon Stories*,
> Garrison Keillor)

In the third sentence here, the text cues up an epistemic sub-world that is the hypothetical story of a different writer. The current story is called 'The Killer': the imaginary sub-world varies a character – the pitchfork man – but leaves the time, location and other objects of Lake Wobegon intact.

The passage also manipulates the world potential of negation. In the second sentence, it creates a sub-world by alluding to the charm which the town only has in an improbable hypothetical sub-world. It negates the possibility of charm in the very act of mentioning it: text world theory can handle this easily as a created sub-world that does not alter the world-built elements of the framing text world. The passage on the pitchfork man that follows is an elaboration of this technique. The sub-world that is mentioned is already negated (or, strictly, non-asserted) since it is the work of another imagined storyteller. In fact, the story later plays another trick by having the inhabitants of the town go to see a film featuring the only film star Lake Wobegon has ever produced. The film is the story of a mad-eyed pitchfork killer in a small town exactly like Lake Wobegon.

In the course of processing text worlds and sub-worlds, participants (and characters) can switch back and forth between worlds, a process called **toggling**. This is common in thrillers and other popular fiction, where two plot-lines are simultaneously tracked in alternate sections until they converge in an explosive or revelatory climax.

All of the sub-worlds outlined above have some content that is accessible to the participants, and some that is only accessible to the characters. To illustrate this, let us pick up the example of the narrative structure of *Wuthering Heights* (from Chapter 4). Some aspects of the discourse world of the novel (the Yorkshire setting, Emily Brontë's house) are accessible to the participants (Emily and the reader): they are **participant-accessible**. All face-to-face conversations and much non-fictional writing is participant-accessible. The two participants live in the same world and stated facts are available for checking and verification in the discourse world.

By contrast, the text world within the novel, most simply, is Lockwood's conversation with Nelly Dean. The content of that text world is inaccessible to the participants: it is only a **character-accessible** text world. What Lockwood sees and what Nelly Dean says to him cannot be verified by the reader, since we all exist logically on different world levels. Further sub-worlds within Nelly's account (such as overheard conversations that are then reported, speculations, comparisons, diary entries, and so on) take the inaccessibility even further. It is an important feature of the novel that Lockwood's world location allows him accessibility to some of the narrated sub-worlds but not others. Heathcliff's character is verified to Lockwood by direct contact: they can be said to exist in the same text world and so are accessible to each other. However, the first Cathy and the world in the past that she lived in is inaccessible to Lockwood, and only reachable by him through Nelly Dean. As readers we need to keep track of all these persectives in order to piece together the 'real' story at the heart of the novel.

Discussion

Before proceeding, you might like to consider some of the implications of text world theory, in particular in relation to the other cognitive linguistic frameworks that you have read about so far.

* Compare the workings of the various approaches to 'world-formation' offered within cognitive poetics. Text world theory, schema theory, possible worlds and discourse worlds theory, mental space theory, and the notion of parable all have points of significant overlap but also different strengths and weaknesses in particular applications. The best method of comparison would be to try out each approach on different sorts of

texts. For example, which approach do you find most satisfactorily accounts for the effects of dream visions, science fictional alternativity, fantasy writing, spy thrillers, autobiography, confessional poetry, love poetry, song lyrics, magical realism, absurdism, and so on?

- How could the main concerns of deictic shift theory (Chapter 4) be assimilated with the deictic sub-world element in text world theory? Do they make different and incompatible assumptions, or could text world theory benefit from the psychological input offered by DST?

- In a similar line of thought, work out how the notion of current text world, or text world and sub-world, or accessibility and non-accessibility could be understood as yet another specification of foreground and background (see Chapter 2)?

Cognitive poetic analysis

In order to illustrate some very simple distinctions using text world theory, I will draw out the text world parameters from two passages that I hope you agree have a very different intuitive 'feel' to them. The first is from a novel mainly concerned with the First World War.

> The Boulevard du Cange was a broad, quiet street that marked the eastern flank of the city of Amiens. The wagons that rolled in from Lille and Arras to the north made directly to the tanneries and mills of the Saint Leu quarter without needing to use this rutted, leafy road. The town side of the boulevard backed on to substantial gardens which were squared off and apportioned with civic precision to the houses they adjoined. On the damp grass were chestnut trees, lilac and willows, cultivated to give shade and quietness to their owners. The gardens had a wild, overgrown look and their deep lawns and bursting hedges could conceal small clearings, quiet pools, and areas unvisited even by the inhabitants, where patches of grass and wild flowers lay beneath the branches of overhanging trees.
>
> (*Birdsong*, Sebastian Faulks, 1994)

If you were to draw a text world diagram (see p. 139) of this passage, the world-building elements would probably include the following:

- t   unspecified, though early twentieth century by inference from the 'rutted' road and 'wagons', or from discourse world knowledge about the novel's setting;
- l   Boulevard du Cange, Amiens (in northern France if this is part of background knowledge);
- c   none in the text world;
- o   gardens, houses, grass, trees, hedges.

There are a number of sub-worlds, some of which are very fleeting. The second sentence offers a deictic sub-world marked by subordination and a past participle: 'The wagons that rolled in … '. This sub-world shifts location to Lille and Arras, adding a specific locative expression 'to the north'. The 'wagons' themselves are objects in the sub-world, not the text world, since they are mentioned in order to draw attention to the fact that they do not use this rutted road and belong in a different, more noisy deictic sub-world. Here is the use of negation as a means of foregrounding the absence of wagons. This one-sentence sub-world contains a further sub-world, this time a hypothetical epistemic one: 'without needing to use this rutted, leafy road'. Again, at a new sub-world level of embedding, the wagons on the Boulevard du Cange are mentioned but negated from the current text world scene. Their noise is removed elsewhere, foregrounding the sense of quietness of the boulevard.

Further deictic sub-worlds have the effect of embedding any discordant activity into the past. Again using past participles and subordination to distance the action, the substantial gardens 'which were squared off' were at some past point 'apportioned'. Similarly, the cultivation worked at by the owners of the houses is embedded in a brief deictic sub-world flashback, 'cultivated to give shade' and those 'owners' themselves are also embedded as characters in that sub-world. Even the clearings, pools and other areas are removed from the current text world by the epistemic sub-world shifter 'could conceal', and a further embedded deictic sub-world shift renders these areas 'unvisited'. The final subordinate clause in the passage describes a scene, therefore, that is so quiet that no one has even seen it.

Drawing this out into all the function-advancing propositions, it is likely that you would find that all of the predicates at the text world level are drawn with horizontal arrows: that is, the text world is dominated by descriptive attribution and relational predications ('The Boulevard du Cange was … ', 'The town side backed on to … ', 'On the grass were chestnut trees', and 'The gardens had … '). The capital letters here also indicate that these expressions are in the foregrounded theme position in the sentence. By contrast, all the actional function-advancers (the vertical arrows) are embedded in the various sub-worlds ('that marked', 'that rolled in', 'made directly', 'to use', 'were squared off and apportioned', 'cultivated to give', 'could conceal', 'unvisited', 'lay'). These are all in grammatically subordinate positions as well as forming sub-worlds. The scene described is one of utter peace and quietness, devoid of people or commerce, in which literally nothing happens.

By absolute contrast, the following passage is from a pulp science fiction story. Rod Blake is struggling with simulacra creatures that can mimic images of anything he is thinking about:

> Blake went, slow-footed. The first thing he did was to close the lock-door, so that he was safely alone in the ship. Blake went into the control room, donned an air-suit complete with helmet, and pushed a control handle over. Then a second. Presently he heard curious bumpings and thumpings, and strange floppings and whimperings. He went back rapidly, and rayed a supply chest and two crates of Venusian specimens that

had sprouted legs and were rapidly growing arms to grasp ray pistols. The air in the ship began to look thick and greenish; it was colder.

Contentedly Blake watched, and opened all the room doors. Another slithering, thumping noise attracted him, and with careful violet-gun work he removed an unnoticed, extra pipe that was crawling from the crossbrace hangers. It broke up into lengths that rolled about unpleasantly. Rod rayed them till the smallest only, the size of golf balls with curious blue-veined legs, staggered about uncertainly. Finally even they stopped wriggling.

(*The Brain-Stealers of Mars*, John W. Campbell, 1936)

The world-building elements here, carried over from the previous part of the text, include:

t the science-fictional future;

l Mars, specifically in the ship, moving into the control room, then all the rooms;

c Rod Blake, (the Martian creatures);

o (the Martian creatures), lock-door, ship, control room, air-suit, helmet, control handle, second control handle, supply chest, crates, air, room doors, violet-gun, pipe, crossbrace hangers.

Of course, my problem in classifying the Martian shape-changers as either characters or objects is a significant thematic feature in this story. Many of the objects mentioned above are actually Martians in disguise. In any other form of fiction, this uncertainty between beings and objects would represent two sub-worlds, contrasting attitudinally along a dimension of belief: someone would believe they were Martians, someone else would believe this was a delusion. In science fiction, however, there is only one asserted text world: the objects *are* Martians.

At the level of function-advancers, almost every predication is a (vertical) action predication, with the text even drawing attention explicitly to the 'actionality' of the action: 'The first thing he did was ... '. All of the actions performed by Blake happen in the text world. There is a sense that we are following his point of view, in that any sub-worlds are those of his belief system: 'so that he was safely alone in the ship' is an attitudinal sub-world of purpose; 'that had sprouted legs and were rapidly growing arms to grasp ray pistols' expresses a speculation by Rod as to the Martians' attitudinal intentions. Notice, though, that these sub-worlds are all present only in order to explain the immediate reason for an action. The emphasis throughout is on activity and the action remains focused in the current text world.

These two passages are obviously from different genres, and you do not require a text world analysis to draw out crude differences between lyricism and action in these sorts of texts. However, text world theory offers a principled means of exploring the detail of these differences, and a framework for understanding exactly how the rich worlds of embedding and accessibility are worked out through literature.

To close this chapter, here is a poem which relies on sub-worlds for its primary structure.

> When I have fears that I may cease to be
>   Before my pen has glean'd my teeming brain,
> Before high-piled books, in charact'ry,
>   Hold like rich garners the full-ripen'd grain;
> When I behold, upon the night's starred face,
>   Huge cloudy symbols of a high romance,
> And think that I may never live to trace
>   Their shadows, with the magic hand of chance;
> And when I feel, fair creature of an hour,
>   That I shall never look upon thee more,
> Never have relish in the faery power
>   Of unreflecting love! – then on the shore
> Of the wide world I stand alone, and think
>   Till Love and Fame to nothingness do sink.
>
> (John Keats)

Initially, we come across a problem with the terminology of text world theory. There is no problem with identifying the participants in the discourse world here: Keats and you. However, the assumption that the next level down in terms of accessibility is the text world is problematic in this poem, since the form of the first sentence seems to evoke a sub-world. Specifically, 'When I have fears that I may cease to be' cues up first a deictic sub-world that shifts the time to those occasions, presumably at several recurring points in the past, when the poetic persona has certain fears. What those fears are in the first line are further embedded in a modalised epistemic sub-world 'that I may', followed by an implicit negation 'cease to be'.

This is further complicated by the first-person presentation, creating a counterpart relationship between the discourse world participant, John Keats, and the poetic persona, 'John Keats'. The identification is also supported by the function-advancing predicates which are all to do with writing literature. The recurring 'When ... ' structure creates a new sub-world each time, but in each sub-world we again find yet another counterpart of John Keats, writing literature in further embedded hypothetical worlds. Since the resolution of the 'When ... ' conditional keeps being deferred, we are presented with increasingly complex and incompleted open-ended sub-worlds. In short, over eleven and a half lines we never flash out to a text world, because we were never built one in the first place.

The problem in calling these 'sub-worlds' is that we never start with a text world, so we don't know to what exactly we are subordinate. I could easily transform any novel into a sub-world by beginning, 'I fell asleep and dreamt that ... ', and this would render a completely different text world analysis without really changing anything fundamental about the novel. Perhaps a better solution is to adapt the manoeuvre apparent in deictic shift theory (in Chapter 4) and see movements between discourse, text and sub-worlds simply as **world-switches** up or down an embedded hierarchy. This would preserve the structural advantages of the theory while acknowledging that the point of entry is not always straightforward.

To explore more detail of this, consider the first four lines. As described above, 'cease to be' represents a third level of sub-world embedding. The second line returns to the second level of sub-world by further specifying the deictically indicated point ('Before') that occurs within the sub-world first introduced by 'may'. However, we are instantly plunged into a further sub-world, parallel to the 'cease to be' world. This sub-world is a hypothetical epistemic world in which the writer has created high piles of books with richly imagined characters, the product of his fertile mind. This world, however, is not expressed purely literally, but through a metaphorical identification along the lines of WRITING IS HARVESTING. In text world theory, a metaphor creates a further sub-world, in which the meanings of mappings such as MY PEN IS A SICKLE, THE WRITER'S MIND IS A FERTILE FIELD, BOOKS ARE HAYSTACKS, POEMS ARE GRAINS OF WHEAT, and LITERARY VALUE IS RIPENESS are apparent and accessible to the discourse participants.

Without offering a resolution for the highest level 'When' sub-world, the next four lines create an equally complex but different pattern of embedded sub-worlds. Again a deictic sub-world is created at repeated points in the past, expressed as a generic present tense, 'When I behold … '. It seems likely, given the non-closure of the first sub-world, that this deictic sub-world co-refers to the same deictic point at which 'I have fears'. Here, though, the metaphor is different: literary imagination is out there on the face of the heavens, rather than inside the writer's mind. Instead of further embedded sub-worlds, this time we get a parallel attitudinal sub-world ('And think'), but this is instantly made very complex with a hypothetical modal and then a negation and then another speculated world ('I may never live to trace').

The next three and a half lines complete the complexity, this time through repeated negative sub-worlds ('never look', 'Never have relish'). Only at the end of this are all the parallel and embedded sub-worlds gathered up and placed into what should be the text world ('then … '). All of this deferred structure would ordinarily lead us to expect a resolving frame, a final assertion of the text world that offers a means of contextualising the fears and anxious thoughts and feelings. What we get instead is a text world that in fact has a similar structure to all the chaotic complexity and depth of the sub-worlds. A deictic shift, encapsulating a metaphorical shift ('on the shore of the wide world'), and then a further attitudinal shift ('and think'), leaves the world-status of the final line ambiguous.

The final line can be read at two different world levels, and the outcome is radically different depending on which one you pursue. Read at the same level as the literal text world, at the same level as 'then', with the sub-world metaphor of the world's edge set aside, the final line offers a sort of stoical resignation. The writer thinks about his position and comes to realise that Love and

Fame, in their (capitalised) literary pretensions, no longer matter as much as the lived experience. Literary elaboration and verbosity, the over-repetition and mixing of metaphors culminating in an exclamatory shriek, all shrink into insignificance, and are shown up as the pretensions that they are. However, if the same line is read within the metaphorical sub-world created 'on the shore of the wide world', the reading is much more bleak. Then, the loneliness of the metaphorical sub-world is where we end up, in a place where Love and Fame, strongly asserted and embodied for posterity in this very sonnet, are left as less than nothing, as 'nothingness', the essence of negation.

Explorations

1   You could use the text world theory description of the discourse world level and the discourse participants to examine texts which are radically different depending on the participants. For example, there are several stories that are parallel in both the Bible and the Koran (such as the story of Joseph and his coat). The respective belief worlds of readers affect the way the discourse world is constituted. In the Koran, the text comes from the prophet Mohammed speaking the word of God through the angel Gabriel, if you have a Muslim belief world. A Christian or Jewish belief world does not accord with this view. Taking a specific story, consider how different religious and cultural belief worlds alter the text worlds, especially the commitment to epistemic and attitudinal sub-worlds.

2   Text world theory is a useful means of exploring texts in which world-switches and sub-world structures are thematically significant. You could use it as a way of investigating the following texts:

> 'Ode on a Grecian Urn', John Keats
> 'La Figlia che Piange', T.S. Eliot
> 'Out on the lawn I lie in bed', W.H. Auden
> 'The Lake Isle of Innisfree', W.B. Yeats
> *The Man in the High Castle*, Philip K. Dick
> *The Third Policeman*, Flann O'Brien
> *The Magus*, John Fowles
> *Feersum Endjinn*, Iain M. Banks
> *The Golden Notebook*, Doris Lessing
> *Slaughterhouse 5*, Kurt Vonnegut

3   All of the examples I have given in this chapter – as in the major works of text world theory itself – are from poetry and prose. In principle, text world theory should also be able to account for dramatic performance. Consider the relationships between participants in the discourse world, text world and sub-worlds of a play, or a film, or a television drama.

4 Text world theory offers a means of describing constraints on interpretation. That is, it specifies the necessary knowledge that is required by the text to build the text world from direct propositions and inferences. It can account in this way for a range of readings, but this also means that a reading which is not accountable in the theory is, by definition, an impossible or 'wrong' reading. In order to test this, you should be able to think of an absurd or ridiculous reading of a literary work and then use text world theory to demonstrate the gaps in evidence or the unwarranted inferential leaps that need to be made to assert the reading.

Further reading and references

The text world approach is most fully outlined in Werth (1999). Most of this chapter is compiled from this source. The table of function-advancing types is taken from Werth (1999: 191), the description of worlds from Werth (1999: 180–209), and the account of sub-worlds from Werth (1999: 210–58). Earlier applications of the approach include Werth (1987, 1994, 1995a, and 1995b).

The notion of world-switches as a way of understanding embedding and the use of the term **text world theory** are from Gavins (2001). For cognitive poetic applications of text world theory see Gavins (2000) and Hidalgo Downing (2000). The notions of autonomy and heteronomy come from Ingarden (1973a, 1973b).

11 The comprehension of literature

Preview

The experience of literature, as described so far throughout this book, is one of rational decision-making and creative meaning construction. However, reading literature can also often be an emotional process, a felt experience, even offering a bodily frisson of excitement and pleasure, the prickling of the hairs on the back of your neck and a line or an idea or a phrase or an event that makes you catch your breath, and remember it for a long time afterwards.

In this chapter, we explore the cognitive poetic notion of being 'transported' by literature. It is an imaginative projection that is both cognitive and emotional, integrated under the general notion of **comprehension**. The stages of comprehension-building are outlined, and I will try to indicate how a framework for understanding this is emerging that encompasses many of the different aspects of cognitive science outlined through this book. It is appropriate, though, at this stage of the book to point out that the cognitive poetic understanding of how all these issues are integrated is still in its early stages. In this chapter, I turn from the abstract modelling of consciousness and comprehension to a practical and specific means of understanding the comprehension of narrative. Cognitive poetics has suggested ways of accounting for how readers monitor and track contexts in literary reading. The model is applied to a dramatic text, and an experience of its performance.

Links with literary critical concepts

Character, engagement, immersion, memory, plot, suspension of disbelief

Most everyday discussion of literature is not concerned with the intricacies of technical description nor the archaeological environment of the text. These matters are the dusty concern of literary critics. For the most part, they alienate readers of literature outside the academies by exclusive and introverted discussions: 'ordinary' readers do not easily get to see the fascinating complexity of academic connections with psychology or history or social theory. Instead, the vast majority of people read literature because they enjoy it, love it even; because it takes them away from their lives as escapism, or because it enriches their lives by adding a textured edge to their thinking and emotional experience.

Many voices within cognitive poetics are passionate about the emergence of the field because it offers an opportunity of reuniting the academic with the everyday. Though literature itself is obviously an artifice, literary readings are natural phenomena, and it is this that cognitive poetics sets out to investigate. Many pieces of literary criticism have also tried to capture the aesthetic texture of emotional experience produced by literature, but have gone about the task impressionistically, either using ill-defined terms or producing personal responses that are often poetic and insightful in their own right but hardly analytical or accessible for discussion.

Cognitive poetics aims to extend its coverage to encompass sensations such as feeling moved by a literary work, feeling immersed in the world of a text that seems almost as real as real life. The psychologising of character that has been a prestigious feature of valued literature for the past two hundred years relies on readerly reconstructions of character that include identification and empathy, ethical agreement and sympathy, and other forms of emotional attachment that readers defend very strongly. The post-Romantic view of literary value also presents fiction and imagination as the 'willing suspension of disbelief' (Samuel Taylor Coleridge). Cognitive poetics tries to account for this by seeing reality and fiction not as cognitively separate, but as phenomena that are processed fundamentally in the same way. The consequence of this view is a principled recognition of the fact that literary works – whether fictional or not – have an emotional and tangible effect on readers and on the real world in which we live with literature.

Experiencing literary narratives

The process of using a text to build and then experience a literary world has been discussed in cognitive poetics using the metaphor of **transportation**. This is a conceptual metaphor – essentially READING IS A JOURNEY – that is often used by people when describing their literary experiences: 'I was carried away by it', 'It swept me off my feet', 'It was like another world', 'I can lose myself in a book', and so on. There are several consequences of this understanding of literary reading as 'being transported'.

First, there must be a reader (traveller) who is transported. This involves the reader adapting themselves to new conditions, taking on assumed characteristics and attitudes, even assumed perceptions and beliefs, in order to make sense of the literary scene. In order to engage in the simple deictic projection (see Chapter 4) that allows us to track a character's point of view, we must take on an imagined model of that other point of perception and belief. This ranges from a very simple adjustment, such as understanding that 'you' addressed to a character is not really a direct address to the reader, right up to being able to model and make predictions about views and beliefs that we do not actually hold. Even in extreme cases (such as reading Hitler's *Mein Kampf*), part of the sense of distaste and revulsion for most people comes from the sense of having to engage with ideas that are not naturally their own and feeling too close to them for comfort. It is the same cognitive process that makes reading literary narratives or lyrical expressions of a poetic persona attractive and pleasurable, since it involves an aspect of 'dressing up' in another's ideas.

The consequence of this is often that readers return changed by the literary experience. The nature of the text (its architecture of formal patterns and genre characteristics) is the means of transport, and readers scale their evaluations of literary texts partly by how well they are seen to operate as vehicles of imaginary transportation. Books judged to have failed receive comments like, 'I just couldn't get on with it', 'It didn't seem to go anywhere'. Of course, it is readers who actively travel, and cognitive poetics sees reading as a process in which the reader **performs** the act of reading. Reading is certainly not passive, as we have seen in previous chapters by outlining all the active cognitive processes that compose it; nevertheless, it is an experience that can often seem effortless.

Clearly, the measurement of travelling is the sense that the place arrived at is different from the starting point. As we saw in Chapter 7, the distance between worlds can be measured in terms of their divergence along a set of parameters, but we assume that real-world conditions hold unless the text explicitly tells us otherwise (**minimal departure**). Because of this disjunction, we have a basic understanding that we cannot affect the people and events in literary worlds, though we can talk about them and extrapolate from them as if they were real. A further consequence of our immersion in the literary world is that certain aspects of the non-literary world, such as particular knowledge that is tied only to the real world, is inaccessible while we are 'in' the literature. We are still anxious for the hero even though our known conventions of the thriller are that he will triumph; we don't want Humbert in Nabokov's *Lolita* to be caught, though in real life we probably would; we cannot save Romeo or Juliet by wondering why they didn't carry mobile phones.

Though we want to express a **participatory response** (silently shouting 'Look out! He's got a gun!', feeling sad, feeling excited, feeling our senses heightened), we also know that these emotions render us as readers in the role of **side-participants**. As in traditional theatre, the audience is behind an invisible fourth wall, overhearing the literary world rather than actually participating in it. However, the sense of potential participation is strong.

One way that this process of comprehension has been explained in cognitive poetics is in terms of the satisfaction of constraints set up by the microprocess of a literary text reading. This is understood as the **construction–integration** (CI) model of comprehension. Essentially, the model is a development of the notion of *macrorules* and *macrostructures* outlined in Chapter 9. Comprehension is seen as a two-stage process. The first stage is a construction phase in which a macrostructural representation is created. This is an approximation (the 'gist') of the propositional content of the text. It is constructed from the textbase together with inferences made at the local level of the reading process, and is at this stage incoherent.

The representation achieves coherence by the second phase of comprehension: the **integration** phase. Cognitive constraints of coherence, relevance and significance have to be satisfied by rejecting local incoherences in favour of a globally coherent representation. The resolution is produced out of a tension between the detail of the textbase (the readerly word-by-word encounter) and the situation model (the reader's understanding of context). The overall comprehension is thus a representation not simply of the propositional content of the literary work, but also its social and personal impact, its felt experience. The aim of the CI model of comprehension is to reintegrate cognition with emotional and motivational aspects of experience and behaviour.

Its mechanism for achieving this is to suggest a different form of knowledge structure than script- or schema-based knowledge. These approaches (see Chapter 6) model knowledge as a retrieval system which is 'looked up' in a directory or pre-existing schematised representation. Instead of infinitely sub-dividing meaningfulness into numerous different tracks through a schema, the CI model suggests that meaning is a construction, and claims that knowledge retrieval seems to work as much by association as by making logical or schematised connections within a domain.

Therefore it offers a framework for understanding in terms of an associative **knowledge net**, comprising propositions, schemas and frames, which is more loose and chaotically organised by associations. The meaning of any single element is a consequence of the number and strength of its links with other elements, and these associations arise differently on each occasion in each new act of context. The substructure out of which meaning is constructed is relatively stable and permanent, but the meaning of any given concept is highly flexible and constructed anew on each occasion of use. The illusion of stable meanings arises because meaning construction is based on the same (or a slightly experientially modified) substructure. It might take a radically different context or circumstance to shift the meaning of a familiar item.

The approach sets out the different levels of mental representation in terms of distance from the stimulating environment:

- **direct representation** – the most basic perceptual and innate system, including the sensory and motor skills of viewing the world, and repetitive physical tasks which can be learned. All animals share this level.
- **episodic representation** – event memory which is available for recall. This level is still heavily dependent on the environment, but is closer to script-like knowledge. Higher animals, such as apes, share this level.
- **image and action representation** – non-verbal representations, such as body-language and facial expressions. A social community is required for this level.
- **narrative representation** – verbal representations that are linear and propositional, including semantic processing, inferencing and induction.

- **abstract representation** – also linguistic or semiotic, where abstract thought, hypothesis-formation, analysis, deduction and logical thought happen.

The lower-level capacities (the first on the list) are encapsulated by each subsequent higher-level capacity. The scale reminds us that human cognition is not simply a higher-level or purely linguistic function, and it draws a continuity with our biological inheritance. This view of language does not require a separate 'language module' in the brain, but understands language as being in a continuum with biological embodiment.

Narrative comprehension

To return the discussion in this chapter to a practically applicable level, I will outline a specific framework of the comprehension of narrative. **Contextual frame theory** was developed in order to understand how readers track reference to characters and events through the process of reading. The basic notion involves the idea of a **contextual frame**, a mental representation of the circumstances containing the current context. This is built up from the text itself as well as from inferences drawn directly from the text.

Information in the frame can be **episodic** or **non-episodic**. For example, some facts about a character in a literary work will apply to them at one point in the narrative but not at others. In Coleridge's *The Rime of the Ancient Mariner*, the mariner tells his story to the narrating wedding guest: inside his story, he tells of a journey in which he shot an albatross, and was then visited by a sequence of bad luck. The reader has to keep track of the fact that the mariner at the beginning of his story does not possess the same knowledge as the mariner at the end of the story. The attachment of this knowledge is episodic. However, the mariner remains a mariner throughout, and this knowledge is thus non-episodic in the narrative.

A reader must thus keep track of which information applies in any particular context, and this knowledge is arranged in terms of contextual frames. These are not simply 'snapshots' of successive moments across the narrative, however, but are a series of ongoing and shifting mental representations of the world of the literary work. How are these frames monitored by the reader?

Though readers need to hold several contextual frames in mind, the current point of reading forms the main frame in focus. Readers monitor this contextual frame by a variety of means. First, characters and objects are bound into the frame in which they appear, and they are bound out when they leave. They remain bound to that frame at that particular time, but are unbound from different contextual frames unless the text explicitly binds them in. Both movements of **binding** have to be explicitly cued by the text. A sense of incoherence is produced when elements simply appear or disappear, or turn up unannounced in another frame without being directly referenced or their entrance or exit predicated with a verb. Exceptions include ghost stories or science fiction settings, in which characters can materialise at will, but even here there are specific circumstances explicitly described to mitigate the oddity.

It is usual for objects to be bound only to one frame at a time, with explicit binding out of one frame preceding a binding in to another. Cognitively, the character remains bound to the first scene at that point in time, and then bound into other, later scenes. This cognitive organisation is so strong that if a scene changes to a later or spatially different one in a narrative, and a character appears who was in an earlier scene, we assume they have been bound out of that previous frame even if this was not explicitly done. Exceptions, again, are usually tricks such as doppelgangers, disguises or deceptions, that are thematised as such.

As the narrative moves on, different contexts move into the primary focus: the current frame that is being monitored is said to be **primed**. Characters, objects and the location of the main context currently being monitored are all bound to that frame and primed too. When the reader's attention is taken elsewhere, that frame and all its contents become unprimed. In *The Rime of the Ancient Mariner*, by the middle of the mariner's story, the surrounding narrative situation featuring the wedding guest is unprimed and the primed frame is the mariner's adventures on his ship.

At any specific point in a narrative, characters and objects might be bound to a context and that context might also be primed in the reader's attention, but a specific character might not be mentioned in the current sentence. At this point they are **textually covert**, though of course since they are still bound and primed the reader is still aware they are in the scene. If a character or object is currently being mentioned, then they are not only bound and primed but are also **textually overt**. Altogether, the tracking of bound, primed and overt factors in relation to contextual framing is held for the reader in the **central directory**.

In the process of shifts in binding, priming and overtness, frames are modified while ongoing. **Frame modification** occurs when, for example, a character enters or leaves a frame. This is a modification since all the other monitored knowledge about the context remains constant. As well as explicit binding and priming by verbs of movement or by direct reference to characters or objects, frames can be modified by retrospective action. As mentioned above, if a character is bound into and primed in the current scene, it is assumed that they are bound out and unprimed from the previous scene.

It would be possible, for example in a one-act play which did not have any flashbacks or flashforwards, for the entire text to consist of a single contextual frame, modified by comings and goings but constantly primed. The frame at the end might look very different from the frame at the beginning, but it would be essentially the same modified frame. However, most literature does not observe these unities of action, time and space. Most literary narratives include **frame switch** as a feature apparent in their structural organisation. The frame is switched in a reader's mind by a change in location, most typically realised linguistically by a spatial locative (see Chapter 4). Large jumps in time, realised by temporal locatives, also create frame switches, since it would be assumed that the characters have become unbound in the intervening time.

Frame switches such as these are **instantaneous**. By contrast, the location of a context can be switched by an explicit account of a character moving from location to another. The previous frame, with its characters and objects still bound to it (except for the travelling character), is left behind unprimed, and the narrative switches to a new primed frame into which the travelling character is bound first. These switches are **progressive**.

Where a frame switch occurs over a short or parallel period of time, the unprimed frame is potentially available for **frame recall**. Narratives sometimes switch back and forth in this way, or characters within a frame think back to a previous scene, before the reader is returned to the present. In these cases, the recalled frame does not have to be rebuilt again from scratch: a brief reference is often enough to cue it up for priming.

Sometimes the reader has to keep track not only of the context of the narrative, but also of the different framed thoughts of characters within the narrative. In other words, the reader has also to monitor the **belief frames** of certain characters. Since the states of knowledge and even of ideological opinion of characters often alter throughout a story, the reader must bind each character's belief frame to the contextually appropriate point at which it was held in the course of the narrative. At the same time, sometimes the flashback to a previous frame is so fleeting as hardly to merit a frame recall, especially where the narrative focus is moving around character's beliefs or is swiftly considering different possibilities or memories. In these cases, the term **frame mixing** seems more appropriate.

In order to keep track of the different states of mind of characters as they progress through a narrative, the notion of **enactors** has been developed. A character might consist of several enactors of that character: versions of the character at different points in the narrative. When a primed and currently textually overt character recalls her younger self, or imagines herself in a different hypothetical situation, then a new enactor of that character becomes available for reference. Enactors are bound to different frames, and cannot exist in the same frame at once except in supernatural, fantasy or science-fictional stories.

So far this framework accounts for the behaviour of a model reader. Of course, sometimes readers make mistakes and sometimes texts provide cues that deliberately mislead the reader in order to provide suspense, shock or a satisfying plot resolution. In all these cases, a **frame repair** is made. An element of a frame is reinterpreted and the frame is modified retrospectively. Sometimes this will also involve the retrospective modification of linked frames that are affected by the repair. Sometimes the repair would need to be radical in order to maintain the coherence of the narrative. This typically happens with large-scale surprise endings, or twists in the tale. There are numerous narratives in which almost on the last page the narrator turns out to have been dead, or dreaming, or living inside a hallucination or simulation, or discovers that a character is actually their mother, father, brother or sister, or their world view has been fundamentally mistaken in some other way. For these, 'repair' hardly seems adequate, and I have called such contexts cases of **frame replacement**.

Discussion

Before proceeding to the final analysis in this book, you might like to consider some of the implications of the ideas presented in this chapter.

- The question of how and how far literature has the power to change individuals has been discussed for a long time. Using the metaphor of literature as transportation, consider the case of a text that is familiar to you. Think of a literary work in which you evidently do not share the ideological viewpoint of the main narrator or prominent character. Examples that come to my mind include the extreme neo-fascist libertarianism of Robert Heinlein's *Starship Troopers*, the paedophile narrator of Vladimir Nabokov's *Lolita*, or the psychotic serial killer in Brett Easton Ellis' *American Psycho*. You might have less extreme examples. How far do you have to enter the cognitive environment of the narrative in order to read these texts?
- Cognitive psychological models of comprehension have to square the circle between common human faculties and individually idiosyncratic responses. This is an even sharper issue for cognitive poetics in dealing with the literary context. Can you formulate an opinion on the difficult question of whether cognitive poetics is flexible enough to encompass the eccentric readings which can be the most interesting? A further question would be to consider how, in the terms set out in this chapter, eccentric but socially powerful readings are diffused to other people, and come to be the accepted reading. In general, does cognitive psychology also need a more social psychological dimension?
- Cognitive poetics aspires to encompass emotional and motivational dimensions of reading as well as the monitoring and negotiation of propositional content. Based on your, now quite extensive, knowledge of the current state of the field, do you think this aspiration is achievable?

Cognitive poetic analysis

Of poetry, prose and drama, the last of these is qualitatively different in that, for the most part, its primary purpose is its literal performance in a theatre. We can use the metaphor to talk of readers performing the processing of poetry or prose, and can also talk of the performative aspects in these modes of writing, but drama is literally performed and is closer to a pre-literate existence. This was not always the case, of course. Much of the poetry of the world that is still in print was written for and by a literate elite, and recited aloud for the enjoyment or edification of the illiterate. In the western world, universal mass literacy has been a recent phenomenon of the past 150 years, coinciding with the rise of the novel as a form of literature. But drama has always been around for the illiterate masses.

The relationship between cognitive poetics and drama needs some specific adaptation. The visual, aural, aromatic and tactile senses become more prominent than in purely documentary literary reading. Any schematisation of the text is already accomplished and presented by the director and the actors. Matters of local interpretation can be disambiguated by the actor's choices of expression, and matters of global interpretation can be constrained by the director's choices of staging and lighting. In short, much of the cognitive work that is usually done by the reader of a literary work is already done and up there on the stage. Of course, the experience of watching a play is not passive because of this, and still involves cognitive monitoring and comprehension. Though the models presented in this chapter were not designed explicitly for dramatic analysis, I think they are adaptable for this purpose.

One play in which it is important for the audience to keep a close track of enactors and belief frames is *The Importance of Being Earnest*, by Oscar Wilde, first performed on St Valentine's Day, 14 February, 1895. Briefly, the plot is as follows. Two young men, John Worthing (Jack) and Algernon Moncrieff (Algy) are leading double lives. Jack is in love with Gwendolen (Algy's cousin), and calls himself Ernest (a name she loves) while with her in town. He is a guardian to Cecily, to whom he is 'Jack' with a wicked brother, 'Ernest', whom he has to visit often in the country. Algy is in love with Cecily. However, Algy also has an imaginary country friend, Bunbury, whose ill-health provides him with frequent excuses to escape awkward situations, especially in avoiding his terrifying aunt, Lady Bracknell. It emerges that Jack is named 'Worthing' because he was found as a baby abandoned in a black leather handbag at the London terminus of the railway from Worthing, a seaside town in Sussex. His unknown parentage makes him unsuitable, in Lady Bracknell's view, for marriage to Gwendolen, and this is compounded by the fact that Gwendolen discovers Jack's real name is not Ernest but 'John'.

Before completing the plot, let us track the contextual monitoring apparent at the beginning of the play. The written script opens with a list of 'The persons of the play', and then:

ACT ONE

Scene: *Morning-room in Algernon's flat in Half-Moon Street, London, W.*
Time: *The present. The room is luxuriously and artistically furnished. The sound of a piano is heard in the adjoining room.*
Lane *is arranging afternoon tea on the table, and after the music has ceased,* Algernon *enters.*

A dialogue on marriage and bachelorhood follows.

For the reader of the play, the opening list binds the set of characters to the world of the play. However, this general world is instantly focused by the priming of the scene described above. The servant, Lane, is bound into the scene by being mentioned, and as the only human is primed in attention. Algy is then bound in by entering, and is primed. The opening line of the play is Algy's, which keeps him primed and textually overt. The textual overtness and covertness switches back and forth between Algy and Lane as they exchange lines. For the reader, this is marked by their name, followed by their scripted speech.

For the audience experiencing a performance, however, the contextual monitoring is different. The audience do not have a list of characters, and so they do not know the names of Lane or Algy until these names are used in direct address by characters later in the scene. Whatever is on the stage in front of the audience is the primed scene. The bare description in the stage directions will have been filled out by the director and set-designer to offer far more visual information to the audience. In the initial dialogue we meet the first obstacle to the straightforward application of a *narrative* comprehension framework: since there is no narrator in the play, we must decide how to treat contextual monitoring when a speaking character switches frame. For example, Lane says, 'I have only been married once. That was in consequence of a misunderstanding between myself and a young person'. Here is a frame switch to a previous time and location in which the earlier enactor of Lane was married. However, for the audience there is a clash of priming. Visually, the stage set remains primed on Algy and Lane in the morning-room; verbally, Lane's speech primes a different frame. This cannot happen in narrative prose, so perhaps for the dramatic application we need to speak of 'visual priming' and 'verbal priming', the latter of which is accessible from the characters, and is monitored as part of their belief frames?

The scene continues:

> *Enter* Lane.
> Lane: Mr. Ernest Worthing.
> *Enter* Jack. Lane *goes out.*
> Algernon: How are you, my dear Ernest?

For the audience, this textual joke does not appear. 'Ernest Worthing' is announced, a man is bound into the primed scene, and Algy addresses him appropriately to confirm the contextual monitoring assumptions. Ernest (labelled, unknown to the audience, 'Jack' in the script) then speaks.

For the reader, there is confusion here, since 'Ernest Worthing' is bound into the frame just beyond the door, and you would expect the next line '*Enter* Ernest' to bind him out of that frame and into the current primed frame. Not only does the stage direction contradict this, but then Algy's address reconfirms that 'Ernest' has been bound in. Some local frame repair is needed here, but it does not emerge until later in the scene:

[Algy has found a cigarette case inscribed by Cecily to 'Uncle Jack']
Algernon: [...] Besides, your name isn't Jack at all; it is Ernest.
Jack: It isn't Ernest; it's Jack.
Algernon: You have always told me it was Ernest. I have introduced you to everyone as Ernest. You look as if your name was Ernest. You are the most earnest-looking person I ever saw in my life. It is perfectly absurd your saying that your name isn't Ernest. It's on your cards [...]
Jack: Well, my name is Ernest in town and Jack in the country, and the cigarette case was given to me in the country.

This is straightforward for the audience, who are simply introduced to the notion that the central character has two enactors, 'Jack' (also called 'John') and Ernest, bound respectively to country and town frames. In fact, Jack's contextual monitoring is apparent in his final line here, too. The reader has to engage in a little more extensive frame repair.

This pattern of miscues and repairs of the identities and relationships between enactors continues throughout the play. Algy's double life is revealed; Cecily is actually Jack's aunt, though she is younger than him and calls him 'uncle', and so on. Eventually, both Cecily and Gwendolen believe they are in love with 'Ernest', and discover Algy and Jack's real names while Algy is unsuccessfully pretending to be Jack's imaginary brother. In order to correct things, the men offer to be christened with different names.

Keeping track of all of these facts is quite a feat for an audience. Not only do enactors proliferate as different permutations of relationships emerge or are disconfirmed, but the audience has to monitor each particular permutation and identify it correctly within the belief frame of the appropriate character. Even more complexly, they have to remember different apparent belief frames as held by the enactors 'Jack' and 'Ernest', and also have to recall different points in the ongoing frame modification at which different belief frames were held earlier in the play.

The resolution of the play sweeps all of this complexity aside, replacing the entire existing frame with all its embedded belief frames with a final single true frame. It turns out that Jack was abandoned as a baby by Miss Prism, who was a nurse for Algy's mother, and Jack is in fact Algy's brother. Furthermore, he had been christened after his father, who was called 'Ernest'. This means he is finally eligible to marry Gwendolen, and in fact has been called 'Ernest' all along. 'Gwendolen', he declares, 'it is a terrible thing for a man to find out that all his life he has been speaking nothing but the truth'. Since all of the characters are on stage in this final scene, all of their belief frames can be overlaid into a single belief frame. The play ends:

Jack: Gwendolen! (*Embraces her.*) At last!
Lady Bracknell: My nephew, you seem to be displaying signs of triviality.
Jack: On the contrary, Aunt Augusta, I've now realised for the first time in my life the vital Importance of Being Earnest.

The audience can hear the pun in the final phrase, set up equally between 'Ernest' and 'Earnest'. For the reader, the pun is reinforced by the capitalisation but the spelling privileges one side of the pun over the other. At the end, the reader's sight gag is visual, while the audience's punchline works because it is verbally constructed.

My account so far imagines an idealised performance. However, consider now a real performance of the play staged during the summer of 2001 by the Library Theatre of Manchester. The director, Lawrence Till, set the play in a 1950's camp coffee bar, and played up all the homosexual subtext without altering a word. The audience framed the opening of the play not with the list of characters, but having read the programme in which their frame knowledge was informed by the fact that 'Ernest' was a Victorian euphemism for homosexual, 'Cecily' a code for a rent-boy, and the play is staged on the centenary of the death of Wilde, exiled in Paris and broken after his trial and imprisonment for homosexual offences. Furthermore, the actors cross-dressed to emphasise the reversals in belief frame, and they even swapped characters during the interval.

In this performance, a separate belief frame is overlaid across the play (that of the director's understanding of Wilde's estimated intention). In the 'straight' version of the play, the audience only had to keep track of the complexity set out above. At least the character's faces stayed the same, in order to assist the anchoring of belief frames to enactors. In the subverted staging, even this stability is removed, and I would suggest that the ensuing complexity becomes so chaotic that it is just about impossible to keep track of the enactor reversals. If this was real life, the observer would abandon the attempt at cognitive resolution at this point, I think. However, in the theatre, the projected belief frame of the director replaces the chaos, and the incoherence becomes the theme. At this point, the dramatic staging has reached the limits of our theoretical model, perhaps, and we should end.

Explorations

1   In the account of a dramatic staging above, I had to make a new distinction in the contextual monitoring framework to account for the different circumstances of drama. Can you think of any other ways in which the general theory would need to be applied with special circumstances for drama? The best way of trying to answer this is to think of a dramatic performance and try to account for it using the framework.

2   The theory of contextual monitoring can be seen as a specification of other, more general frameworks for comprehension, such as those set out initially in this chapter and in Chapters 9 and 10. You might try to elaborate at the even more specific level by investigating, using a play-text, the precise linguistic realisations of binding, priming, overtness, and various patterns in frame manipulation.

3 Many cognitive poetic frameworks outlined in this book have tried to reconcile individual psychologised readings with socially collective readings. The question of what is the 'reader' and what is a 'reading' is complicated by the fact of performance in front of an audience, in drama. Consider the key issues here and try to set out as precisely as you can what constitutes a 'reading' of a performance.

4 The framework set out in this chapter was designed primarily to account for *narrative* comprehension, so it is in that area that it should also be applied. Consider examples of narrative literature which rely on enactor manipulation (such as science fiction time-paradox stories, or ghost stories), or multiple frame switching (thriller or crime fiction), or multiple frame repairs, or contradictory belief frames, or frame replacement, or which seem to break the conventions of binding and priming.

Further reading and references

The view of the 'transporting' power of literature is from Gerrig (1993); see also Boruah (1988), Martindale (1988), Coles (1989), Currie (1990), Maclean (1988), and Novitz (1987) for other discussions specifically on the comprehension of literature.

The CI model of comprehension is taken from Kintsch (1998), which develops the process model of understanding from Kintsch (1977) and van Dijk and Kintsch (1983). See also Just and Carpenter (1976) and Pylyshyn (1984).

Contextual frame theory is taken from Emmott (1997), but see also Emmott (1992, 1994, 1995, 1996) for more detail especially on enactors. The notion of *frame replacement* was adapted for science-fictional climaxes in Stockwell (2000a: 163–5).

12 The last words

Review

Cognitive poetics is not the study of texts alone, nor even specifically the study of literary texts; it is the study of literary reading. Using Ingarden's (1973a) distinction, literary texts are **autonomous** objects, having a material existence in the world, but literature is a **heteronomous** object, existing only when activated and engaged by the animating consciousness of the reader (see Chapter 10). This textbook works on a similar principle. On its own, it is an autonomous but lonely little thing. If it had a user's manual, the first instructions would be to attach yourself as reader, plug in your central nervous system, and engage your mind.

To this end, I have tried to make it as clear and usable as possible, setting out frameworks and ideas as explicitly as I can, and offering examples and illustrations of cognitive poetic applications throughout. Sometimes the generic demands of the textbook form have dictated that clarity and exemplification have taken precedence over the depth or intricacy of the analysis. This has been unavoidable, I think, but the book was not intended to be either a manifesto or a master-class. (For a manifesto, see Turner (1991) and for masterly analyses, see Gavins and Steen's (2003) companion volume to this book.)

In order to emphasise heteronomy, I have scattered the chapters with discussions and explorations. These are designed to make the book as interactive as a book can be. Stylistically, they feature questions and commands; they encode my voice and try to engage your thinking and collective discussions. They should not be seen as 'add-on' textbook paraphernalia, but as essential features of cognitive poetics. The way forward is not to read the book on your own but to engage it as a conversation, answer the questions in your own thinking and generate new questions – and solutions – in return. Many of the discussions are intended not for introspection but for real conversations with other people. Try this too. Literary reading itself might be a personal activity, but its study is enriched by being turned over and around by several minds talking to each other.

The book itself is only the first part of a process of learning. Some chapters might seem like long schematic lists of keywords and terminology – I know the glossarial index reinforces this idea. However, the worst thing you could do with this book would be to treat its outlines as mechanical devices through which to press literary texts. It would be easy simply to describe textual features and even parts of the reading process using these terms, but little is to be gained by this. It is not what cognitive poetics is about. The key concepts and checklists are merely the first stage, to be joined by intelligent thinking and exploration. You need not just other readers but a teacher, and I have tried to write the book with space for teachers to teach. I would have liked the book to have been sold with a free artificial intelligence teacher included, but technology and time are against me. In any case, human interaction is the better alternative. The key ideas do not work as an isolated mechanism, but need human imagination and enthusiasm to be applied. In I.A. Richards' (1924: i) famous phrase, the 'book is a machine to think with'.

Cognitive poetics itself embodies the principle of application. It is under application – the practical exploration of a cognitive framework – that approaches are tested and achieve any sort of value. In this book I have tried to encourage you to take insights from cognitive science and engage in new analyses of other literary readings. It is important to be able to feel that this sort of innovation is not only permitted but should be encouraged. It is how new ideas are formed and how existing understanding is modified and revised. And it is too important to be left only to academic authorities and eminent professors. I have always encouraged my students to develop their own thinking and argue with books and articles and especially with me, and this textbook should be no exception to that invitation.

Fortunately, cognitive poetics is in the position as a new discipline to offer rapid access to the frontier of exploration. By this point in the book, you should have a good understanding of a wide range of different approaches. More importantly, you should also possess the schematic patterns that will allow you to extend the method to other cognitive frameworks and other literary works. Though this is the final chapter of the book, it is where the process of exploration really begins.

No doubt some of the areas addressed in this book will come to be regarded as resolved, or fade from interest, or will give way to new ways of thinking about cognitive poetics. I have been struck while putting the book together how various and vigorous are the different strands within the discipline, and it is inconceivable that all this energy will not cause movements in the clusters of interest and research. The landscape of cognitive poetics is shifting fast already – resolving itself as a discipline rather than an interdiscipline for some people, multiplying into new interdisciplinary connections for others. Either way, my simple map over the previous chapters will almost certainly become less and less navigable as time goes by. I hope that you become responsible for some of that remoulding.

Before I give up the book to the world, however, I feel I should at least outline some of the emergent strands of the moment. In the rest of this chapter, then, I offer a few last words that seem to me to be important and worth some thought. They are words that have all been mentioned throughout this book, in a variety of contexts and in the work of many different writers within cognitive poetics. The words are: *texture, discourse, ideology, emotion* and *imagination*. I am raising them here, not in order to develop further investigation in this book, but to leave them in your mind.

Texture

The word **texture** reminds us of the etymological origin of concepts of text and textuality in weaving. If there is one thing that is common to many different attempts to describe or characterise literariness, it is the notion that there is a texture to a text, a sense that the materiality of the object is noticeable alongside any content that is communicated through it. Literature draws attention to its own condition of existence, which is its texture.

We can understand conceptual texture by extending our understanding of visual and other perceptual textures. In literary texts, it is often the smallest items or features that can seem disproportionately significant, beyond any measure of their objective status in terms, for example, of frequency or position alone. Prominence is thus a factor in texture. It also seems to be the case that prominent small items in our visual field receive attention and focus, become the figure in the ground, and seem to be 'closer' to us than other objects. This sense of a text having a relief of depth, proximity and intimacy is also its texture.

It might even be said that the power of literary works to attract the time and effort necessary for their engagement lies in the perceived texture not only of the work itself but also of the experience. The connections between the stylistic texture of the literary work and the felt experience of the reader can be explored in cognitive poetics. Both are textural, and both are necessary in the holistic picture of literary cognition. Texture concerns variation and unevenness. Flat, undistinguished fields of perception do not have texture, or at least have only an unattractive default texture that is monotonous. However, our perceptual ability to create figure and ground, and scales of depth, all involve the experience of texture that is extended into the conceptual domain of reading.

Similarly, we seem to perceive difference and variation as motion, perhaps because in the natural environment the only change we can see immediately is when things move. Long-term decay is understood as a change from one state to another (note even here the motion metaphor) if it is too slow for us to see in one perceptual session. By contrast, the difference between, say, upright trees and fallen trees is an assumption of movement from one to the other. It is this apparent motion that allows 'stop-frame' animators to create cartoons.

Change manifests as texture, then, but motion itself also creates textured variation. In the visual field, as an object passes in front of another, we not only throw the objects into a figure and ground relief, we also create texture at the point at which the foreground object eclipses the background, and at the point where the background emerges again. This texture at the boundaries shifts with the moving object. In literary works, this motion is *style*.

Interesting unevenness (the one entails the other) is captured by the style of a literary work and the process of reading. Both of these involve movement in the sense that reading is a movement through a text. In cognitive poetics, we have various means of understanding textured motion. We can explore stylistic variation by looking at the microstructures of images, metaphors, grammar and semantic domains. We can explore the textured sensation of moving with the reading through a shifting mental space, parable, text world or schema. Above all, cognitive poetics can allow us to understand how we negotiate the *continuities* through texts and readings – the moving textured boundaries as one stylistic feature moves into focus over another.

However, we can only do any of this if we remain sufficiently faithful to the essentially *dynamic* nature of the reading process. Though almost all cognitive theories state as a principle the procedural and dynamic dimensions of the reading or comprehension process, in practice a solidification of the process is often a consequence of the fact that accounts have to be written down. The process of reading then appears more like a fossil record, or at best a series of snapshots which are then assembled like a cinematic reel to give only the cartoon illusion of motion. In remembering this essential distortion when we create theories and frameworks, we should also be reminded that these models are best understood as heuristic tools for improving our insight. When the models themselves become the occasion for argument, rather than the literary reading for which they were developed, we are no longer applying anything to anything; this would no longer be cognitive poetics at all.

There are several ways of exploring texture, but the notion captures the primacy of the reader in the exploration. Cognitive poetics must keep sight of the reader and the reading process if it is to remain cognitive poetics. If we focus on the text as object, we are doing linguistics. If we focus on the reader alone, we are doing psychology. Neither of these fields have anything in themselves to say about literary reading. Cognitive poetics, then, is essentially an applied discipline, interested in the naturalistic process of literary reading.

Discourse

Cognitive poetics did not arise in a vacuum, fully sprung in adult form. It has brought with it several of the preoccupations and assumptions of its parent disciplines, not only within psychology and linguistics but also from the historical development of literary critical studies. Some of the arguments and debates being fought out today are the rag-tag ends of older skirmishes in other disciplines. However, one preoccupation common to many of the debates over recent decades remains a powerful and important focus of thinking: the concept of **discourse**.

Many of the earlier approaches within cognitive linguistics, in spite of their direct concern for context, restricted their explorations to simple single sentences.

Some of these were taken from literary texts, often without it mattering very much how the surrounding co-text affected a reading of the sentence in focus. Sometimes the sentences were simply invented for the purposes of illustrating a cognitive linguistic point. Sometimes assumptions have been made about how language speakers or communities would use and process a particular term, without any actual empirical evidence being produced.

These all seem to me to be flawed or fatally partial ways of doing cognitive poetics. Essentially, and in spite of cognitive scientific principles, they treat language as an object in its own right. Even in a simple sense of the term, *discourse* points to the notion of a text in use, and is a reminder that any approach that tries to treat language decontextually is doomed to failure. Most plainly, this is because language out of context is no longer language at all. (A consequence of this view is that much theoretical linguistics simply lacks an object of investigation and is, literally, pointless).

This simple definition of *discourse* foregrounds the communicativeness and functionality that are essential defining features of language itself. Cognitive science has tended to focus on the individual and personal aspects of mind and paid only implicit attention to the social and interactive dimensions of human cognition. This is a bias that has persisted in cognitive poetics, perhaps understandably given the personal focus of the solitary reader in literary criticism. However, it is a tendency that must be resisted.

It would be worth revisiting many of the approaches outlined in this book and evaluating them for their sense of social and discoursal interaction. In schema theory, to take the most obvious example, the model is focused very firmly on the perceptions, plans, goals and scripted strategies of the individual (see Chapter 6). Other people are regarded almost as actors simply speaking their lines. It may be that a reconception of schema poetics can be imagined which encompasses the social negotiation of situations through interactive discourse. It might be up to cognitive poetics to produce such a revision, and I think that it could be achieved by exploring schema theory in dramatised forms of literature, where expectations and disruptions are modelled on stage.

Some cognitive poetic approaches, such as text world theory (Chapter 10), arise directly out of discourse analysis and have a more discoursal awareness as a result. Discursive negotiations obviously inform the **discourse world**, at the level of discourse participants, their social situations in relation to each other and the wider community. Nevertheless, a further problem arises when models such as this are applied to literary texts, since the dialogue with the text is virtual rather than real. Normal books do not literally speak to us, but are understood to be metaphorically **dialogic** in various senses: they represent another voice; they often traverse chronological periods and cultures; they often encompass a range of characters and viewpoints; they often situate themselves intertextually with other writers, readers and literary works. The fact that all of these senses of *discourse* are metaphorical, of course, should mean that cognitive poetics is relatively easily able to evolve discoursal models for literary reading.

Some features of some cognitive poetic frameworks are evidently amenable to a discoursal dimension. Work in literary comprehension (see Chapter 11) is necessarily interactive and social. Elements such as narrative tracking, world building and frame repair are all essentially dialogic and socially negotiated, even if the social dimension involved is local to the text and the reader's cognition. It is noticeable, though, that it is approaches from within cognitive poetics which tend to regard this as an issue, whereas for cognitive psychologists it seems in general not to be a concern. In this area, it is out of cognitive poetics that solutions are being found.

A more radical understanding of *discourse* regards it not simply as a text in its situation of use but as the essential defining feature of language. This view foregrounds a wider view of the social dimensions of language than simple face-to-face interaction. Language itself is socially negotiated, right down to particular lexicogrammatical choices of style, register, accent and dialect. Social negotiation (and sometimes social conflict) is the place where cultural models and cognitive models come from. It is not enough to emphasise the embodied nature of cognition and language, without also recognising the various discursive practices that structure both society and language inextricably. Cognitive poetics must address this too.

Ideology

I am arguing for cognitive linguistics to be more sociolinguistic, and the means of doing this is by being more critically aware of **ideology** in language. By this I mean not only the ordinary sense of political ideology but also the social scientific sense of ideology as a set of beliefs which inform practice. Our cognition is embodied and experiential, but cognitive science has paid insufficient attention to the social and ideological roots of shared human conditions and experiences. This is not because of any incapacity in the method of cognitive science; rather it is again simply because the focus of its origins is psychological and individual rather than social and economic.

Cognitive poetics – as an essentially applied form of cognitive science – is ideally positioned to take up this challenge. In adopting a more critically sophisticated approach, we would also necessarily make connections between microstructural matters of word and grammar choice and the macrostructural matters of global ideology and viewpoint. We would be forced to reconnect individual sentences with co-text and context, and we would have to address the natural occurrence of the text in relation to the social conditions of its readership and projected world.

In Chapter 5, I suggested one possible means of achieving this. The cognitive dimension of grammatical analysis (for both Langacker and Halliday) provides a method for exploring the social relations between participant roles in forms of expression. Hallidayan systemic-functional linguistics has been the basis for a **critical discourse analysis** (CDA), investigating the discursive practices of socially situated groups in relation to each other. For example, the manipulations of power through language have been explored in the forms of discourse used by politicians, newspapers, television and other media, advertisers, corporations and institutions such as universities and colleges.

One method within CDA, for example, has been to examine the differences between different discourses in war reporting. Some reports blend registers and metaphors from different domains to construct a particular view on events: military jargon, children's games, fairy tales, folk fables, and toy advertising used in a newspaper to describe a military action, for example. It is argued that such metaphorical blends of different discourses eventually become naturalised by customary usage, and lose their sense of ideological spin altogether.

It is obvious even from this simple example that cognitive linguistics has a lot to offer an analysis like this. The notion of blending, and its emergent structure (Chapter 7), would be a very precise means of tracking the development of metaphorical reasoning in such political usage. Cognitive linguistics, too, would benefit from a greater sophistication in awareness of critical theory and the philosophy of ideology. A critical cognitive linguistics is long overdue.

It seems to me that cognitive poetics is the natural ground for developments in this direction. Much literary criticism has been thoroughly concerned with the political, social and ideological aspects of literary texts, production and readings, and a method of analysis rooted in cognitive principles would bridge the gap between two disciplines that sorely lack each other's insight. In the notion of schematic projection, common to several frameworks, cognitive poetics already offers the means of tracking ideological differences between characters, narrators, authors and readers. We have very precise ways of delineating different viewpoints. All that is missing is an element of critical theory to connect the reading process with wider social concerns.

It might also be a salutary experience for some in cognitive science to discover precursors of basic principles in other critical disciplines. For example, the notion of language as essentially embodied and experiential is hardly new to feminism, having been discussed at least as far back as Virginia Woolf and expressed in literary texts such as Charlotte Perkins Gilman's *Herland* (1914), for example. Cognitive poetics offers a principled means of understanding the expression of such experiences and intuitions.

Emotion

The concept of **emotion** is an obvious point where literature and cognition meet. There have been many recent calls in cognitive poetics for greater attention to be paid to the phenomenon, and it seems likely that the study of emotion and affect will assume an even higher profile in cognitive poetics in the future.

Oatley (1992) was one of the first within the modern field to highlight the view of emotion as something that could be decomposed and understood analytically: emotion is regarded as a cognitive phenomenon. According to Oatley (1992: 18), emotions are 'mental states with coherent psychological functions'. In contrast to mystical or poetic views of emotions, they are seen within cognitive psychology as being basically communicative. This view foregrounds cognitive, functional and communicative aspects in a way that is easily applicable to the literary context through cognitive poetics.

Throughout history, the educational, moral, didactic, or the escapist, entertaining, artistic aspects of literature have been discussed and explored in literary criticism. The emotional 'content' of a literary work has almost been regarded as a coincidental side-effect, or simply part of the rhetorical trickery involved in putting a moral message over on a reader under the guise of entertainment. The text is seen as responsible for emotional cues, but the actual emotions which are evoked have been regarded as within the bounds only of readerly whim. This is unanalysable and has been of little interest to literary critics. However, the emotional dimension of a text is not solely an extra-textual feature but is often a reason for the attraction of readers to particular works in the first place. The cognitive poetic cues in the text can be explored.

In Oatley's view, emotions have two components. First, they have the functional aspect of marking readiness for action, or a point at which the readiness for action changes. Second, emotional states have a phenomenological **tone** that is a felt experience, often with a bodily reaction or expression. The readiness for action is understood in relation to **plans** and **goals**, and different emotions follow upon the maintenance of plans, the achievement of goals, their frustration or failure.

Emotions as seen in this framework are the human experience of signals that arise when there are variations in plans or goals which are being monitored. We use emotions to communicate within ourselves in this way. We also use expressions of direct emotion to communicate with others, and we have linguistic systems for categorising and representing emotions so that we can talk about them explicitly with other people.

It is not difficult to see how this approach could be adapted to the literary affective context. Oatley even provides a number of worked-out literary examples for illustration. Literary empathy or the sorts of vicarious emotions generated during literary reading feel as real as genuine directly generated emotions. This is a result of the **simulation** (another sort of projection) that readers often set up when they engage with text worlds. We can identify with a character, often encouraged by the patterns of focalisation and point of view that we negotiate through a text. *Identifying* means the process of constructing that character's plans and goals and then feeling an emotional consequence at points of juncture in the evolution of the plan, as in real life. Of course, this empathy in literature is the same as the feeling of empathy for other people in real life: in both cases a similar simulation is involved.

Many cognitive frameworks emphasise the fact that cognition is ongoing and developmental. Cognitive models adapt and change in response to experience and usage. Since cognition is intimately tied up with identity and personality, the changes in cognitive models are deeply felt and often regarded as 'life-changing' or seen as new personal perspectives. The empathetic understanding engendered with literature relies on the same processes as our lives in general, except that in literature certain aspects of emotional responses are permitted to be discussed within institutional frameworks like universities. Oatley (1992: 412) regards the cognitive psychological model of emotions as a system that occupies the whole of consciousness, and so requires an integrated model to account for it: 'we are indeed systems that write new pieces of ourselves'.

One way that insights like this generate new ways of understanding is simply by changing the metaphor that structures our framework. Seeing the mind not as a computer but as an integrated network, or as a sponge, or as a shifting ocean, are all conceptual metaphors which can suggest new ideas. This can have profound effects, such as offering a cognitive poetic approach to emotional engagement that is not coldly rational, but that seems to match more satisfactorily our sense of why we read and enjoy happy, passionate, serious or even sad, frightening, or angry literature.

Imagination

A talismanic word especially for the Romantics, **imagination** is of course at the core of cognitive poetics, and our great challenge is to be able to explore its workings and understand its mysterious processes more richly. It has been used to invoke the creative act of literary production, but of course imagination is required of the reader just as much as empathy or projection. Here perhaps is where we need the most radical deliberate shifts in metaphor. Recent work which has moved in this direction includes that by Scarry (2001), as she explores our human capacity for invoking mental images, making them move, and moving around within them.

She offers five ways of moving mental pictures, each a variation of metaphor and each highly suggestive. **Radiant ignition** captures the sense of imagined vividness that literature can produce. Like blinding lights or a sudden shining image, this way of making mental pictures move is the most dynamic, containing the notion of speed and energy. Again, this is a sort of foregrounding of a bright, attractive or moving element as an attractor of attention. Countless poems, prose and dramas create energy and vividness by making the centres of attention bright, or gold and silver coloured, or simply more colourful and active than anything around them.

Scarry next offers **rarity** as part of the cognitive scaffolding of imagination. This is to do with the delicacy or loss of solidity of an image. The thing is focused on so closely and intimately that it becomes almost transparent, as every element and connection within it is turned over in our imagination, and the essence of the thing can be felt and discerned. Parts of the image are magnified and described in ways that go far beyond the focus of everyday consideration. Delicate and barely substantial things can be moved in our mental imagery very easily. Much literature stays with things – feelings, sensations, tastes, tones, atmosphere – that are intangible and barely perceptible. Narratives are suspended while the lyrical moment or scene is rendered.

The third pattern is **addition and subtraction**, in which an image is built and then removed. The effect is of having the thing move away, just as in negation (see the example from Garrison Keillor in Chapter 10). The imagined sensation serves to move elements around in your mind, either by letting them fade from consciousness or by explicitly and directly removing them using a predication. Addition and subtraction (or world-building, maintenance and negation, if you prefer) are ways of making motionless images appear to move, simply by the text moving on from one to another, which of course is really the reader moving their imagination on. The character or object, which appears in place of the previously mentioned object, seems to move into position as the older object moves out of sight.

The fourth way of imaginary motion involves seeing the text as a cloth (the textile origins of texture, again), which can **stretch** out, **fold** and **tilt** images according to the shifting perspective of the focaliser. Images that characters or narrators see are manipulated in this way so as to be human in size and manageable, but the effect is of the character and their perspective in motion. Scarry's final pattern, **floral supposition**, is the most idiosyncratic of all, I think. She imagines all four previous metaphors wrapped up in her mental image of a flower, and tracks examples of flowers through literary moments involving motion. The textured boundary where figure moves across ground is seen as a floral blurring, as all the patterns of imaginary motion come into play.

Beginning cognitive poetics

By this point I think we have come a long way from static schematised models, and have reached the boundaries of speculation. It will be interesting to see whether adventurous approaches like Scarry's, with its wild leaps of and into the imagination, lead to a more thorough understanding of a wide range of literary experiences. Of course, it is only by engaging with all such ideas and trying them out in literary reading that we will ever hope to resolve the issues for ourselves.

It is with that thought that I want to leave you, with this book in hand in the country of the mind. We have reached the edge of the discipline, or at least of this map of a landscape that is forming and reforming even as you read and think. At the moment, the territory has many uncharted areas, some false signposts, and some roads which were only recently begun and are only half-finished. Some of the people who live in this country have grand plans for an integrated communications system, and they are busy trying to raise money and persuade other people that their vision is the right one. Others simply want to cultivate small fields and be left alone to perfect their methods and let their ideas mature. Already there are some small signs of civilisation, with local customs and conventions. There are a few small societies, but few factions as yet. There is even talk of putting together some laws though no one is quite sure yet what the laws would be, nor even how to enforce them.

All that is in the future, though. For the moment, this little book is simply a guide to the lie of the land, and an introduction to a field that so far has borders only where you want to draw them. I am certain that other, grander works will follow, and eventually render parts of the map outdated; but if from here you go and help to move that work along, then it will have served its purpose.

References

For a view on the consequences of taking all of the factors of context, cognition, emotion and felt experience seriously, see Toolan (1996). Edwards (1997) argues persuasively for the prominence of discourse in cognition. The radical view of language as discourse is offered by McCarthy and Carter (1994); see also Carter (1999). Critical discourse analysis is best exemplified in the work of Fairclough (1995); see also Caldas-Coulthard and Coulthard (1996) for a collection of analyses, and Simpson (1993) on ideology and point of view from a literary perspective. In Stockwell (2001) I tried to sketch out a picture of a critical cognitive linguistics, using an exemplary piece of political analysis by Lakoff (1992). On dialogism in literature (and many other proto-cognitive ideas ahead of their time) see Bakhtin (1968, 1984). On emotions, see Miall (1989; Miall and Kuiken 1994), Oatley (1992, 1994), Kneepkens and Zwaan (1994), LeDoux (1999) and Burke (2002). Scarry (2001) closes the section above on imagination.

Key readings in cognitive poetics

Now you have finished thinking your way through this book, you are well equipped to continue your exploration of the field of cognitive poetics. In the further reading at the end of each chapter, you will find quick routes into the heart of the country. However, there is a vastness of books and articles to be explored. While being aware that the following list is bound to be personal and partial, these for me are the key books which you ought to have read if you want to take this journey.

Tony Bex, Michael Burke and Peter Stockwell (eds) (2000) *Contextualised Stylistics: In Honour of Peter Verdonk*, Amsterdam: Rodopi.

Guy Cook (1994) *Discourse and Literature*, Oxford: Oxford University Press.

Derek Edwards (1997) *Discourse and Cognition*, London: Sage.

Catherine Emmott (1997) *Narrative Comprehension: A Discourse Perspective*, Oxford: Clarendon Press.

Gilles Fauconnier (1997) *Mappings in Thought and Language*, Cambridge: Cambridge University Press.

Richard Gerrig (1993) *Experiencing Narrative Worlds: On the Psychological Activities of Reading*, New Haven, CT: Yale University Press.

Ray Gibbs (1994) *The Poetics of Mind: Figurative Thought, Language and Understanding*, Cambridge: Cambridge University Press.

Mark Johnson (1987) *The Body in the Mind: The Bodily Basis of Meaning, Imagination, and Reason*, Chicago, IL: University of Chicago Press.

Philip Johnson-Laird (1983) *Mental Models: Towards a Cognitive Science of Language, Inference and Consciousness*, Cambridge: Cambridge University Press.

Philip Johnson-Laird (1988) *The Computer and the Mind: An Introduction to Cognitive Science*, London: Fontana.

Walter Kintsch (1998) *Comprehension: A Paradigm for Cognition*, Cambridge: Cambridge University Press.

George Lakoff (1987) *Women, Fire and Dangerous Things: What Categories Reveal About the Mind*, Chicago, IL: University of Chicago Press.

Ronald Langacker (1987) *Foundations of Cognitive Grammar, Vol. I: Theoretical Prerequisites*, Stanford, CA: Stanford University Press.

Ronald Langacker (1991) *Foundations of Cognitive Grammar, Vol. II: Descriptive Application*, Stanford, CA: Stanford University Press.

Marvin Minsky (1986) *The Society of Mind*, London: Heinemann.

Keith Oatley (1992) *Best Laid Schemes: The Psychology of Emotions*, Cambridge: Cambridge University Press.

Andrew Ortony (ed.) (1993) *Metaphor and Thought* (second edition), Cambridge: Cambridge University Press.

Marie-Laure Ryan (1991a) *Possible Worlds: Artificial Intelligence and Narrative Theory*, Bloomington and Indianapolis, IN: Indiana University Press.

Elena Semino (1997) *Language and World Creation in Poems and Other Texts*, London: Longman.

Gerard Steen (1994) *Understanding Metaphor*, London: Longman.

Reuven Tsur (1992) *Toward a Theory of Cognitive Poetics*, Amsterdam: North-Holland.

Reuven Tsur (1998) *Poetic Rhythm: Structure and Performance*, Berne: Peter Lang.

Mark Turner (1987) *Death is the Mother of Beauty: Mind, Metaphor, Criticism*, Chicago, IL: University of Chicago Press.

Mark Turner (1991) *Reading Minds: The Study of English in the Age of Cognitive Science*, Princeton, NJ: Princeton University Press.

Mark Turner (1996) *The Literary Mind: The Origins of Thought and Language*, Oxford: Oxford University Press.

Friedrich Ungerer and Hans-Jörg Schmid (1996) *An Introduction to Cognitive Linguistics*, London: Longman.

Paul Werth (1999) *Text Worlds: Representing Conceptual Space in Discourse* (edited by M. Short), Harlow: Longman.

Bibliography

Abelson, R. (1987) 'Artificial Intelligence and literary appreciation: how big is the gap?' in L. Hálàsz (ed.) *Literary Discourse: Aspects of Cognitive and Social Psychological Approaches*, Berlin: de Gruyter, pp. 1–37.

Abrams, M.H. (1953) *The Mirror and the Lamp: Romantic Theory and the Critical Tradition*, Oxford: Oxford University Press.

Aldiss, Brian (1973) *Frankenstein Unbound*, London: Jonathan Cape.

—— (1987) *Cracken at Critical*, London: Kerosina Books.

Allen, S. (ed.) (1989) *Possible Worlds in Humanities, Arts and Sciences*, Berlin: de Gruyter.

Baddeley, A.D. and Weiskrantz, L. (eds) (1993) *Attention: Awareness, Selection, and Control*, Oxford: Oxford University Press.

Bakhtin, Mikhail (1968) *Rabelais and his World* (trans. Helene Iswolsky), Cambridge, MA: MIT Press.

—— (1984) *Problems of Dostoevsky's Poetics* (ed. and trans. Caryl Emerson, *Problemy Tvorchestva Dostoyevskogo*, 1929), Manchester: Manchester University Press.

Bal, Mieke (1985) *Narratology: Introduction to the Theory of Narrative*, Toronto: University of Toronto Press.

Ballard, J.G. (1970) *The Atrocity Exhibition*, London: Jonathan Cape.

Barsalou, Lawrence (1982) 'Context-independent and context-dependent information in concepts', *Memory and Cognition* 10: 82–93.

—— (1983) 'Ad hoc categories', *Memory and Cognition* 11: 211–27.

Barthes, Roland (1977) *Image Music Text* (ed. S. Heath), London: Fontana.

Bartlett, F.C. (1932) *Remembering: A Study in Experimental and Social Psychology* (reprinted 1995), Cambridge: Cambridge University Press.

Bates, Elizabeth and MacWhinney, Brian (1982) 'Functionalist approaches to grammar', in L. Gleitman and E. Wanner (eds) *Language Acquisition: The State of the Art*, Cambridge: Cambridge University Press, pp.173–218.

Beardslee, David C. and Wertheimer, Max (eds) (1958) *Readings in Perception*, Princeton, NJ: Van Nostrand.

Berry, Margaret (1977) *Introduction to Systemic Linguistics* (2 vols), London: Batsford.

Bex, Tony (1996) *Variety in Written English*, London: Routledge.

Bex, Tony; Burke, Michael, and Stockwell, Peter (eds) (2000) *Contextualised Stylistics: In Honour of Peter Verdonk*, Amsterdam: Rodopi.

Black, Max (1962) *Models and Metaphors*, Ithaca, NY: Cornell University Press.

——— (1990) *Perplexities*, Ithaca, NY: Cornell University Press.

Booth, Wayne C. (1961) *A Rhetoric of Fiction*, Chicago, IL: University of Chicago Press.

Boring, Edwin (1950) *A History of Experimental Psychology* (second edition), New York: Appleton Century Crofts.

Boruah, B.H. (1988) *Fiction and Emotion*, Oxford: Oxford University Press.

Bradley, R. and Swartz, N. (1979) *Possible Worlds: An Introduction to Logic and its Philosophy*, Indiana: Hackett Publishing Co.

Brooke-Rose, Christine (1958) *A Grammar of Metaphor*, London: Mercury Books.

Brown, P. and Levinson, S.C. (1987) *Politeness: Some Universals in Language Usage*, Cambridge: Cambridge University Press.

Bruder, Gail A. and Wiebe, Janyce M. (1995) 'Recognizing subjectivity and identifying subjective characters in third-person fictional narrative', in J.F. Duchan, G.A. Bruder and L.E. Hewitt (eds) *Deixis in Narrative: A Cognitive Science Perspective*, Hillsdale, NJ: Lawrence Erlbaum, 341–56.

Bühler, K. (1982) 'The deictic field of language and deictic worlds', in R.J. Jarvella and W. Klain (eds) *Speech, Place and Action: Studies in Deixis and Related Topics* (translated from *Sprachtheorie*, 1934), Chichester: John Wiley, pp.9–30.

Burke, Michael (2002) *The Oceanic Mind: Charting Emotive Cognition in Literary Texts*, (unpublished PhD thesis), University of Amsterdam.

Caldas-Coulthard, Carmen-Rosa and Coulthard, Malcolm (eds) (1996) *Texts and Practices: Readings in Critical Discourse Analysis*, London: Routledge.

Cameron, L. and Low, G. (eds) (1999) *Researching and Applying Metaphor*, Cambridge: Cambridge University Press.

Carter, Ronald (1997) *Investigating English Discourse: Language, Literacy, Literature*, London: Routledge.

——— (1999) 'Common language: corpus, creativity and cognition', *Language and Literature* 8(3): 195–216.

Carter, Ronald and Nash, Walter (1990) *Seeing Through Language: A Guide to Styles of English Writing*, Oxford: Basil Blackwell.

Chatman, Seymour (1978) *Story and Discourse*, Ithaca, NY: Cornell University Press.

——— (1990) *Coming to Terms: The Rhetoric of Narrative in Fiction and Film*, Ithaca, NY: Cornell University Press.

Chilton, P. (ed.) (1985) *Language and the Nuclear Arms Debate*, London: Pinter.

——— (1986) 'Metaphor, euphemism, and the militarization of language'. Paper presented at the Biannual Meeting of the International Peace Research Association, Sussex.

——— (1988) *Orwellian Language and the Media*, London: Pluto Press.

Cockcroft, Robert (2002) *Renaissance Rhetoric: Reconsidered Passion – The Interpretation of Affect in Early Modern Writing*, London: Palgrave.

Coles, R. (1989) *The Call of Stories*, Boston, MA: Houghton Mifflin.

Cook, Guy (1989) *Discourse*, Oxford: Oxford University Press.

——— (1992) *The Discourse of Advertising*, London: Routledge.

——— (1994) *Discourse and Literaure*, Oxford: Oxford University Press.

Culler, Jonathan (1975) *Structuralist Poetics*, London: Routledge & Kegan Paul.

Culpeper, Jonathan (2001) *Language and Characterisation*, London: Longman.

Currie, G. (1990) *The Nature of Fiction*, Cambridge: Cambridge University Press.

de Beaugrande, Robert (1980) *Text, Discourse and Process: Toward an Interdisciplinary Science of Texts*, Hillsdale, NJ: Lawrence Erlbaum.

—— (1987) 'Schemas for literary communication', in L. Hálàsz (ed.) *Literary Discourse: Aspects of Cognitive and Social Psychological Approaches*, Berlin: de Gruyter, pp.49–99.

Dolezel, L. (1976) 'Narrative modalities', *Journal of Literary Semantics*, 5 (1): 5–14.

—— (1988) 'Mimesis and possible worlds', *Poetics Today*, 9 (3): 475–97.

—— (1989) 'Possible worlds and literary fictions', in S. Allen (ed.) *Possible Worlds in Humanities, Arts and Sciences*, Berlin: de Gruyter, pp. 223–42.

Duchan, J.F.; Bruder, G.A. and Hewitt, L.E. (eds) (1995) *Deixis in Narrative: A Cognitive Science Perspective*, Hillsdale, NJ: Lawrence Erlbaum.

Eco, Umberto (1976) *A Theory of Semiotics*, Bloomington: Indiana University Press.

—— (1981) *The Role of the Reader: Explorations in the Semiotics of Texts*, London: Hutchinson.

Edwards, Derek (1997) *Discourse and Cognition*, London: Sage.

Egan, Greg (1996) *Axiomatic*, London: Millennium.

—— (1998) *Diaspora*, London: Millennium.

Emmott, Catherine (1992) 'Splitting the referent: an introduction to narrative enactors', in M. Davies and L.J. Ravelli (eds) *Advances in Systemic Linguistics: Recent Theory and Practice*, London: Pinter, pp.221–8.

—— (1994) 'Frames of reference: contextual monitoring and narrative discourse', in R.M. Coulthard (ed.) *Advances in Written Text Analysis*, London: Routledge, pp.157–66.

—— (1995) 'Consciousness and context-building: narrative inferences and anaphoric theory', in Keith Green (ed.) *New Essays in Deixis*, Amsterdam: Rodopi, pp.81–97.

—— (1996) 'Real grammar in fictional contexts', *Glasgow Review* 4: 9–23.

—— (1997) *Narrative Comprehension: A Discourse Perspective*, Oxford: Clarendon Press.

Erlich, V. (1965) *Russian Formalism: History, Doctrine*, Berlin: Mouton.

Fairclough, Norman (1995) *Critical Discourse Analysis*, London: Longman.

Fauconnier, G. (1994) *Mental Spaces* [original in French as *Espaces Mentaux*, 1984, Paris: Editions de Minuit], Cambridge: Cambridge University Press.

—— (1997) *Mappings in Thought and Language*, Cambridge: Cambridge University Press.

—— (1998) 'Conceptual integration networks', *Cognitive Science* 22(2): 133–87.

Fauconnier, G. and Sweetser, E. (eds) (1996) *Spaces, Worlds and Grammar*, Chicago, IL: University of Chicago Press.

Fauconnier, G. and Turner, M. (1996) 'Blending as a central process of grammar', in Adele Goldberg (ed.) *Conceptual Structure, Discourse, and Language*, Stanford: Center for the Study of Language and Information.

Fillmore, Charles (1975) 'An alternative to checklist theories of meaning', in C. Cogen, H.Thompson, G. Thurgood and K. Whistler (eds) *Proceedings of the Berkeley Linguistics Society*, Berkeley, CA: Berkeley Linguistics Society, pp. 123–31.

—— (1976) 'The need for a frame semantics within linguistics', *Statistical Methods in Linguistics* 14: 5–29.

—— (1977) 'The case for case reopened', in P. Cole and J.M. Sadock (eds) *Syntax and Semantics, Vol. 8: Grammatical Relations*, New York: Academic Press, pp. 59–81.

—— (1985) 'Frames and the semantics of understanding', *Quaderni di Semantica* 6: 222–54.

Fish, Stanley (1970) 'Literature in the reader: affective stylistics', *New Literary History* 2: 123–62.

—— (1973) 'What is stylistics and why are they saying such terrible things about it?' in S. Chatman (ed.) *Approaches to Poetics*, New York: Columbia University Press.

—— (1980) *Is There a Text in this Class?* Cambridge, MA: Harvard University Press.

Fleischman, S. (1982) *The Future in Thought and Language: Diachronic Evidence from Romance*, Cambridge: Cambridge University Press.

—— (1990) *Tense and Narrativity: From Medieval Performance to Modern Fiction*, London: Routledge.

Forceville, C. (1995a) '(A)symmetry in metaphor: the importance of extended context', *Poetics Today* 16(4): 679–708.

—— (1995b) 'IBM is a tuning fork: degrees of freedom in the interpretation of pictorial metaphors', *Poetics* 23: 189–218.

—— (1996) *Pictorial Metaphor in Advertising*, London: Routledge.

Fowler, Roger (1977) *Linguistics and the Novel*, London: Methuen.

—— (1996) *Linguistic Criticism* (second edition), Oxford: Oxford University Press.

Freeman, D (1996) 'According to my bond: *King Lear* and re-cognition', in J.J. Weber (ed.) *The Stylistics Reader*, London: Arnold, pp.280–97 [and in *Language and Literature* 2(2), 1993].

Freundlieb, D. (1982) 'Understanding Poe's tales: a schema-theoretic view', *Poetics* 11: 25–44.

Gadamer, Hans-Georg (1989) *Truth and Method* (trans. Joel Weinsheimer and Donald G. Marshall, second edition, from *Wahrheit und Methode*, 1960), New York: Crossroad Press.

Galbraith, Mary (1995) 'Deictic shift theory and the poetics of involvement in narrative', in J.F. Duchan, G.A. Bruder and L.E. Hewitt (eds) *Deixis in Narrative: A Cognitive Science Perspective*, Hillsdale, NJ: Lawrence Erlbaum, pp.19–59.

Garvin, P.L. (ed.) (1964) *A Prague School Reader on Aesthetics, Literary Structure and Style*, Washington, DC: Georgetown University Press.

Gavins, Joanna (2000) 'Absurd tricks with bicycle frames in the text world of *The Third Policeman*', *Nottingham Linguistic Circular* 15: 17–34.

—— (2001) *Text World Theory: a Critical Exposition and Development in Relation to Absurd Prose Fiction* (unpublished PhD thesis), Sheffield Hallam University.

Gavins, Joanna and Steen, Gerard (eds) (2003) *Cognitive Poetics in Practice*, London: Routledge.

Genette, Gérard (1980) *Narrative Discourse*, Ithaca, NY: Cornell University Press.

—— (1995) *Mimologics* (trans. Thaïs Morgan), Lincoln, NE: University of Nebraska Press.

—— (1997a) *Palimpsests: Literature in the Second Degree* (trans. Channa Newman and Claude Doubinsky), Lincoln, NE: University of Nebraska Press.

—— (1997b) *Paratexts: Thresholds of Interpretation* (trans. Jane Lewin), Cambridge: Cambridge University Press.

Gentner, D. (1982) 'Are scientific analogies metaphors?' in David S. Miall (ed.) *Metaphor: Problems and Perspectives*, Brighton: Harvester, pp.106–32.

Gerrig, R.J. (1993) *Experiencing Narrative Worlds: On the Psychological Activities of Reading*, New Haven, CT: Yale University Press.

Gibbs, R. (1994) *The Poetics of Mind: Figurative Thought, Language and Understanding*, Cambridge: Cambridge University Press.

Gibbs, Ray and Colston, Herbert (1995) 'The cognitive psychological reality of image schemas and their transformations', *Cognitive Linguistics* 6: 347–78.

Gibson, William and Sterling, Bruce (1990) *The Difference Engine*, London: Victor Gollancz.

Gladsky, R.K. (1992) 'Schema theory and literary texts: Anthony Burgess's Nadsat', *Language Quarterly* 30 (1–2): 39–46.

Goatly, Andrew (1997) *The Language of Metaphors*, London: Routledge.

Goldberg, Adele (ed.) (1996) *Conceptual Structure, Discourse, and Language*, Stanford, CA: Center for the Study of Language and Information.

Green, Keith (1992) 'Deixis and the poetic persona', *Language and Literature* 1(2): 121–34.

—— (ed.) (1995) *New Essays in Deixis: Discourse, Narrative, Literature*, Amsterdam: Rodopi.

Haber, Ralph and Hershenson, Maurice (1980) *The Psychology of Visual Perception* (second edition), New York: Holt, Rinehart & Winston.

Halliday, M.A.K. (1985) *An Introduction to Functional Grammar*, London: Edward Arnold.

Heinlein, Robert (1959a) *The Menace from Earth*, New York: Signet.

—— (1959b) *6 x H*, New York: Pyramid Books.

Hidalgo Downing, Laura (2000) *Negation, Text Worlds, and Discourse: The Pragmatics of Fiction*, Stamford, CT: Ablex.

Hoban, Russell (1982) *Riddley Walker*, London: Picador.

Hook, G. (1983) 'The nuclearization of language', *Journal of Peace Research* 21(3): 259–75.

Hoy, David C. (1997) 'Post-Cartesian interpretation: Hans-Georg Gadamer and Donald Davidson', in Lewis Edwin Hahn (ed.) *The Philosophy of Hans-Georg Gadamer*, Chicago, IL: Open Court, pp.111–28.

Hughes, Ted (1994) *Elmet* (edition with photographs by Fay Godwin, revised from *Remains of Elmet*, 1979), London: Faber & Faber.

Hutcheon, Linda (1985) *A Theory of Parody: The Teachings of Twentieth-Century Art Forms*, New York: Methuen.

Ingarden, Roman (1973a) *The Literary Work of Art: An Investigation on the Borderlines of Ontology, Logic, and Theory of Literature* (trans. George Grabowics, from the third edition of *Das literarische Kunstwerk*, 1965; after a Polish revised translation, 1960; from the original German, 1931), Evanston, IL: Northwestern University Press.

—— (1973b) *The Cognition of the Literary Work of Art* (trans. Ruth Ann Crowley and Kenneth Olson, from the German *Vom Erkennen des literarischen Kunstwerks*, 1968; original Polish *O poznawaniu dziela literackiego*, 1937), Evanston, IL: Northwestern University Press.

Iser, Wolfgang (1974) *The Implied Reader: Patterns of Communication in Prose Fiction from Bunyan to Beckett*, Baltimore, MD: Johns Hopkins University Press.

—— (1978) *The Act of Reading: A Theory of Aesthetic Response*, Baltimore, MD: Johns Hopkins University Press.

Jarvella, R.J. and Klein, W. (eds) (1982) *Speech, Place and Action: Studies in Deixis and Related Topics*, Chichester: John Wiley.

Johnson, Mark (1987) *The Body in the Mind: The Bodily Basis of Meaning, Imagination, and Reason*, Chicago, IL: University of Chicago Press.

Johnson-Laird, P.N. (1983) *Mental Models: Towards a Cognitive Science of Language, Inference and Consciousness*, Cambridge: Cambridge University Press.

—— (1988) *The Computer and the Mind: An Introduction to Cognitive Science*, London: Fontana.

Just, Marcel A. and Carpenter, Patricia A. (1976) *Cognitive Processes in Comprehension*, Hillsdale, NJ: Lawrence Erlbaum.

Kintsch, Walter (1977) *Memory and Cognition*, New York: Wiley.

—— (1998) *Comprehension: A Paradigm for Cognition*, Cambridge: Cambridge University Press.

Kittay, Eva (1987) *Metaphor: Its Cognitive Force and Linguistic Structure*, Oxford: Clarendon Press.

Kneepkens, E.W.E.M. and Zwaan, R.A. (1994) 'Emotions and literary text comprehension', *Poetics* 23: 125–38.

Kövecses, Z. (1986) *Metaphors of Anger, Pride and Love*, Amsterdam: John Benjamins.

—— (1988) *The Language of Love*, Lewisburg, PA: Associated University Press.

—— (1990) *Emotion Concepts*, New York: Springer.

Kuester, Martin (1992) *Framing Truths: Parodic Structures in Contemporary English-Canadian Historical Novels*, Toronto: University of Toronto Press.

Lakoff, George (1987) *Women, Fire and Dangerous Things: What Categories Reveal about the Mind*, Chicago, IL: University of Chicago Press.

—— (1990) 'The invariance hypothesis: is abstract reason based on image-schemas?', *Cognitive Linguistics* 1 (1): 39–74.

—— (1992) 'Metaphors and war: the metaphor system used to justify the Gulf War', in M. Pütz (ed.) *Thirty Years of Linguistic Evolution. Studies in Honour of René Dirven on the Occasion of his Sixtieth Birthday*, Amsterdam: John Benjamins.

Lakoff, G. and Johnson, M. (1980) *Metaphors We Live By*, Chicago, IL: University of Chicago Press.

—— and —— (1999) *Philosophy in the Flesh*, Chicago, IL: University of Chicago Press.

Lakoff, G. and Turner, M. (1989) *More Than Cool Reason: A Field Guide to Poetic Metaphor*, Chicago, IL: University of Chicago Press.

Langacker, Ronald (1987) *Foundations of Cognitive Grammar, Vol. I: Theoretical Prerequisites*, Stanford, CA: Stanford University Press.

—— (1990) *Concept, Image, and Symbol: The Cognitive Basis of Grammar*, Berlin: Mouton de Gruyter.

—— (1991) *Foundations of Cognitive Grammar, Vol. II: Descriptive Application*, Stanford, CA: Stanford University Press.

LeDoux, J. (1999) *The Emotional Brain*, London: Phoenix.

Leech, Geoffrey (1981) *Semantics* (second edition), Harmondsworth: Penguin.

Leech, Geoffrey and Short, Mick (1981) *Style in Fiction*, London: Longman.

Lehnert, W.G. and Vine, E.W. (1987) 'The role of affect in narrative structure', *Cognition and Emotion* 1 (3): 299–322.

Lemon, L. and Reis, M.J. (eds) (1965) *Russian Formalist Criticism*, Lincoln, NE: University of Nebraska Press.

Levinson, S.C. (1983) *Pragmatics*, Cambridge: Cambridge University Press.

Lewis, D. (1973) *Counterfactuals*, Cambridge: Cambridge University Press.

—— (1986) *On the Plurality of Worlds*, Oxford: Blackwell.

Logan, G.D. (1995) 'Linguistic and conceptual control of visual spatial attention', *Cognitive Psychology* 28: 103–74.

—— (1996) 'The CODE theory of visual attention: an integration of space-based and object-based attention', *Psychological Review* 103: 603–49.

Lyons, John (1977) *Semantics, Vols I and II*, Cambridge: Cambridge University Press.

McCarthy, Michael and Carter, Ronald (1994) *Language as Discourse: Perspectives for Language Teaching*, London: Longman.

Maclean, M. (1988) *Narrative as Performance*, London: Routledge.

Maitre, D. (1983) *Literature and Possible Worlds*, London: Middlesex University Press.

Mandler, J.M. (1984) *Scripts, Stories and Scenes: Aspects of a Schema Theory*, Hillsdale, NJ: Lawrence Erlbaum.

Martindale, C. (ed.) (1988) *Psychological Approaches to the Study of Literary Narratives*, Hamburg: Buske.

Matejka, L. and Pomorska, K. (eds) (1971) *Readings in Russian Poetics: Formalist and Structuralist Views*, Cambridge, MA: MIT Press.

Mervis, Carolyn and Rosch, Eleanor (1981) 'Categorization of natural objects', *Annual Review of Psychology* 32: 89–115.

Meutsch, D. and Viehoff, R. (1989) *Comprehension of Literary Discourse*, Berlin: de Gruyter.

Miall, David S. (1988) 'Affect and narrative: a model of response to stories', *Poetics* 17: 259–72.

—— (1989) 'Beyond the schema given: affective comprehension of literary narratives', *Cognition and Emotion* 3 (1): 55–78.

Miall, David S, and Kuiken, D. (1994) 'Beyond text theory: understanding literary response', *Discourse Processes* 17: 337–52.

Minsky, Marvin (1975) 'A framework for representing knowledge', in P.E. Winston (ed.) *The Psychology of Computer Vision*, New York: McGraw-Hill, pp.221–77.

—— (1986) *The Society of Mind*, London: Heinemann.

More, (St) Thomas (1910) *Utopia*, London: Dent [1516, in Latin, translated by R. Robinson, 1561].

Müller, Beate (ed.) (1997) *Parody: Dimensions and Perspectives*, Amsterdam: Rodopi.

Müske, E. (1990) 'Frame and literary discourse', *Poetics* 19: 433–61.

Nash, Walter (1985) *The Language of Humour*, London: Longman.

—— (1992) *An Uncommon Tongue: The Uses and Resources of English*, London: Routledge.

Novitz, D. (1987) *Knowledge, Fiction and Imagination*, Philadelphia, PA: Temple University Press.

Oatley, Keith (1992) *Best Laid Schemes: The Psychology of Emotions*, Cambridge: Cambridge University Press.

—— (1994) 'A taxonomy of the emotions of literary response and a theory of identification in fictional narrative', *Poetics* 23: 53–74.

Ortony, Andrew (ed.) (1993) *Metaphor and Thought* (second edition), Cambridge: Cambridge University Press.

Paprotte, W. and Dirven, R. (eds) (1985) *The Ubiquity of Metaphor*, Amsterdam: John Benjamins.

Posner, M.I. (ed.) (1989) *Foundations of Cognitive Science*, Cambridge, MA: MIT Press.

Prince, Gerald (1982) *Narratology: The Form and Function of Narrative*, Amsterdam: Mouton.

Putnam, H. (1990) *Realism with a Human Face*, Cambridge, MA: Harvard University Press.

Pylyshyn, Z.W. (1984) *Computation and Cognition*, Cambridge, MA: Massachusetts Institute of Technology Press.

Rauh, G. (ed.) (1983) *Essays on Deixis*, Tübingen: Gunter Narr Verlag.

Rescher, N. (1975) *A Theory of Possibility*, Pittsburgh, PA: Pittsburgh University Press.

Richards, I.A. (1924) *Principles of Literary Criticism*, London: Routledge & Kegan Paul.

Ricoeur, Paul (1977) *The Rule of Metaphor: Multidisciplinary Studies of the Creation of Meaning in Language* (trans. R. Czerny), Toronto: University of Toronto Press.

Riffaterre, M. (1959) 'Criteria for style analysis', *Word* 15: 154–74.

—— (1966) 'Describing poetic structures: two approaches to Baudelaire's "Les Chats"', *Yale French Studies* 36/7: 200–42.

Ronen, R. (1994) *Possible Worlds in Literary Theory*, Cambridge: Cambridge University Press.

Rorty, R. (1982) *Consequences of Pragmatism (Essays 1972–1980)*, Minneapolis, MN: University of Minnesota Press.

Rosch, Eleanor (1975) 'Cognitive representations of semantic categories', *Journal of Experimental Psychology: General* 104: 193–233.

—— (1977) 'Human categorization', in Neil Warren (ed.) *Studies in Cross-Cultural Psychology, Vol. I*, London: Academic Press, pp.1–49.

—— (1978) 'Principles of categorization', in Eleanor Rosch and Barbara Lloyd (eds) *Cognition and Categorization*, Hillsdale, NJ: Lawrence Erlbaum, pp.27–48.

—— (1988) 'Coherence and categorization: a historical view', in F.S. Kessel (ed.) *The Development of Language and Language Researchers: Essays in Honour of Roger Brown*, Hillsdale, NJ: Lawrence Erlbaum, pp.373–92.

Rosch, Eleanor and Lloyd, B.B. (eds) (1978) *Cognition and Categorization*, Hillsdale, NJ: Lawrence Erbaum.

Rosch, Eleanor and Mervis, Carolyn (1975) 'Family resemblances: studies in the internal structure of categories', *Cognitive Psychology* 7: 573–605.

Rosch, Eleanor; Mervis, Carolyn; Gray, Wayne; Johnson, David and Boyes-Braem, Penny (1976) 'Basic objects in natural categories', *Cognitive Psychology* 8: 382–439.

Rose, Margaret (1993) *Parody: Ancient, Modern and Post-Modern*, Cambridge: Cambridge University Press.

Rumelhart, David E. (1975) 'Notes on a schema for stories', in D.G. Bobrow and A. Collins (eds) *Representation and Understanding*, New York: Academic Press, pp. 211–36.

—— (1980) 'Schemata: the building blocks of cognition', in R.J. Spiro, B. Bruce and W. Brewer (eds) *Theoretical Issues in Reading Comprehension: Perspectives from Cognitive Psychology, Linguistics, Artificial Intelligence and Education*, Hillsdale, NJ: Lawrence Erlbaum, pp. 33–58.

—— (1984) 'Schemata and the cognitive system', in R.S Wyer and T.K. Srull (eds) *Handbook of Social Cognition, vol. 1*, Hillsdale, NJ: Lawrence Erlbaum, pp. 161–88.

Rumelhart, David E. and Norman, D.A. (1978) 'Accretion, tuning and restructuring: three modes of learning', in J.W. Cotton and R.L. Klatzky (eds) *Semantic Factors in Cognition*, Hillsdale, NJ: Lawrence Erlbaum, pp. 37–53.

Ryan, M.L. (1991a) *Possible Worlds: Artificial Intelligence and Narrative Theory*, Bloomington and Indianapolis, IN: Indiana University Press.

—— (1991b) 'Possible worlds and accessibility relations: a semantics typology of fiction', *Poetics Today*, 12 (3): 553–76.

Ryder, Mary Ellen (1998) 'I met myself (me?) coming and going: co(?)-referential noun phrases and point of view in time travel stories', Paper presented at the eighteenth Poetics and Linguistics Association Conference, University of Berne, April 1998.

Sanford, A.J. and Garrod, S.C. (1981) *Understanding Written Language*, New York: Wiley.

Scarry, Elaine (2001) *Dreaming by the Book*, Princeton, NJ: Princeton University Press.

Schank, R.C. (1982a) *Dynamic Memory: A Theory of Reminding and Learning in Computers and People*, Cambridge: Cambridge University Press.

—— (1982b) *Reading and Understanding: Teaching from the Perspective of Artificial Intelligence*, Hillsdale, NJ: Lawrence Erlbaum.

—— (1984) *The Cognitive Computer*, Reading, MA: Addison-Wesley.

—— (1986) *Explanation Patterns*, Hillsdale, NJ: Lawrence Erlbaum.

Schank, R.C. and Abelson, R. (1977) *Scripts, Plans, Goals and Understanding*, Hillsdale, NJ: Lawrence Erlbaum.

Searle, John (1975) 'The logical status of fictional discourse', *New Literary History* 6(2): 319–32.

Segal, Erwin M. (1995a) 'Narrative comprehension and the role of deictic shift theory', in J.F. Duchan, G.A. Bruder and L.E. Hewitt (eds) *Deixis in Narrative: A Cognitive Science Perspective*, Hillsdale, NJ: Lawrence Erlbaum, pp. 3–17.

—— (1995b) 'A cognitive-phenomenological theory of fictional narrative', in J.F. Duchan, G.A. Bruder and L.E. Hewitt (eds) *Deixis in Narrative: A Cognitive Science Perspective*, Hillsdale, NJ: Lawrence Erlbaum, 61–78.

Semino, Elena (1997) *Language and World Creation in Poems and Other Texts*, London: Longman.

Short, Mick (1996) *Exploring the Language of Poems, Plays and Prose*, London: Longman.

Simpson, Paul (1993) *Language, Ideology and Point of View*, London: Routledge.

—— (2002) *Satire*, Amsterdam: John Benjamins.

Smyth, M.M.; Collins, A.F.; Morris, P.E. and Levy, P. (1994) *Cognition in Action* (second edition), Hove: Lawrence Erlbaum.

Spiro, R.J. (1980) 'Prior knowledge and story processing: integration, selection and variation', *Poetics* 9: 313–27.

—— (1982) 'Long-term comprehension: schema-based versus experiential and evaluative understanding', *Poetics* 11: 77–86.

Spiro, R.J.; Bruce, B. and Brewer, W. (eds) (1980) *Theoretical Issues in Reading Comprehension: Perspectives from Cognitive Psychology, Linguistics, Artificial Intelligence and Education*, Hillsdale, NJ: Lawrence Erlbaum.

Stapledon, Olaf (1937) *Star Maker*, London: Methuen.

Steen, Gerard (1994) *Understanding Metaphor*, London: Longman.

Stephenson, Neal (1995) *The Diamond Age, or A Young Lady's Illustrated Primer*, Harmondsworth: Penguin.

Stockwell, Peter (1990) 'Scripts, frames and nuclear discourse in the Washington super-power summit, December 1987', *Liverpool Papers in Language and Discourse* 2: 18–39.

—— (1992) 'The metaphorics of literary reading', *Liverpool Papers in Language and Discourse* 4: 52–80.

—— (1994) 'To be or not to be a phagocyte: procedures of reading metaphors', in Roger Sell and Peter Verdonk (eds) *Literature and the New Interdisciplinarity: Poetics, Linguistics, History*, Amsterdam: Rodopi, pp.65–78.

—— (1999) 'The inflexibility of invariance', *Language and Literature* 8(2): 125–42.

—— (2000a) *The Poetics of Science Fiction*, London: Longman.

—— (2000b) '(Sur)real stylistics: from text to contextualizing', in Tony Bex, Michael Burke and Peter Stockwell (eds) *Contextualized Stylistics: in honour of Peter Verdonk*, Amsterdam: Rodopi, pp.15–38.

—— (2001) 'Toward a critical cognitive linguistics?' in Annette Combrink and Ina Biermann (eds) *Poetics, Linguistics and History: Discourses of War and Conflict*, Potchefstroom: Potchefstroom University Press, pp. 510–28.

Stroop, J.R. (1935) 'Studies of interference in serial-verbal reaction', *Journal of Experimental Psychology* 18: 643–62.

Styles, Elizabeth (1997) *The Psychology of Attention*, Hove: Psychology Press.

Suvin, Darko (1990) 'Locus, horizon and orientation: the concept of possible worlds as a key to utopian studies', *Utopian Studies* 1(2): 69–83.

Swales, J. (1988) 'Discourse communities, genres and English as an international language', *World Englishes* 7(2): 211–20.

—— (1990) *Genre Analysis*, Cambridge: Cambridge University Press.

Sweetser, Eve (1990) *From Etymology to Pragmatics: Metaphorical and Cultural Aspects of Semantic Structure*, Cambridge: Cambridge University Press.

Talmy, Leonard (1978) 'Figure and ground in complex sentences', in J. Greenberg (ed.) *Universals of Human Language* (vol. 4), Stanford, CA: Stanford University Press, pp. 627–49.

—— (1988) 'Force dynamics in language and cognition', *Cognitive Science* 12: 49–100.

—— (1995) 'Narrative structure in a cognitive framework', in J.F. Duchan, G.A. Bruder and L.E. Hewitt (eds) *Deixis in Narrative: A Cognitive Science Perspective*, Hillsdale, NJ: Lawrence Erlbaum, 421–60.

Tannen, Deborah (1984) 'What's in a frame? Surface evidence for underlying expectations', in R.O. Freedle (ed.) *New Directions in Discourse Processing*, Norwood, NJ: Ablex, pp.137–81.

Taylor, John (1995) *Linguistic Categorization: Prototypes in Linguistic Theory* (second edition), Oxford: Clarendon Press.

Thorndyke, P.W. (1977) 'Cognitive structures in comprehension and memory of narrative discourse', *Cognitive Psychology* 9: 77–110.

Thorndyke, P.W. and Yekovich, F.R. (1980) 'A critique of schema-based theories of human story memory', *Poetics* 9: 23–49.

Toolan, Michael (1996) *Total Speech: An Integrational Linguistic Approach to Language*, Durham, NC: Duke University Press.

—— (2001) *Narrative: A Critical Linguistic Introduction* (second edition), London: Routledge.

Tsur, Reuven (1992) *Toward a Theory of Cognitive Poetics*, Amsterdam: North-Holland.

—— (1998) *Poetic Rhythm: Structure and Performance*, Berne: Peter Lang.

Turner, Mark (1987) *Death is the Mother of Beauty: Mind, Metaphor, Criticism*, Chicago, IL: University of Chicago Press.

—— (1990) 'Aspects of the invariance hypothesis', *Cognitive Linguistics* 1 (2): 247–55.

—— (1991) *Reading Minds: The Study of English in the Age of Cognitive Science*, Princeton, NJ: Princeton University Press.

—— (1996) *The Literary Mind: The Origins of Thought and Language*, Oxford: Oxford University Press.

Turner, Mark and Fauconnier, G. (1995) 'Conceptual integration and formal expression', *Metaphor and Symbolic Activity* 10(3): 183–203.

—— and — (1999) 'A mechanism of creativity', *Poetics Today* 20(3): 397–418.

Ungerer, Friedrich and Schmid, Hans-Jörg (1996) *An Introduction to Cognitive Linguistics*, London: Longman.

van Dijk, Teun A. (1977) *Text and Context*, London: Longman.

—— (1980) *Macrostructures*, Hillsdale, NJ: Lawrence Erlbaum.

van Dijk, Teun A. and Kintsch, Walter (1983) *Strategies of Discourse Comprehension*, New York: Academic Press.

Van Oosten, Jeanne (1984) *Subject, Topic, Agent, and Passive* (PhD thesis), San Diego, CA: University of California.

van Peer, Willie (1986) *Stylistics and Psychology: Investigations of Foregrounding*, New York: Croom Helm.

Verdonk, Peter and Weber, Jean-Jacques (eds) (1995) *Twentieth Century Fiction: From Text to Context*, London: Routledge.

Walton, K.L (1978) 'How remote are fictional worlds from the real world?' *Journal of Aesthetics and Art Criticism* 37: 11–23.

Warnke, Georgia (1987) *Gadamer: Hermeneutics, Tradition and Reason*, Stanford, CA: Stanford University Press.

Werth, Paul (1987) 'Understanding understanding', *Journal of Literary Semantics*, XVI: 129–53.

—— (1994) 'Extended metaphor: a text world account', *Language and Literature* 3(2): 79–103.

—— (1995a) 'How to build a world (in a lot less than six days, and using only what's in your head)', in Keith Green, (ed.) *New Essays in Deixis*, Amsterdam: Rodopi, pp.49–80.

—— (1995b) '"World enough and time": deictic space and the interpretation of prose', in Peter Verdonk and Jean Jacques Weber (eds) *Twentieth Century Fiction: From Text to Context*, London: Routledge, pp.181–205.

—— (1999) *Text Worlds: Representing Conceptual Space in Discourse* (edited by M. Short), Harlow: Longman.

Wiebe, Janyce M. (1995) 'References in narrative text', in J.F. Duchan, G.A. Bruder and L.E. Hewitt (eds) *Deixis in Narrative: A Cognitive Science Perspective*, Hillsdale, NJ: Lawrence Erlbaum, pp. 263–86.

Wilson, John (1990) *Politically Speaking: The Pragmatic Analysis of Political Language*, Oxford: Blackwell.

Wimsatt, W.K. and Beardsley, Monroe C. (1954) *The Verbal Icon*, Lexington, KY: University of Kentucky Press.

Wittgenstein, Ludwig (1958) *Philosophical Investigations* (second edition trans. G.E.M. Anscobe), Oxford: Blackwell.

Womack, Jack (2000) *Going Going Gone*, London: HarperCollins.

Zubin, David A. and Hewitt, Lynne E. (1995) 'The deictic center: a theory of deixis in narrative', in J.F. Duchan, G.A. Bruder and L.E. Hewitt (eds) *Deixis in Narrative: A Cognitive Science Perspective*, Hillsdale, NJ: Lawrence Erlbaum, pp. 129–55.

Glossarial index

All keywords which are written in the text in **bold** appear in the glossarial index. **Bold** page numbers in the list below indicate the place where a definition is given in context. Other page numbers point to places where the term is also used.